Front cover
*Bab al-Mansur al-'Alj, entrance bag,
detail of the frame decorated in ceramic, Meknes.*

Museum With No Frontiers *Exhibition Trails*

ISLAMIC ART IN THE MEDITERRANEAN | MOROCCO

Andalusian Morocco
A Discovery in Living Art

Museum With No Frontiers

EUROPEAN UNION
Euromed Heritage

The realisation of the MWNF Exhibition Trail
ANDALUSIAN MOROCCO: A Discovery in Living Art
has been co-financed by the **European Union** within the framework
of the **Euromed Heritage** programme
and has received the support of the following Moroccan institutions:

MINISTRY OF CULTURAL AFFAIRS

Ministry of Cultural Affairs of the Kingdom of Morocco

MINISTRY OF TOURISM OF THE KINGDOM OF MOROCCO

NATIONAL MOROCCAN TOURIST OFFICE

Ministry of Tourism of the Kingdom of Morocco

National Moroccan Tourist Office

First edition
© 2001 Ministry of Cultural Affairs of the Kingdom of Morocco, Rabat, Morocco & Museum With No Frontiers
  (texts and illustrations)
© 2001 Electa (Grijalbo Mondadori S.A.), Madrid, Spain & Museum With No Frontiers

Second edition
© 2010 Ministry of Cultural Affairs of the Kingdom of Morocco, Rabat, Morocco & Museum With No Frontiers
  (texts and illustrations)
© 2010 Museum With No Frontiers

ISBN: 978-3-902782-08-3

All rights reserved.

Information
www.museumwnf.org
www.mwnfbooks.net

Museum With No Frontiers
Idea and overall concept
Eva Schubert

Head of Project
Abdelaziz Touri, Rabat

Curatorial Committee
Mhammad Benaboud, Tétouan
Naïma El-Khatib Boujibar, Casablanca
Kamal Lakhdar, Rabat
Mohamed Mezzine, Fez
Abdelaziz Touri, Rabat

Catalogue

Introductions
Abdelaziz Touri
Naïma El-Khatib Boujibar
Mohamed Mezzine

Presentation of Itineraries
Curatorial Committee

Technical Texts
Nadia Hachimi Alaoui, Casablanca

Photography
Khalil Nemmaoui, Casablanca

General Map
José Antonio Dávila Buitrón, Madrid

Sketches
Rachid Tedjini, Casablanca
Sergio Viguera, Madrid

Monument plans
Curatorial Committee

General Introduction
Islamic Art in the Mediterranean
Jamila Binous, Tunis
Mahmoud Hawari, East Jerusalem
Manuela Marín, Madrid
Gönül Öney, Izmir

Plans
Şakir Çakmak, Izmir
Ertan Daş, Izmir
Yekta Demiralp, Izmir

Translation
Maria Leonidas Vlotides, London

Copy editor
Mandi Gomez, London

Layout and design
Augustina Fernández,
Electa España, Madrid
Christian Eckart,
MWNF, Vienna (2nd edition)

Local coordination

Production Manager
Nadia Hachimi Alaoui, Casablanca
Nouria Cherradi, Casablanca

Secretariat
Lamia Moukhliss, Casablanca

International cordination

Overall coordination
Eva Schubert

Curatorial committees, translations, editing and production of the catalogues (1st edition)
Sakina Missoum, Madrid

Acknowledgements

We thank the following institutions for their support:

The archives of the Ministry of Cultural Affairs, Rabat
Association Ader-Fez
General Library and Archives, Rabat
Royal al-Hassania Library, Rabat
Crossroads of the Arts (Le Carrefour des Arts), Casablanca
The American Delegation in Tangier
The Villa of the Arts (La Villa des Arts), ONA Foundation, Casablanca
The local communities
The regional delegates from the Ministry of Tourism and from the Ministry of Cultural Affairs

as well as the curators from the following museums:
Dar Jamaï Museum, Meknès
Batha Museum, Fez
Ethnographic Museum, Chefchaouen
Ethnographic Museum, Tétouan
Archaeological Museum, Tétouan
The College of Arts and Crafts, Tétouan
The Kasbah Museum, Tangiers
The Udayas Museum, Rabat
Archaeological Museum, Rabat

and Royal Air Maroc

We would also like to thank:

The Spanish Ministry of Foreign Affairs and Cooperation, Spanish Agency for International Development Cooperation
The Spanish Ministry of Culture

The Federal Ministry of Foreign and European Affairs, Austria
The Ministry of Cultural Heritage and Cultural Activities (National Museum for Oriental Arts, Rome), Italy
The Secretary of State for Tourism, Portugal
The Museum of Mediterranean and Near-Eastern Antiquities, Stockholm, Sweden

as well as:
The Regional Government of Tyrol (Austria), where the MWNF Exhibition Trails pilot project was set up

Photographic references
See page 5, and
Ann & Peter Jousiffe (London), page 20 (Aleppo)
Oronoz Photographic Archives (Madrid), page 23 (Alhambra, Granada)
Cambridge University Library, page 141 (Maïmonides's Letter).

Plan references
R. Ettinghaussen and O. Grabar (Madrid, I, 1997), page 26 (Mosque of Damascus)
Z. Sönmez (Ankara, 1995), page 27 (Mosque of Divrişi and Istanbul) and page 28 (Mosque of Sivas)
Sergio Viguera (Madrid), page 28 (Minaret styles)
Blair, S. S., and Bloom, J. M. (Madrid, II, 1999), page 29 (Mosque and Madrasa Sultan Hassan).
R. Ettinghaussen and O. Grabar (Madrid, I, 1997), page 30 (Qasr al-Khayr al-Sharqi)
A. Kuran (Istanbul, 1986), page 31 (Khan Sultan Aksaray)

The opinions expressed in this work do not necessarily reflect the opinions of either the European Union or of its Member States.

Preface

In 1996 Museum With No Frontiers (MWNF) initiated a comprehensive programme to research, document and increase knowledge and public awareness of the history and cultural legacy of Islam in the countries surrounding the Mediterranean basin. This book is one of the outcomes of this programme, which involves hundreds of scholars and is carried out in cooperation with institutions from all the countries concerned. Important initial funding from the European Union made it possible to set the basis for a sustainable network of public and private partners implementing attractive projects in the field of culture, education and tourism.

When the MWNF programme was first launched, the topic of Islamic art and architecture was familiar only to experts and there was an implicit understanding that cultural heritage in the Mediterranean meant the legacy of the classical civilisations. Thanks to the launch coinciding with the establishment at the end of 1995 of the Euro-Mediterranean Partnership, a joint initiative of the European Union and its Mediterranean neighbours, the MWNF programme took off quickly and became a pioneering venture to disseminate knowledge about the world contribution of Islam.

The initial focus on the Mediterranean region was determined by its place at the centre stage of Islamic history and the economic and cultural interdependence of its shores throughout that history. However, we look forward to extending the programme to other areas of the Islamic and Arab world.

In connection with our Exhibition Trails and related thematic guides, MWNF also offers the possibility to participate in themed tours organised in cooperation with specialised local travel agencies in each country. For further details and virtual tours to the Exhibition Trails please visit *www.mwnftravels.net*.

Our Virtual Museum – *www.discoverislamicart.org* – offers access to a large collection of Islamic artefacts and monuments, with descriptions for all items regularly updated in Arabic, English, French and Spanish. A series of Virtual Exhibitions enables visitors to locate the topics of the Exhibition Trails within the relevant regional context.

All MWNF publications are compiled, written and illustrated by scholars and photographers from the country concerned and convey the cultural and historical context of the featured sites from a local perspective. 'We appreciate only what we see and we understand only what we know.' It was with this idea in mind that our Egyptian colleagues who designed the visit and wrote the text for this book paid particular attention to providing information that usually remains undisclosed to tourists.

On behalf of the whole MWNF team I wish you an enjoyable visit to Andalusian Morocco and look forward to meeting you soon in another part of our Euro-Mediterranean museum with no frontiers.

Eva Schubert
Chairperson and CEO
Museum With No Frontiers

Advice

Transliteration of the Arabic

We have retained standard spelling for Arabic words in common use and included those in the English dictionary. We have used phonetic spellings for the various dialects spoken within different regions of Morocco as provided by the authors themselves. For all other words, we have simplified the transcription. We do not transcribe the initial *hamza* nor do we distinguish between long and short vowels, which have been transcribed as *a, i, u*.
The *ta' marbuta* has been transcribed as *a* (in its absolute), and as *at* (when followed by a genitive). The transcription for the 28 Arabic consonants is as follows:

ء	'	ح	h	ز	z	ط	t	ق	q	ه	h
ب	b	خ	kh	س	s	ظ	z	ك	k	و	u/w
ت	t	د	d	ش	sh	ع	'	ل	l	ي	y/i
ث	th	ذ	dh	ص	s	غ	gh	م	m		
ج	j	ر	r	ض	d	ف	f	ن	n		

Words in italic in the text without an accompanying translation or explanation can be found in the glossary.

The Muslim Era

The Muslim era began with the exodus of the Prophet Muhammad from Mecca to Yathrib. Then the name was changed to Madina, "The City" or "the town of the Prophet". With his small community of followers (70 people including members of his family) recently converted to Islam, the Prophet undertook the *al-hijra* (literally "the emigration") and the new era began.
The date of the emigration is the first of the month of *Muharram* in year 1 of the *Hijra*, which corresponds to the 16th July of the year 622 of the Christian era. The Muslim year is made up of twelve lunar months, each month having 29 or 30 days. Thirty years form a cycle in which the 2nd, 5th, 7th, 10th, 13th, 16th, 18th, 21st, 24th, 26th and 29th are leap years having 355 days; the others are normal years with 354 days. The Muslim lunar year is 10 or 11 days shorter than the Christian solar year. Each day begins immediately after sunset, i.e. at dusk rather than after midnight. Most Muslim countries use both the *Hijra* Calendar (which marks all the religious events) and the Christian Calendar.

Dates

Dates are given according to the *Hijra* calendar followed by their equivalent date in the Christian calendar after an oblique stroke.
The *Hijra* date is not indicated in references derived from Christian sources, European historical events or those that have occurred in Europe, Christian dynasties, those prior to the Muslim era or after the signature of the Treaty of 1856, which obliged Morocco to recognise, among other things, the Regime of the Protectorate.
Exact correspondence between years in one calendar and another is only possible when the day and month are given. To facilitate reading, we have chosen to avoid intermediate years and, in the case of *Hijra* dates falling between the beginning and end of a century, both centuries are mentioned.

Abbreviations:
AD = Anno Domini, BC = before Christ, b. = born, d. = died, r. = reigned.

Practical Advice

Each of the Itineraries which make up *ANDALUSIAN MOROCCO: A Discovery in Living Art* exist independently of each other, and it is therefore possible to undertake them in whichever order one wishes. Itinerary VII, entitled "The Ports of the Strait", is spread over three days, and this has been done for the geographical reason that substantial distances separate each stage of the itinerary. On the other hand, Itinerary VIII, "Ebb and Flow, Shine and Eclipse" spreads itself over two days as there are a significant number of monuments to visit.

For the Itineraries in the Medina of Fez, Itineraries II, III and IV, the instructions given to locate a monument are but suggestions, the chosen route being, more often than not, the simplest rather than the shortest way there. It is possible to opt for another route or, even, to alter the sequencing of your visits to particular monuments.

Since Morocco poses the problem of translating Arabic nouns, orientation can be difficult, as a monument can be signposted in various ways.

In Morocco, generally speaking, only persons belonging to the Muslim faith can enter places of worship, with the particular exception of the Mausoleum of Mulay Isma'il in Meknès. Information concerning this rule is reiterated in the instructive texts within the guidebook.

The instructions concerning the visits to monuments correspond vigorously to those correct at the time of writing this catalogue. During our visit, certain monuments were closed to the public, and this information is reiterated in the instructive texts within the guidebook. Museum With No Frontiers does not take responsibility for possible changes that may arise subsequent to publication.

However, it is important to note that on Fridays, the opening times of certain monuments can change at around 12.00 hours so that the guardian can reach the mosque. Due to the variations in this change, the times cannot be stated in the instructive texts within the guidebook and we ask you to be aware of this during your visit.

National Museums are closed on Tuesdays, and those on the premises of administrative buildings are closed at the weekend.

Museum With No Frontiers does not take any responsibility for incidents that could arise during your visit to the Exhibition Trail.

Nadia Hachimi Alaoui
Production Manager

INDEX

- 15 **Islamic Art in the Mediterranean**
  Jamila Binous, Mahmoud Hawari, Manuela Marín, Gönül Öney

- 35 **Historical Introduction**
  Abdelaziz Touri

- 50 **Andalusian Morocco**
  Naïma El-Khatib Boujibar
  Mohamed Mezzine

- 64 **Itinerary I**
  The Royal City
  Mulay Isma'il
  Mohamed Mezzine

- 86 **Itinerary II**
  A Day in the Life of a *Taleb* in Fez
  Calligraphy
  Mohamed Mezzine

- 110 **Itinerary III**
  A Day in the Life of an Artisan in Fez
  Naima El-Khatib Boujibar, Mohamed Mezzine
  Ceramics
  Naïma El-Khatib Boujibar

- 130 **Itinerary IV**
  A Day in the Life of a Jew in Fez
  Maimonides
  Mohamed Mezzine

- 142 **Itinerary V**
  Chefchaouen: The Holy City of the Rif Mountains
  Saïda El-Horra, Princess of Chefchaouen
  Naïma El-Khatib Boujibar

- 162 **Itinerary VI**
  Tétouan: The Patio of a Civilisation
  Andalusian Music
  Mhammad Benaboud

- 182 **Itinerary VII** (3 days)
  The Ports of the Strait
  Ibn Battuta
  Naïma El-Khatib Boujibar

- 214 **Itinerary VIII** (2 days)
  Ebb and Flow, Shine and Eclipse
  Zellij - The Rugs of Rabat
  Kamal Lakhdar

- 249 **Glossary**

- 253 **Historical Personalities**

- 258 **Further Reading**

- 259 **Authors**

ISLAMIC DYNASTIES IN THE MEDITERRANEAN

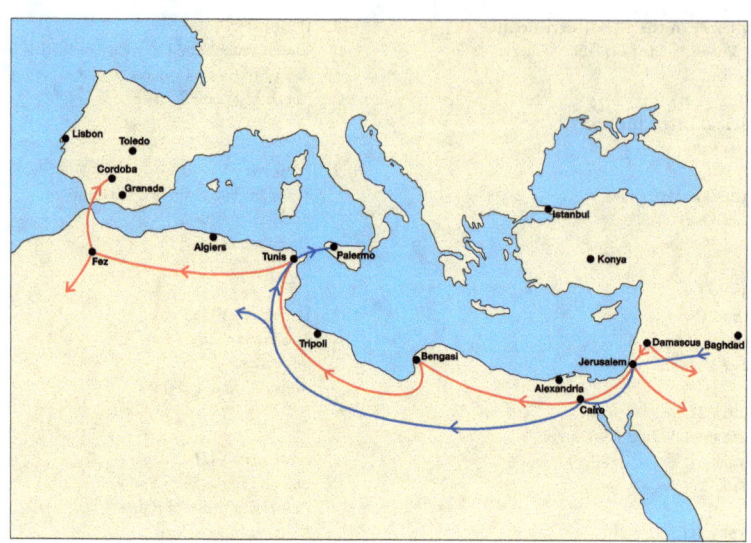

← The Umayyads (41/661-132/750)   Capital: Damascus
← The Abbasids (132/750-656/1258)   Capital: Baghdad

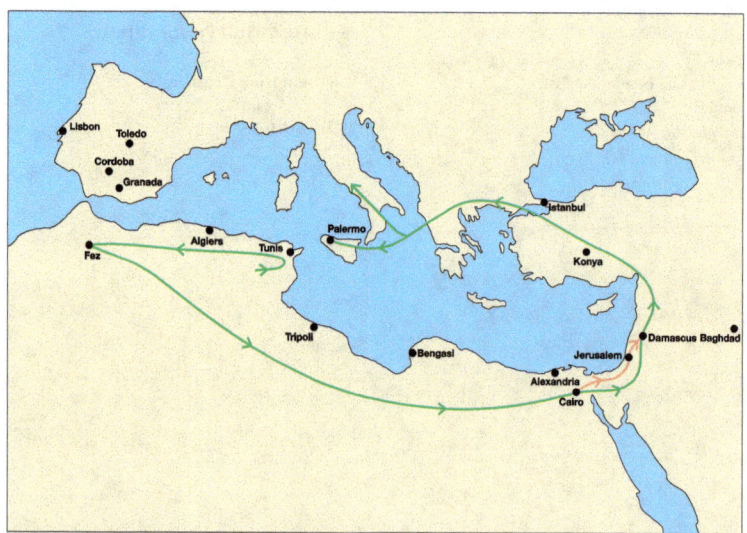

← The Fatimids (296/909-567/1171)   Capital: Cairo
← The Mamluks (648/1250-923/1517)   Capital: Cairo

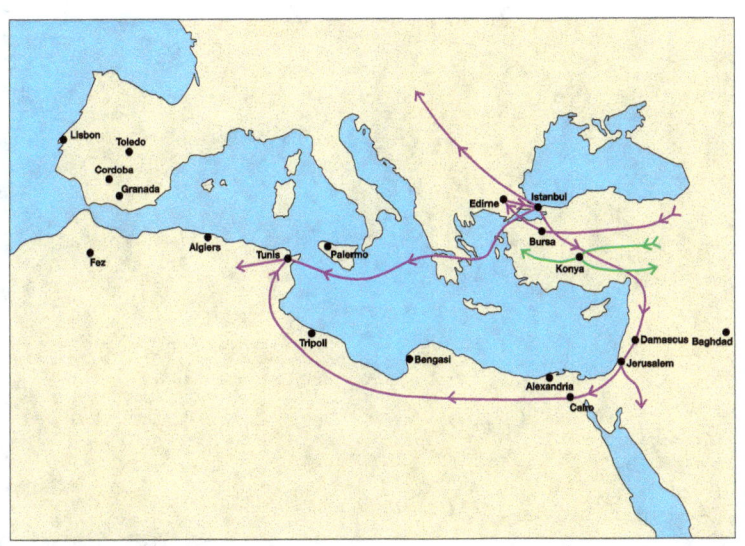

← The Seljuqs (571/1075-718/1318)   Capital: Konya
← The Ottomans (699/1299-1340/1922)   Capital: Istanbul

← The Almoravids (427/1036-541/1147)   Capital: Marrakesh
← The Almohads (515/1121-667/1269)   Capital: Marrakesh

Qusayr 'Amra, mural in the Audience Hall, Badiya of Jordan.

ISLAMIC ART IN THE MEDITERRANEAN

Jamila Binous
Mahmoud Hawari
Manuela Marín
Gönül Öney

The Legacy of Islam in the Mediterranean

Since the first half of the 1st/7th century, the history of the Mediterranean Basin has belonged, in remarkably similar proportion, to two cultures, Islam and the Christian West. This extensive history of conflict and contact has created a mythology that is widely diffused in the collective imagination, a mythology based on the image of the other as the unyielding enemy, strange and alien, and as such, incomprehensible. It is of course true that battles punctuated those centuries from the time when the Muslims spilled forth from the Arabian Peninsula and took possession of the Fertile Crescent, Egypt, and later, North Africa, Sicily, and the Iberian Peninsula, penetrating into Western Europe as far as the south of France. At the beginning of the 2nd/8th century, the Mediterranean came under Islamic control.

This drive to expand, of an intensity seldom equalled in human history, was carried out in the name of a religion that considered itself then heir to its two immediate antecedents: Judaism and Christianity. It would be a gross oversimplification to explain the Islamic expansion exclusively in religious terms. One widespread image in the West presents Islam as a religion of simple dogmas adapted to the needs of the common people, spread by vulgar warriors who poured out from the desert bearing the *Qur'an* on the blades of their swords. This coarse image does away with the intellectual complexity of a religious message that transformed the world from the moment of its inception. It identifies this message with a military threat, and thus justifies a response on the same terms. Finally, it reduces an entire culture to only one of its elements, religion, and in doing so, deprives it of the potential for evolution and change.

The Mediterranean countries that were progressively incorporated into the Muslim world began their journeys from very different starting points. Forms of Islamic life that began to develop in each were quite logically different within the unity that resulted from their shared adhesion to the new religious dogma. It is precisely the capacity to assimilate elements of previous cultures (Hellenistic, Roman, etc.), which has been one of the defining characteristics of Islamic societies. If one restricts one's observations to the geographical area of the Mediterranean, which was extremely diverse culturally at the time of the emergence of Islam, one will discern quickly that this initial moment does not represent a break with previous history in the least. One comes to realise that it is impossible to imagine a monolithic and immutable Islamic world, blindly following an inalterable religious message.

If anything can be singled out as the *leitmotiv* running through the area of the Mediterranean, it is diversity of expression combined with harmony of sentiment, a sentiment more cultural than religious. In the Iberian Peninsula – to begin with the western perimeter of the Mediterranean – the presence of Islam, initially brought about by military conquest, produced a society clearly differentiated from, but in permanent contact with Christian society. The importance of the cultural expression of this Islamic society was felt even after it ceased to exist as such, and gave rise to perhaps one of the most original components of Spanish culture, Mudejar art. Portugal maintained strong Mozarab traditions throughout the Islamic period and there are many imprints from this time that are still clearly visible today. In Morocco and Tunisia, the legacy of al-Andalus was assimilated into the local forms and continues to be evident to this day. The western Mediterranean produced original forms of expression that reflected its conflicting and plural historical evolution.

Lodged between East and West, the Mediterranean Sea is endowed with terrestrial enclaves, such as Sicily, that represent centuries-old key historical locations. Conquered by the Arabs established in Tunisia, Sicily has continued to perpetuate the cultural and historical memory of Islam long after the Muslims ceased to have any political presence on the island. The presence of Sicilian-Norman aesthetic forms preserved in architectural monuments clearly demonstrates that the history of these regions cannot be explained without an understanding of the diversity of social, economic and cultural experiences that flourished on their soil.

In sharp contrast, then, to the immutable and constant image alluded to at the outset, the history of Mediterranean Islam is characterised by surprising diversity. It is made up of a mixture of peoples and ethnicities, deserts and fertile lands. As the major religion has been Islam since the early Middle Ages, it is also true that religious minorities have maintained a presence historically. The Classical Arabic language of the *Qur'an,* has coexisted side-by-side with other languages, as well as with other dialects of Arabic. Within a setting of undeniable unity (Muslim religion, Arabic language and culture), each society has evolved and responded to the challenges of history in its own characteristic manner.

The Emergence and Development of Islamic Art

Throughout these countries, with ancient and diverse civilisations, a new art permeated with images from the Islamic faith emerged at the end of the $2^{nd}/8^{th}$ century, which successfully imposed itself in a period of less than 100 years. This art, in its own particular manner, gave rise to creations and innovations based on unifying regional formulas and architectural and decorative processes, and was simultaneously inspired by the artistic traditions that proceeded it: Greco-Roman and Byzantine, Sasanian, Visigothic, Berber or even Central Asian.

The initial aim of Islamic art was to serve the needs of religion and various aspects of socio-economic life. New buildings appeared for religious purposes such as mosques and sanctuaries. For this reason, architecture played a central role in Islamic art because a whole series of other arts are dependent on it. Apart from architecture a whole range of complimentary minor arts found their artistic expressions in a variety of materials, such as wood, pottery, metal, glass, textiles and paper. In pottery, a great variety of glaze techniques were employed and among these distinguished groups are the lustre and polychrome painted wares. Glass of great beauty was manufactured, reaching excellence with the type adorned with gold and bright enamel colours. In metal work, the most sophisticated technique is inlaying bronze with silver or copper. High-quality textiles and carpets, with geometric, animal and human designs, were made. Illuminated manuscripts with miniature paintings represent a spectacular achievement in the arts of the book. These types of minor arts serve to attest the brilliance of Islamic art.

Figurative art, however, is excluded from the Islamic liturgical domain, which means it is ostracised from the central core of Islamic civilisation and that it is tolerated only at its periphery. Relief work is rare in the decoration of monuments and sculptures are almost flat. This deficit is compensated with a richness in ornamentation on the lavish carved plaster panelling, sculpted wooden panelling, wall tiling and glazed mosaics, as well as on the stalactite friezes, or *muqarnas*. Decorative elements taken from nature, such as leaves, flowers and branches, are generally stylised to the extreme and are so complicated that they rarely call to mind their sources of origin. The intertwining and combining of geometric motifs such as rhombus and etiolated polygons, form interlacing networks that completely cover the surface, resulting in shapes often called arabesques. One innovation within the decorative repertoire is the introduction of epigraphic elements

Islamic Art in the Mediterranean

Dome of the Rock, Jerusalem.

in the ornamentation of monuments, furniture and various other objects. Muslim craftsmen made use of the beauty of Arabic calligraphy, the language of the sacred book, the *Qur'an*, not only for the transcription of the Qur'anic verses, but in all of its variations simply as a decorative motif for the ornamentation of stucco panelling and the edges of panels.

Art was also at the service of rulers. It was for patrons that architects built palaces, mosques, schools, hospitals, bathhouses, *caravanserais* and mausoleums, which would sometimes bear their names. Islamic art is, above all, dynastic art. Each one contributed tendencies that would bring about a partial or complete renewal of artistic forms, depending on historical conditions, the prosperity enjoyed by their states, and the traditions of each people. Islamic art, in spite of its relative unity, allowed for a diversity that gave rise to different styles, each one identified with a dynasty.

The Umayyad Dynasty (41/661-132/750), which transferred the capital of the caliphate to Damascus, represents a singular achievement in the history of Islam. It absorbed and incorporated the Hellenistic and Byzantine legacy in such a way that the classical tradition of the Mediterranean was recast in a new and innovative mould. Islamic art, thus, was formed in Syria, and the architecture, unmistakably Islamic due to the personality of the founders, would continue to bear a relation to Hellenistic and Byzantine art as well. The most important of these monuments are the Dome of the Rock in Jerusalem, the earliest existing monumental Islamic sanctuary, the Great Mosque of Damascus, which served as a model for later mosques, and the desert palaces of Syria, Jordan and Palestine.

When the Abbasid caliphate (132/ 750-656/1258) succeeded the Umayyads, the political centre of Islam was moved from the Mediterranean to Baghdad in Mesopotamia. This factor would influence the development of Islamic civilisation and the entire range of culture, and art would bear the mark of that change. Abbasid art and architecture were influenced by three major traditions: Sassanian, Central Asian and Seljuq. Central Asian influence was already present in Sassanian architecture, but at Samarra this influence is represented by the stucco style with its arabesque ornamentation that would rapidly spread throughout the Islamic world. The influence of Abbasid monuments can be observed in the buildings constructed during this period in the other regions of the empire, particularly Egypt and Ifriqiya. In Cairo, the Mosque of Ibn Tulun (262/876-265/879) is a masterpiece, remarkable for its plan and unity of conception. It was modelled after the Abbasid Great Mosque of Samarra, particularly its spiral minaret. In Kairouan, the capital of Ifriqiya, vassals of the Abbasid caliphs, the Aghlabids (184/800-296/909) expanded the Great Mosque of Kairouan, one of the most venerable congregational mosques in the Maghrib. Its *mihrab* was covered by ceramic tiles from Mesopotamia.

Kairouan Mosque, mihrab, Tunisia.

Kairouan Mosque, minaret, Tunisia.

Islamic Art in the Mediterranean

Citadel of Aleppo, view of the entrance, Syria.

Complex of Qaluwun, Cairo, Egypt.

The reign of the Fatimids (297/909-567/1171) represents a remarkable period in the history of the Islamic countries of the Mediterranean: North Africa, Sicily, Egypt and Syria. Of their architectural constructions, a few examples remain that bear witness to their past glory. In the central Maghrib the Qal'a of the Bani Hammad and the Mosque of Mahdiya; in Sicily, the Cuba (*Qubba*) and the Zisa (*al-'Aziza*) in Palermo, constructed by Fatimid craftsmen under the Norman King William II; in Cairo, the Azhar Mosque is the most prominent example of Fatimid architecture in Egypt.

The Ayyubids (567/1171-648/1250), who overthrew the Fatimid Dynasty in Cairo, were important patrons of architecture. They established religious institutions *(madrasas, khanqas)* for the propagation of *Sunni* Islam, mausoleums and welfare projects, as well as awesome fortifications pertaining to the military conflict with the Crusaders. The Citadel of Aleppo in Syria is a remarkable example of their military architecture.

The Mamluks (648/1250-923/1517) successors of the Ayyubids, successfully resisted the Crusades and the Mongols, achieved the unity of Syria and Egypt and created a formidable empire. The wealth and luxury of the Mamluk Sultan's court in Cairo motivated artists and architects to achieve an extraordinarily elegant style of architecture. For the world of Islam, the Mamluk period marked a rebirth and renaissance. The enthusiasm for establishing religious foundations and reconstructing existing ones place the Mamluks among the greatest patrons of art and architecture in the history of Islam. The Mosque of Hassan (757/1356), a funerary mosque built with a cruciform plan in which the four arms of the cross were formed by four *iwans* of the building around a central courtyard, was typical of the era.

Anatolia was the birthplace of two great Islamic dynasties: the Seljuqs (571/1075-718/1318), who introduced Islam to the region; and the Ottomans (699/1299-1340/1922), who brought about the end of the Byzantine Empire upon capturing Constantinople, and asserted their hegemony throughout the region.

Selimiye Mosque, general view, Edirne, Turkey.

A distinctive style of Seljuq art and architecture flourished with influences from Central Asia, Iran, Mesopotamia and Syria, which merged with elements deriving from Anatolian Christian and antiquity heritage. Konya, the new capital in Central Anatolia, as well as other cities, were enriched with buildings in the newly developed Seljuq style. Numerous mosques, *madrasas, turbes* and *caravanserais,* which were richly decorated by stucco and tiling with diverse figural representations, have survived to our day.

Tile of Kubadabad Palace, Karatay Museum, Konya, Turkey.

As the Seljuq Emirates disintegrated and Byzantium declined, the Ottomans expanded their territory swiftly changing their capital from Iznik to Bursa and then again to Edirne. The conquest of Constantinople in 858/1453 by Sultan Mehmet II provided the necessary impetus for the transition of an emerging state into a great empire. A superpower that extended its boundaries to Vienna including the Balkans in the West and to Iran in the East, as well

Islamic Art in the Mediterranean

Great Mosque of Cordoba, mihrab, Spain.

Madinat al-Zahra', Dar al-Yund, Spain.

as North Africa from Egypt to Algeria, turning the Eastern Mediterranean into an Ottoman sea. The race to surpass the grandeur of the inherited Byzantine churches, exemplified by the Hagia Sophia, culminated in the construction of great mosques in Istanbul. The most significant one is the Mosque of Süleymaniye, built in the $10^{th}/16^{th}$ century by the famous Ottoman architect Sinan, it epitomises the climax in architectural harmony in domed buildings. Most major Ottoman mosques were part of a large building complex called *kulliye* that also consisted several *madrasa*s, a *Qur'an* school, a library, a hospital (*darussifa*), a hostel (*tabhane*), a public kitchen, a *caravanserai* and mausoleums (*turbe*s). From the beginning of the $12^{th}/18^{th}$ century, during the so-called Tulip Period, Ottoman architecture and decorative style reflected the influence of French Baroque and Rococo, heralding the Westernisation period in arts and architecture.

Al-Andalus at the western part of the Islamic world became the cradle of a brilliant artistic and cultural expression. 'Abd al-Rahman I established an independent Umayyad caliphate (138/750-422/1031) with Cordoba as its capital. The Great Mosque of Cordoba would pioneer innovative artistic tendencies such as the double-tiered arches with two alternating colours and panels with vegetal ornamentation which would become part of the repertoire of al-Andalus artistic forms.

In the $5^{th}/11^{th}$ century, the caliphate of Cordoba broke up into a score of principalities incapable of preventing the progressive advance of the reconquest initiated by the Christian states of the Northwestern Iberian Peninsula. These petty kings, or Taifa Kings, summoned the Almoravids in 479/1086 and the Almohads in 540/1145 in order to repel the Christians and re-established partial unity in al-Andalus. Through their intervention in the Iberian Peninsula, the Almoravids (427/1036-541/1147) came into contact with a new civilisations and were captivated quickly by the refinement of al-Andalus art as reflected in their capital, Marrakesh, where they built a grand mosque and palaces. The influence of the architecture of Cordoba and other capitals such as Seville would be felt in all of the Almoravid monuments from Tlemcen, Algiers to Fez.

Tinmal Mosque, aerial view, Morocco.

Under the rule of the Almohads (515/1121-667/1269), who expanded their hegemony as far as Tunisia, Western Islamic art reached its climax. During this period, artistic creativity that originated with the Almoravid rulers was renewed and masterpieces of Islamic art were created. The Great Mosque of Seville with its minaret the Giralda, the Kutubiya in Marrakesh, the Mosque of Hassan in Rabat and the Mosque of Tinmal high in the Atlas Mountains in Morocco are notable examples.

Ladies Tower and Gardens, Alhambra, Granada, Spain.

Upon the dissolution of the Almohad Empire, the Nasrid Dynasty (629/1232-897/1492) installed itself in Granada and was to experience a period of splendour in the $8^{th}/14^{th}$ century. The civilisation of Granada would become a cultural

Islamic Art in the Mediterranean

Mertola, general view, Portugal.

model in future centuries in Spain (Mudejar Art) and particularly in Morocco, where this artistic tradition enjoyed great popularity and would be preserved until the present day in the areas of architecture and decoration, music and cuisine. The famous palace and fort of *al-Hamra'* (the Alhambra) in Granada marks the crowning achievement of al-Andalus art, with all features of its artistic repertoire.

Decoration detail, Abu Inan Madrasa, Meknes, Morocco.

At the same time in Morocco, the Merinids (641/1243-876/1471) replaced the Almohads, while in Algeria the 'Abd al-Wadid's reigned (633/1235-922/1516), as did the Hafsids (625/1228-941/1534) in Tunisia. The Merinids perpetuated al-Andalus art, enriching it with new features. They embellished their capital Fez with an abundance of mosques, palaces and *madrasa*s, with their clay mosaic and *zellij* panelling in the wall decorations, considered

Qal'a of the Bani Hammad, minaret, Algeria.

Sa'adian Tomb Marrakesh, Morocco.

to be the most perfect works of Islamic art. The later Moroccan dynasties, the Sa'adians (933/1527-1070/1659) and the 'Alawite (1077/1659 – until the present day), carried on the artistic tradition of al-Andalus that was exiled from its native soil in 897/1492. They continued to build and decorate their monuments using the same formulas and the same decorative themes as had the preceding dynasties, adding innovative touches characteristic of their creative genius. In the early 11th/17th century, emigrants from al-Andalus (the *Moriscos*), who took up residence in the northern cities of Morocco, introduced numerous features of al-Andalus art. Today, Morocco is one of the few countries that has kept traditions of al-Andalus alive in its architecture and furniture, at the same time modernising them as they incorporated the architectural techniques and styles of the 15th/20th century.

ARCHITECTURAL SUMMARY

In general terms, Islamic architecture can be classified into two categories: religious, such as mosques, *madrasas*, mausoleums, and secular, such as palaces, *caravanserais*, fortifications, etc.

Religious Architecture

Mosques

The mosque for obvious reasons lies at the very heart of Islamic architecture. It is an apt symbol of the faith that it serves. That symbolic role was understood by Muslims at a very early stage, and played an important part in the creation of suitable visual markers for the building: minaret, dome, *mihrab*, *minbar*, etc.

The first mosque in Islam was the courtyard of the Prophet's house in Medina, with no architectural refinements. Early mosques built by the Muslims as their empire was expanding were simple. From these buildings developed the congregational or Friday mosque (*jami'*), essential features of which remain today unchanged for nearly 1400 years. The general plan consists of a large courtyard surrounded by arched porticoes, with more aisles or arcades on the side facing Mecca (*qibla*) than the other sides. The Great Umayyad Mosque in Damascus, which followed the plan of the Prophet's Mosque, became the prototype for many mosques built in various parts of the Islamic world.

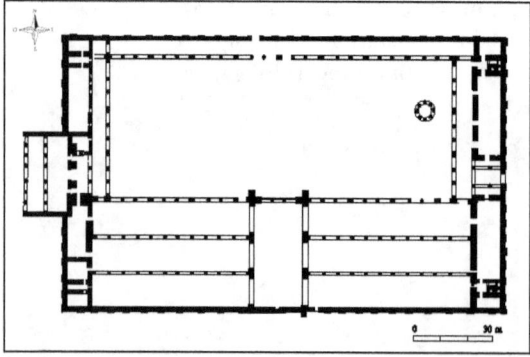

Umayyad Mosque of Damascus, Syria.

Two other types of mosques developed in Anatolia and afterwards in the Ottoman domains: the basilical and the dome types. The first type is a simple pillared hall or basilica that follows late Roman and Byzantine Syrian traditions, introduced with some modifications in the $5^{th}/11^{th}$ century. The second type, which developed during the Ottoman period, has its organisation of interior space under a single dome. The Ottoman architects in great imperial mosques created a new style of domed construction by merging the Islamic mosque tradition with that of dome building in Anatolia. The main dome rests on a hexagonal support system, while lateral bays are covered by smaller domes. This emphasis on an interior space dominated by a single dome became the starting point of a style that was to be introduced in the 10th/16th century. During this period, mosques became multipurpose social complexes consisting of a *zawiya*, a *madrasa*, a public kitchen, a bath, a *caravanserai* and a mausoleum of the founder. The supreme monument of this style is the Sülaymeniye Mosque in Istanbul built in 965/1557 by the great architect Sinan.

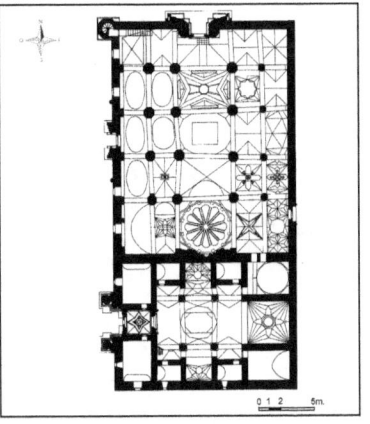

Great Mosque, Divriği, Turkey.

The minaret from the top of which the *muezzin* calls Muslims to prayer, is the most prominent marker of the mosque. In Syria the traditional minaret consists of a square-plan tower built of stone. In Mamluk Egypt minarets are each divided into three distinct zones: a square section at the bottom, an octagonal middle section and a circular section with a small dome on the top. Its shaft is richly decorated and the transition between each section is covered with a band of *muqarnas* decoration. Minarets in North Africa and Spain, that share the square-tower form with Syria, are decorated with panels of motifs around paired sets of windows. During the Ottoman period the octagonal or cylindrical minarets replaced the square tower. Often these are tall pointed minarets and although mosques generally have only one minaret, in major cities there are two, four or even six minarets.

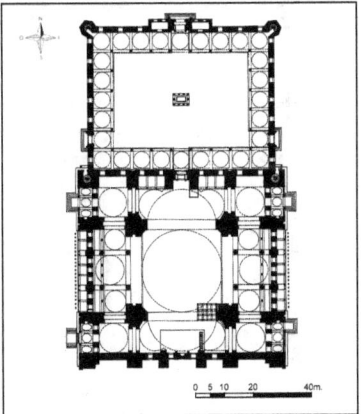

Sülaymeniye Mosque, Istanbul, Turkey.

Typology of minarets.

Madrasas

It seems likely that the Seljuqs built the first *madrasas* in Persia in the early $5^{th}/11^{th}$ century when they were small structures with a domed courtyard and two lateral *iwans*. A later type developed that has an open courtyard with a central *iwan* and which is surrounded by arcades. During the $6^{th}/12^{th}$ century in Anatolia, the *madrasa* became multifunctional and was intended to serve as a medical school, mental hospital, a hospice with a public kitchen (*imaret*) and a mausoleum. The promotion of *Sunni* (Orthodox) Islam reached a new zenith in Syria and Egypt under the Zengids and the Ayyubids ($6^{th}/12^{th}$–early $7^{th}/13^{th}$ centuries). This era witnessed the introduction of the *madrasa* established by a civic or political leader for the advancement of Islamic jurisprudence. The foundation was funded by an endowment in perpetuity (*waqf*), usually the revenues of land or property in the form of an orchard, shops in a market (*suq*), or a bathhouse (*hammam*). The *madrasa* traditionally followed a cruciform plan with a central court surrounded by four *iwans*. Soon the *madrasa* became a dominant architectural form with mosques adopting a four-*iwan* plan. The *madrasa* gradually lost its sole religious and political function as a propaganda tool and tended to have a broader civic function, serving as a congregational mosque and a mausoleum for the benefactor.

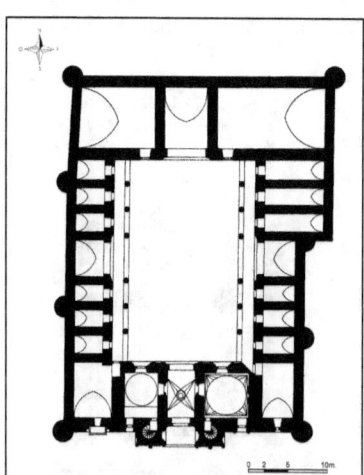

Sivas Gök Madrasa, Turkey.

The construction of *madrasa*s in Egypt, and particularly in Cairo, gathered new momentum with the arrival of the Mamluks. The typical

Cairene *madrasa* of this era was a multifunctional gigantic four-*iwan* structure with a stalactite (*muqarnas*) portal and splendid façades. With the advent of the Ottomans in the 10th/16th century, the joint foundation, typically a mosque-*madrasa*, became a widespread, large complex that enjoyed imperial patronage. The *iwan* disappeared gradually and was replaced by a dominant dome chamber. A substantial increase in the number of domed cells used by students is a characteristic of Ottoman *madrasa*s.

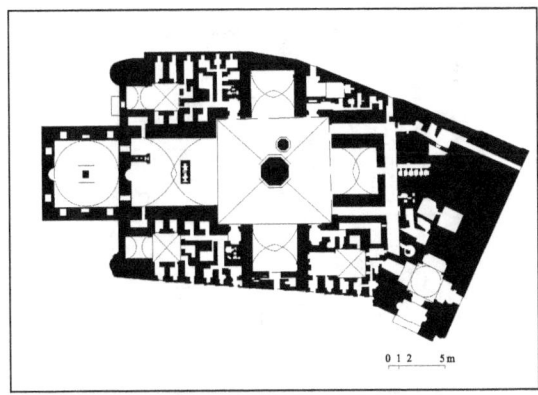

Mosque and Madrasa Sultan Hassan, Cairo, Egypt.

One of the various building types that by virtue of their function and of their form can be related to the *madrasa* is the *khanqa*. The term indicates an institution, rather than a particular kind of building, that houses members of a Muslim mystical (*sufi*) order. Several other words used by Muslim historians as synonyms for *khanqa* include: in the Maghrib, *zawiya*; in Ottoman domain, *tekke*; and in general, *ribat*. Sufism permanently dominated the *khanqa*, which originated in eastern Persia during the 4th/10th century. In its simplest form the *khanqa* was a house where a group of pupils gathered around a master (*shaykh*), and it had the facilities for assembly, prayer and communal living. The establishment of *khanqas* flourished under the Seljuqs during the 5th/11th and the 6th/12th centuries and benefited from the close association between Sufism and the *Shafi'i madhhab* (doctrine) favoured by the ruling elite.

Mausoleums

The terminology of the building type of the mausoleum used in Islamic sources is varied. The standard descriptive term *turbe* refers to the function of the building as for burial. Another term is *qubba* that refers to the most identifiable, the dome, and often marks a structure commemorating Biblical prophets, companions of the Prophet Muhammad and religious or military notables. The function of mausoleums is not limited simply to a place of burial

*Qasr al-Khayr
al-Sharqi, Syria.*

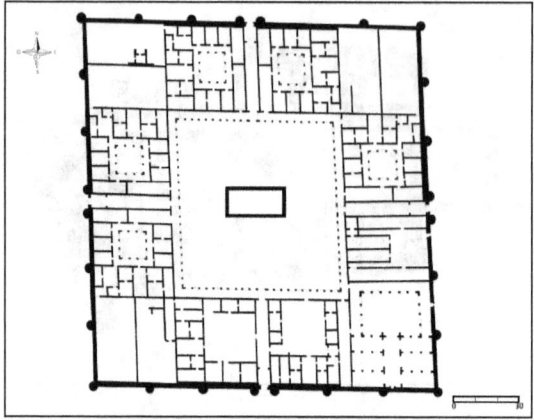

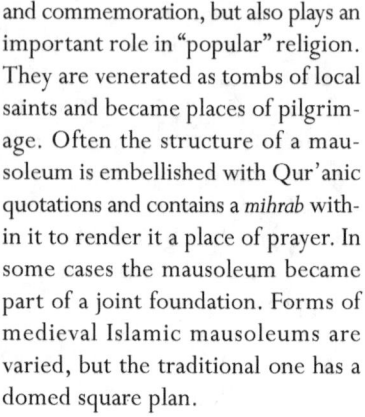

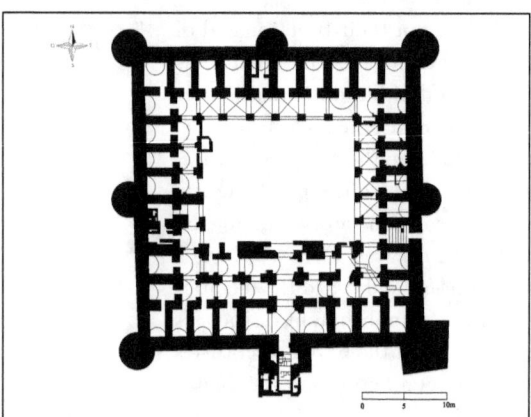

*Ribat of Sousse,
Tunisia.*

and commemoration, but also plays an important role in "popular" religion. They are venerated as tombs of local saints and became places of pilgrimage. Often the structure of a mausoleum is embellished with Qur'anic quotations and contains a *mihrab* within it to render it a place of prayer. In some cases the mausoleum became part of a joint foundation. Forms of medieval Islamic mausoleums are varied, but the traditional one has a domed square plan.

Secular Architecture

Palaces

The Umayyad period is characterised by sumptuous palaces and bathhouses in remote desert regions. Their basic plan is largely derived from Roman military models. Although the decoration of these structures is eclectic, they constitute the best examples of the budding Islamic decorative style. Mosaics, mural paintings, stone or stucco sculpture were used for a remarkable variety of decorations and themes. Abbasid palaces in Iraq, such as those at Samarra and Ukhaidir, follow the same plan as their Umayyad forerunners, but are marked by an increase in size, the use of the great *iwan*, dome and courtyard, and the extensive use of stucco decorations. Palaces in the later Islamic period developed a distinctive style that was more decorative and less monumental. The most remarkable example of royal or princely palaces is the Alhambra. The vast area of the palace is broken up into a series of separate units: gardens, pavilions and courts. The most striking feature of Alhambra, however, is the decoration that provides an extraordinary effect in the interior of the building.

Caravanserais

A *caravanserai* generally refers to a large structure that provides a lodging place for travellers and merchants. Normally, it has a square or rectangular floor plan, with a single projecting monumental entrance and towers in the exterior walls. A central courtyard is surrounded by porticoes and rooms for lodging travellers, storing merchandise and for the stabling of animals.

The characteristic type of building has a wide range of functions since it has been described as *khan*, *han*, *funduq*, *ribat*. These terms may imply no more than differences in regional vocabularies rather than being distinctive functions or types. The architectural sources of the various types of *caravanserais* are difficult to identify. Some are perhaps derived from the Roman *castrum* or military camp to which the Umayyad desert palaces are related. Other types, in Mesopotamia and Persia, are associated with domestic architecture.

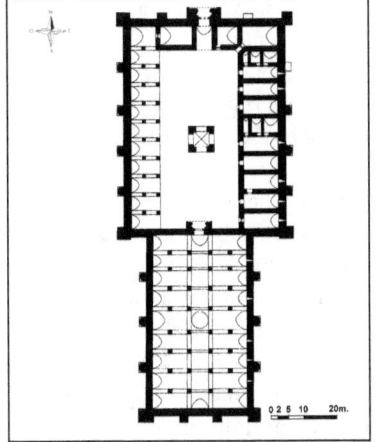

Aksaray Sultan Khan, Turkey.

Urban Organisation

From about the 3rd/10th century every town of any significance acquired fortified walls and towers, elaborate gates and a mighty citadel (*qal'a* or *qasba*) as the seat of power. These are massive constructions built in materials characteristic of the region in which they are found; stone in Syria, Palestine and Egypt, or brick, stone and rammed earth in the Iberian Peninsula and North Africa. A unique example of military architecture is the *ribat*. Technically, this is a fortified palace designated for the temporary or permanent warriors of Islam who committed themselves to the defence of frontiers. The *ribat* of Sousse in

Tunisia bears a resemblance to early Islamic palaces, but with a different interior arrangement of large halls, mosque and a minaret.

The division of the majority of Islamic cities into neighbourhoods is based on ethnic and religious affinity and it is also a system of urban organisation that facilitates the administration of the population. In the neighbourhood there is always a mosque. A bathhouse, a fountain, an oven and a group of stores are located either within or nearby. Its structure is formed by a network of streets, alleys and a collection of houses. Depending on the region and era, the home takes on diverse features governed by the historical and cultural traditions, climate and construction materials available.

The market (*suq*), which functions as the nerve-centre for local businesses, would be the most relevant characteristic of Islamic cities. Its distance from the mosque determines the spatial organisation of the markets by specialised guilds. For instance, the professions considered clean and honourable (bookmakers, perfume makers, tailors) are located in the mosque's immediate environs, and the noisy and foul-smelling crafts (blacksmiths, tanning, cloth dying) are situated progressively further from it. This geographic distribution responds to imperatives that rank on strictly technical grounds.

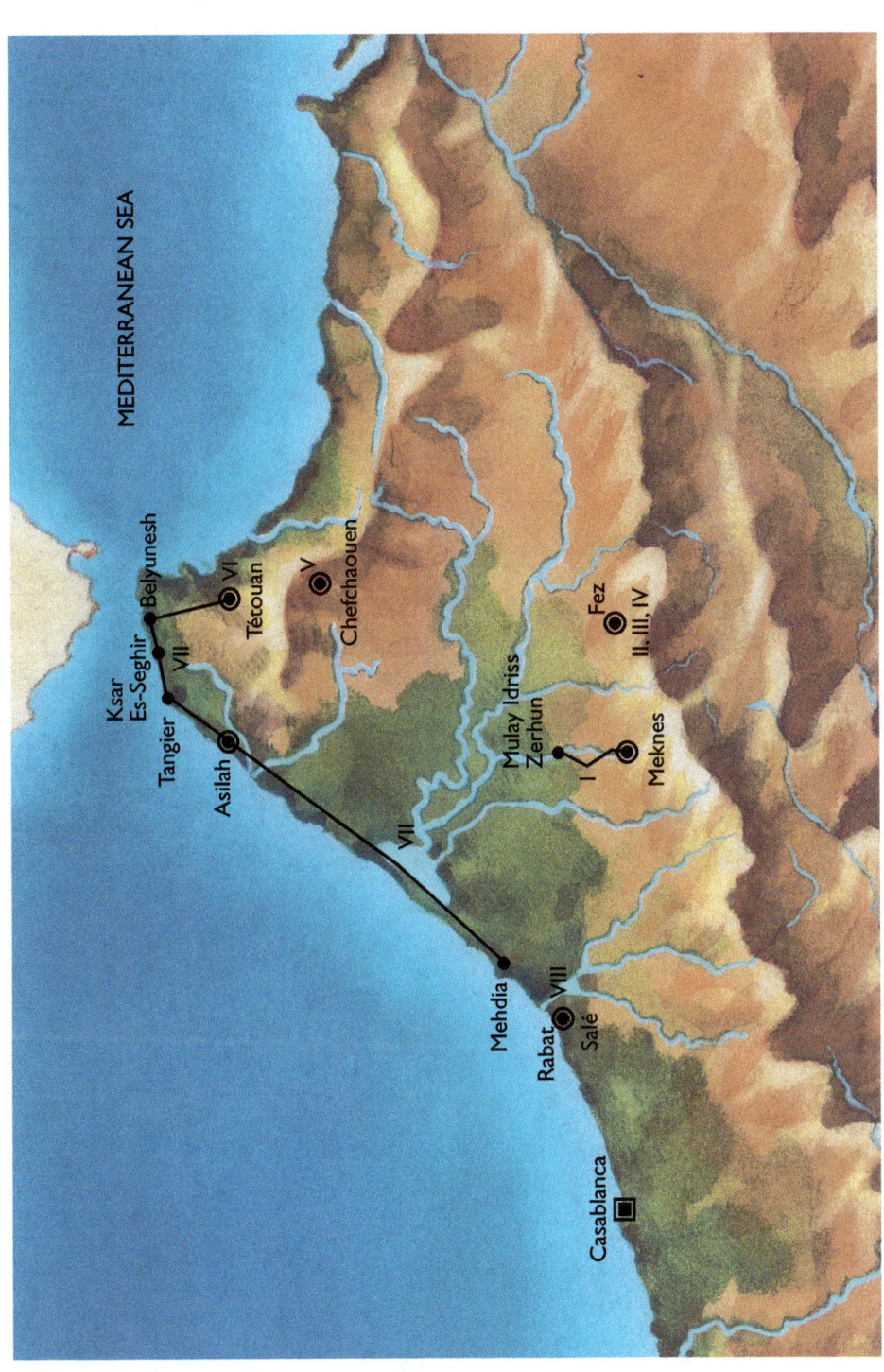

The Strait of Gibraltar seen from Belyunesh.

HISTORICAL INTRODUCTION

Abdelaziz Touri

The Grand saga of Andalusian Morocco is entwined with the epic of western Islam. The establishment of Islam, in North Africa generally, and in Morocco especially, over official or local cults such as Christianity and to an extent Judaism, was neither easy nor quick. The conquests of Egypt and of Spain, for example, hardly lasted more than three months each; that of Iraq took four years and that of Syria six, but the armies of Islam needed over half a century of more or less continuous fighting (26/647–91/710) before they could install themselves definitively in the Maghreb.

The Islamisation of Morocco took a firm step with Musa Ibn Nusayr who, at the beginning of the $2^{nd}/8^{th}$ century, succeeded in converting the inhabitants and integrating them into the army of Allah. In fact, it was with these rough and belligerent conscripts that he established the Muslim conquest of Spain. This political move allowed him to find a favourable outlet for Islam, for, unable to disarm the Berbers, he made them the spearhead of his propagation. Thus the Arab messenger and the Berber neophyte became engaged in an irreversible process which, in this intense far-off region, the Maghreb, gave birth to one of the most brilliant homes of Islamic civilisation, a home which for more than seven centuries, would remain an Hispano-Maghrebic focal point.

As soon as Moroccan Islam took root in its renewed form, it immediately looked over to its neighbouring Iberian peninsula, and resolved to spread itself there. It is now the year 92/711, and Tariq Ibn Ziyad, the recently converted, famous and enigmatic Berber, who is also a general under the orders of Musa Ibn Nusayr, drives the Muslim armies of the West to initiate the conquest of that which would become al-Andalus. Some 40 years later, as the Umayyad caliphate draws its last breath in the East, we see his revival in Spain brought about with the help of the Berbers. From then on, the destinies of the two riverbanks of the strait become entwined, and we witness a period of incessant exchange and interpenetration across the centuries over which the Islam of al-Andalus survives. Between 91/710 and 122/740, Islam advances at a spectacular rate. However, it is the Islam of the Berbers, an Islam which will manifest itself in an increasingly autonomous manner towards the authority of the Damascus Caliphate.

Consequently, for reasons which seem to be based primarily on the exploitative politics of heavy and unpopular taxation, a revolt arose in 122/740 on the plains of the Atlantic side. Known as the Kharijite Revolt, its name derives from its rigid religious parent doctrine which appeared in the East, in 37/658, at the time of the first Grand crisis of the Caliphate. This movement gathered importance before rapidly dividing into several factions, thus scattering itself across other parts of the Empire in order to attain the Maghreb.

In Morocco, a Kharijite principality set itself up in the Tafilalet, in the south-east of the country, and founded Sijilmassa, a caravan-type town of Grand importance, where Saharan commerce retained an active role until the $6^{th}/12^{th}$ century.

The Kharijite revolt which began in Morocco quickly spread across the rest of the Maghreb, thus enabling it to become independent from Eastern guardianship; for, despite the restructuring of the Caliphate undertaken by the Abbassids since the middle of the $2^{nd}/8^{th}$ century, the Muslim East had become sovereign under the iron rule of three dynasties: the Umayyads in Spain, the Idrissids in Morocco, and the Rustemids in Algeria. However, by the end of the 2nd/beginning

Historical Introduction

Mulay Idriss Zerhun, panoramic view.

of 9th century, the image of Morocco is one of a country divided into several different entities. Apart from Sijilmassa, there is the principality of the Nakkur in the Rif, and of the Berghuatas in the Atlantic plains and plateaus, as well as utterly independent tribes and confederations of tribes living in the rest of the country.

It was under these divisive circumstances that the first great Muslim dynasty of Morocco, the Idrissids, was founded in Volubilis. This dynasty brought about, for the first time in history, the unification of the country, and founded the town of Fez. It should be remembered that the accession of the Idrissids is rooted in the crisis which occurred in the Eastern Caliphate. The crisis, brought upon by the supporters of 'Ali, had polarised Muslims into two camps: those who were partisans of 'Ali, the son-in-law of the Prophet, and those who supported his rival, Mu'awiya. Mu'awiya went on to establish the Umayyad dynasty in Damascus before it was supplanted by the Abbassid dynasty in around 132/750.

In 169/786, Idriss Ibn 'Abd Allah escaped Abbassid repression and took refuge in Morocco. He installed himself in Walili, ancient Volubilis, in 171/788, at the centre of a region independent from both the influence of the Kharijites of Sijilmassa, and from that of the Berghuatas from Tamesna. Strengthened by the prestige of his Sherifian origins, as being a descendant of the Prophet, he was very well received by the native Berbers who pledged their allegiance to him and viewed him as *Imam*. He founded the Idrissid dynasty and took the title of Idriss I.

The reign of Idriss I lasted no more than three years (171/788–174/791). However, with a speed which could be viewed as disconcerting, he had managed to establish his authority, see through peace campaigns and rally numerous tribes around him. This led to the creation of a centralised state which, having gained such a swift and mighty reputation, worried the Caliph of Baghdad, so much so that he had the monarch assassinated.

The success of the Idrissids attracted many people to the city of Walili, the kingdom's first capital, which resulted rapidly in it becoming cramped through over population. So, in 172/789, Idriss founded a new capital on the right riverbank of the Fez *wadi*, where in fact the Andalusian neighbourhood was situated: *madinat Fas*, the city of Fez.

Founded as the seat of government, the city established by Idriss had the promise of fulfilling a remarkable destiny. Situated on a crossroads, surrounded by fertile plains, it benefited sufficiently from the arrival of successive Andalusian and Ifriqiyan immigrants to become a great economic, spiritual and religious metropolis. These achievements could be viewed as the inaugural force behind the cyclical dynastic creation of great cities, since, at the instigation of the Idrissids, every Moroccan dynasty went on to found a capital or city: for the Almoravids it was Marrakesh, for the Almohads it was Rabat, for the Merinids it was *Fas Jdid*, otherwise known as Fez Newtown, and for the 'Alawites it was Meknès.

In 193/809, *madinat Fas* would witness the birth of a new city on the left bank of the same Fez *wadi*, known today as the river banks of Kairouans. This split, wished for by Idriss II, the son and successor of the founder of the dynasty, led to rivalry between the two sides of the riverbank. All in all the presence of this rivalry was beneficial, since the "double city" only became larger and more radiant as a result.

On the political front, the first two monarchs were able to undertake a dynamic plan of action and put into place the foundations of a truly state-like organisation. Inspired by eastern models of government, Idriss II (192/808–212/828) in particular, furnished his kingdom with an administration, an army, a new capital and a currency. However, within his 20-year reign, he was still refused the glory of holding authority over the whole of Morocco. His kingdom ended, *grosso modo*, at the borders of ancient Mauretania Tingitania. Nevertheless, he succeeded in bringing numerous Berber tribes under his jurisdiction which until then had remained independent from each other. The mystery surrounding Idriss II's death revealed the fragility of the structures which had been put into place. His son and successor, Mohamed Ibn Idriss (212/828–221/836) committed a fatal mistake: he shared out his father's possessions between his brothers. Thus began a long period of rivalry between them, bringing about power struggles and continuous instability. The fragility of power and weakness of the princes encouraged foreign intervention. Fez is first taken by the Fatimids of Ifriqiya, then by the Umayyads of al-Andalus. The Idrissids oscillate between the two in order to take permanent refuge in the north of the country where they remain entrenched until the arrival of the Almoravids.

The arrival of the latter onto the platform of power, in the $5^{th}/11^{th}$ century, marks an important stage in the history of Morocco and of the whole of North Africa. The Almoravids, natives of *Ribat*, are nomadic Berbers who traversed the great desert, from the oasis in the Moroccan south right across to the "Land of the Blacks", *Bilad al-Sudan*. Their wealth lay in their complete control of caravan trafficking, and from the importance of their herds, as well as from the loot gained through war and raids. Rough warriors, hardly inclined towards discipline, as such, they nevertheless offered a

Panoramic view of the Medina of Fez seen from the roof top of the Qarawiyin Mosque, Fez.

favourable land to whoever could tame and organise them. 'Abd Allah Ibn Yassin did just that. A visionary renowned for his piety, erudition and rigour, he was summoned by the nomadic chieftains to teach Arabic and the principles of Islam to their tribes. With this rare talent for providing unity, he rapidly succeeded in raising an army of "monk-soldiers", and launched Holy Wars against the animistic sub-Saharan tribes.

Hardened and well-organised, the Almoravids turned their gaze onto the northern regions and took Sijilmassa in 445/1053–1054. Thus began one of the most glorious ventures which, in the name of Islam and religious rigour, brought about the first great Berber-Islamic empire in the West.

In capturing Sijilmassa, the Almoravids secured their complete control over the two main routes of sub-Saharan commerce: the western route, which they controlled already, and that which had been recently seized, opening out onto Sijilmassa.

The feeble resistance which they encountered at the beginning encouraged their rulers to undertake a comprehensive conquest of Morocco.

Under the leadership of Yusuf Ibn Tashfin (453/1061–500/1107), they took out one by one the main towns and regions of the time, and pushed their assault as far as the central Maghreb. About 464/1072–466/1074, they had rooted themselves firmly in Morocco and the western half of Algeria.

In 466/1074, when the cavalcade which had allowed him to establish his authority over most of the Maghreb had come to an end, Yusuf Ibn Tashfin received a cry for help from the Kings of *Taifas*. These Spanish Muslim princes, inheritors of the Caliphate of Cordoba, were in real danger of being exterminated by Castillian troops.

Alphonse VI of Castille had in fact mobilised his troops in a first advance of Reconquest and had gained entry to Toledo in 477/1085. This move proved to be decisive in the Almoravids choice to remain on the other side of the Gibraltar strait.

The clash with the Christians took place at Zallaqa, near Badajoz, in 478/1086. The Muslim troops were victorious. Yusuf gained much prestige, enabling him to enter al-Andalus and to conquer, systematically one after the other, the Andalusian principalities which had been undermined by the division and debauchery of their princes.

Masters of both the Maghreb and al-Andalus, the Almoravids oversaw for the first time in history the unification of the greatest area covered by Western Islam. By taking over al-Andalus, these ferocious desert warriors would, in addition, certainly come into contact with a brilliant and refined civilisation. Their capital, Marrakesh, built in about 461/1069 from nothing in order to serve as a base camp for their Moroccan expeditions, became home to the most reputable wise men, the most talented poets and the most highly regarded artists. The strength of the monarchs, coupled with the stability of power and wealth of the Empire, gave birth to a flourishing art scene, from which the most beautiful results would come to see the light of day as creations fashioned from Maghrebin earth.

Around the middle of the $6^{th}/12^{th}$ century, the power of the Almoravids is replaced by that of the Almohads. According to some, the advent of the latter marked "the peak of Moroccan domination" in both the Maghreb and al-Andalus as well as the Islamic West's complete independence from its Eastern tutelage.

Mosque of Tinmel.

In truth, whilst being politically free from all foreign powers, Almoravid Morocco was nonetheless spiritually tied to the power of the Baghdad caliphate. In only taking the honorary title of *Amir al-Muslimin*, Prince of the Muslims, the Almoravid monarchs acknowledged the religious and spiritual supremacy of the Eastern Caliph: only he could possess the glorious title of *Amir al-Mu'minin*, Commander of the Believers. However, this tie was broken by the first monarch of the Almohad dynasty, 'Abd al-Mumen Ibn 'Ali, inaugurating the era of the Maghrebin Caliphate. As soon as he had come to power, having undertaken a series of military campaigns which had brought him beyond the frontiers of Morocco to Spain and the Maghreb, he took the title of Caliph. As with previous dynasties, his successors followed his lead by continuing to take the title. The power of the Almohads, born in the combative thrust for an ideal and a spiritual mission, secured itself straight away due to the personalities of the first three sovereigns: 'Abd al-Mumen (524/1130–558/1163), Abu Yusuf Ya'qub (558/1163–579/1184) and Ya'qub al-Mansur (579/1184–595/1199). Considering themselves responsible for a reformative mission which put claim to the uniqueness of Allah or *tawhid*, these monarchs were all warriors. 'Abd al-Mumen needed to fight for seven years to take control of Morocco and Algeria before venturing into Tunisia in 546/1152. Muslim Spain came under his power, from then on ensuring that his successors need never again surrender in the face of Christian attack. The victory of Alarcos, in 591/1195, marked the culmination of Almohad efforts towards the triumph of Islam. But as well as fighting a Holy War in Spain, the Almohads were required to be fighters of a Holy War in Ifriqiya, which had fallen under Norman influence. In recapturing Tunisia from the Normans and extending their power up to Tripoli, they succeeded for the first time in unifying the entire Muslim West in the name of a single united empire, the centre of which was Morocco and the Atlas mountains.

Historical Introduction

The esplanade of the Hassan Mosque and Tower, Rabat.

A theologian and philosopher, Mohamed Ibn Tumert, whose religious zeal soon secured him a name, stood at the core of this empire. Extremely cultivated, a good public speaker and an astute polemist, he had made himself noticed at every debate and impassioned discussion he undertook in his confrontations with Almoravid lawyers.

But his preference lay in taking his campaign for reformation to the streets, a reformation based on the censure of standards, moral improvements, and the strict lobbying against the growing anthropomorphism which attributed human qualities to God. Ibn Tumert thought of the Almoravids as victims of the syndrome of civilisation – a dependence on material wealth and well-being – which had turned them into "anthropomorphists". They therefore needed to be fought down and replaced by a power who would know to return, in all its actions, to the sources of Islam: the *Qur'an* and the Traditions of the Prophet. In order for this to be done, Ibn Tumert, the "Impeccable *Imam*", had started a Spartan-styled socio-military organisation in Tinmel, at the heart of the Atlas mountains, about a 100 km. away from Marrakesh where he must have taken refuge around 519/1125. There, the first, small community of Almohads grew rapidly, and the origins of its members, like those of her future leaders, were modelled closely on her masters' principles. On his death, in 524/1130, his closest and most faithful disciple, 'Abd al-Mumen, became leader and, with a true talent for tireless and realistic conquering, he fulfilled his master's dream. With the exception of the Balearic Islands, the whole of the Western Muslim hemisphere would come to fully obey the Almohads; and it would be because of this that their era could perhaps be considered to be the true Golden Age of the Maghreb. It would be natural for such a creation of unity, peace and power to favour the birth of a civilisation regarded as magnificent by several authors, even more so because of the harsh reformers who, from the start, knew how to maintain a certain amount of freedom necessary for such a development.

What factors truly contributed to such a development? The first factor was economic wealth. The commercial networks of the time were all under Moroccan control. African riches, gold and slaves, would arrive in Marrakesh, Sijilmassa, Fez or Ceuta before travelling north, towards al-Andalus and Europe, or East. Maritime routes ran all along the lengths of the empire's coast. The $6^{th}/12^{th}$ and $7^{th}/13^{th}$ centuries, which characterise the renewal of economic, and particularly commercial strength in Europe, were dominated by the force of the Almohad empire. The golden dinar, like the Almoravid dinar before it, known as the *morabotin*, was the most wanted currency on European and Mediterranean markets. A second factor was the cultural and artistic patronage offered by the sovereigns themselves and by the notables of the empire. Both intellectuals and artists were encouraged and protected. The Almohad period thus oversaw the rise of great thinkers, philosophers and doctors such as Ibn Tofail, Ibn Roshd, Averroës and Ibn Maimun, otherwise known as Maimonides, as well as reputed geographers like al-Idrissi, etc.

The architectural and urban development projects of the Almohad dynasty were both grandiose and varied, to the inclusion of even penetrating the earth; the most constructive example being the fortress of Tinmel.

This most brilliant civilisation came into decline rapidly. Within 50 years, the empire dissolved into several dynasties. In Morocco itself, the Almohad capital, Marrakesh, is vested with new forces from the Algerian-Moroccan borders in 667/1269, powers which would usher in a new dynasty: that of the Merinids.

Breeders of goats and sheep, the Merinids moved nomadically between the oasis of Figuig in the south-east of Morocco and the plains of Muluya. Its was as nomads in search for new pastures that, in around 610/1214, they began to move further afield, finding themselves as far as the Rif, the Sais, the region of Fez and Meknès, and Taza. These forays, undertaken for reasons of economic necessity and subsistence, had at first nothing to do with political ambition. But a combination of

Chellah, the funeral steles of the Merinid Sultan Abu al-Hassan and his wife, Rabat.

circumstances would bring these desires to the fore.

First of all came the weakness of the Almohad sovereigns who, after Ya'qub al-Mansur and his son al-Nassir (595/1199–609/1213) were manipulated, manoeuvred or just simply deposed by rival factions and tribes. Then came the dissolution of the Empire. In Tunis, the Hafsids reclaim their independence in 626/1229. They are followed by the Bani 'Abd al-Wad who founded their dynasty at Tlemcen. In al-Andalus, the Almohad defeat before the Christian armies at *Las Navas de Tolosa* in 608/1212 destroyed all hope and even brought about the assassination of the Almohad Caliph (609/1213). Finally, the famine and the plague, which hit the country at the same time, succeeded in ruining the remaining forces of the empire.

The Merinid era can be divided into two periods. The first, from 656/1258 (the accession of Abu Yusuf Ya'qub) until 759/1358 (the death of Abu Inan) can be considered as the time of construction and zenith. The second, which starts on the day following the death of Abu Inan and ends a century later, is that of decline, difficulty and dissolution.

During that first century (656/1258–759/1358), the Merinid dynasty succeeds in bringing back to Morocco some of its past glory. The kingdom experiences an important expansion "from the oceanic sea up to Barça". With energetic sovereigns and clairvoyants like Abu Sa'id 'Uthman (709/1310–731/1331), Abu al-Hassan (731/1331–752/1351) and Abu Inan (752/1351–759/1358), it rediscovers relative stability and prosperity which enables important developments to happen.

In intellectual terms, the Merinid era is the era of the *madrasa*s. These religious colleges, where civil servants were formed as men of religious science, flowered more or less everywhere. Morocco remains to this day the country which has kept the largest number of these monuments to be admired in Fez, Meknès or Salé.

The Merinid era is also one in which thought, and cultural and artistic creation, experienced favourable moments. In order to grasp the importance of these endeavours at the time, it is sufficient to know that this is the period of the notable historian Ibn Khaldun, or even that of the great explorer Ibn Battuta.

However, the expansion and well-being which characterised the first century of the Merinid era would become mere souvenirs during the run of the dynasty's second century. A weak centre of power, economic difficulties, and foreign dangers would come to underscore this latter period.

As it happened, internal disputes amongst heads of the court, which always ended in

Buinaniya Madrasa, interior courtyard, Meknès.

Historical Introduction

the deposition of the sovereign, rapidly paralysed all structures of the State. The empire was even broken into pieces, and two kingdoms, independent of Fez, emerged: the kingdom of Marrakesh and that of Tafilalet around Sijilmassa.

Denied trans-Saharan commerce, and fought against at sea by the European powers, the central government found itself empty of resources. The conquering spirit of Europe in the aftermath of the Renaissance was at its doors. Europe lost no time in setting foot in Morocco through the Portuguese debarkation at Ceuta in 817/1415, signifying the end of the Merinids and opening the country up to Christian conquest. From 817/1415 until 947/1541, the Portuguese and the Spanish made their presence known in several towns and strategic points along the coast. Consequently, towns were taken over, such as Ksar Es-Seghir in 862/1458, Anfa in 873/1468–1469, Asilah and Tangier in 875/1471, Melilla in 902/1497 by the Spanish, and so on. The reactive defence put up by Abu Zakariya, the Great Wattassid *vizier*, which succeeded in halting the Portuguese at the Straits, and in defending Tangier in 840/1437, was but a mere spark which was rapidly extinguished. The accession of the Wattassid dynasty, established by the grand Merinid *viziers*, hardly brought about the much hoped for trigger.

However, in the face of Christian attacks and government failure, a popular and religious Moroccan offensive mobilised and organised itself, while being supported by brotherhoods who take the helm of the resistance, a resistance which soon grows into a movement to reclaim power. Thus begins the era of the *zawiya*s. Extolling Holy War, the *jihad*, the movement engendered first and foremost the emergence of a Sherifian power which habitually exploited the strength of the marabouts to reclaim, in the first instance, all those places which had fallen into the hands of the Christians, and to reestablish order inland. This new engendered power was that of the Sa'adians, *shorfa*s from the Draa.

Portuguese bastion, Asilah.

Originating from this south-east region of Morocco, in between Zagora and Tamgrut, they installed themselves in a small village around Tarudant, in about the middle of the 9th/15th century. There, they quickly gained importance thanks to their *shorfa* status and to the renowned leader of the Shadiliya brotherhood next to whom they had settled, who had many followers in the Sous region.

Sa'adian activity began in 916/1511, with a first attack against Agadir. Regardless of the fact that this was not a success, it was perceived as a point of departure for a new era and a new force. In fact, during the following 43 years, the Sa'adian dynasty left a firm mark in national terms by taking Marrakesh from

Historical Introduction

the Wattassids in 931/1525, before claiming Fez in 961/1554.

Meanwhile, several places are won back from the Portuguese: Agadir (947/1541), Safi, and Azemmur. After 957/1550, the only remaining Portuguese were to be found in Ceuta, Tangier and Mazagan, the old town of al-Jadida.

The year 985/1578 marks the turning point of the century. That year, on Moroccan soil, there took place what is known as the Battle of the Three Kings, the consequences of which extended themselves far beyond the proper framework of Moroccan history and are of interest in respect to the whole of the Mediterranean basin. However, Morocco was to benefit from it significantly in terms of material gain and international prestige.

The battle took place at Wadi al-Makhazin, in the Larache region, on the 30th *Jumada I* 985/4th August 1578. It ended in the crushing victory of the Sa'adian armies, led by 'Abd al-Malik and his brother Ahmed, the future al-Mansur, over the Portuguese armies of King Dom Sebastião (1557–1578). Three kings were to meet their deaths: 'Abd al-Malik, Dom Sebastião, and Mohamed al-Muttawakil, nephew of 'Abd al-Malik and ally of the Portuguese.

Portugal lost her king and her independence for she was immediately annexed to the Spanish Crown. In Morocco, Ahmed, brother of and lieutenant to 'Abd al-Malik, became Sultan and took the title of *al-Mansur*, "The Victorious". *"The European Powers are full of respect for the new monarch whom one supposes is particularly wealthy following the acquisition of loot from the war".*

In the Mediterranean, this victory put a stop to the Ottoman desire to occupy Morocco. Al-Mansur could therefore turn his attention towards the control of his gold and his slaves in sub-Saharan Africa, and towards thwarting European supremacy at sea. In 998/1590, the Moroccan armies are at Timbuktu and Gao. Al-Mansur also becomes *al-Dhahbi*, "The Golden One". The caravans, commerce, for a long time derailed towards the East, turns back to retrace the trail of Moroccan towns.

In Europe, Morocco allied itself to Philip II's Spain whilst skilfully playing off Anglo-Spanish opposition. Strong through acquisition, al-Mansur is a monarch fulfilled with satisfaction. His court shines with brilliance. He surrounds himself with poets and wise men, and loves books. The luxury and ceremonial dress in which he is clothed strikes observers and foreign visitors alike.

This rediscovered glory encourages the monarchs to look inland towards the creation of works of art, to inscribe in stone the marks of their sovereignty and souvenirs of their power. They do this more or less everywhere where works are being constructed; but it is most of all in Marrakesh where embellishments of this sort are actively worked upon.

Town and Port of Tangier, engraving, Rabat General Library.

However, the death of al-Mansur (1011/1603) highlights the end of the dynasty's prime as well as the end of a political stability which this monarch so skilfully knew how to preserve. Explosive quarrels between his successors were not far off, dragging Morocco into a period of anarchy which lasted nearly 60 years.

The weak nature of al-Mansur's sons was the main cause for the incompetence of government; but economic problems aggravated the situation. Everything that upheld the Sa'adian economy (sugar, gold, caravans) crumbled within five months in the face of increasing competition from Europe. Whilst Morocco only managed to receive one caravan every three years, each Spanish galleon unloaded up to four tons in Cadiz on arrival from America. Elsewhere, although undermined by the Thirty Years War, Europe remained a menacing threat, with its sights fixed on reoccupying the territories it had lost on Moroccan soil. All this accounts for how Spain came to occupy Larache (1018/1610), Mehdia and the Ma'mora (1023/1614), and how Portugal reclaimed its hold over Tangier and Mazagan (1049/1640).

Meanwhile, the religious brotherhoods, who for a time had been distanced from all aspects of political life, re-emerged and sought to extend their influence. Soon they had devious claimants by their sides who exploited the ideal of a Holy War against the Christian occupying forces in order to come to power.

This provided a backdrop onto which a new Moroccan phenomenon would sew itself: the phenomenon of privateering. The initial causes of this phenomenon can be found in the waves of expulsion affecting Spanish Muslims. Expulsion edicts were imposed on the Muslims of Castille in 1017/1609, of al-Andalus in 1018/1610, of Catalonia in 1019/1611, and of Murcia in 1023/1614. Naturally, those expelled turned towards North Africa to find refuge.

The first immigrants (Moriscos) to arrive on the Moroccan Atlantic coastline are the Hornacheros, from Hornachos, a small town in the Extremadura region. They settled in Rabat, in the actual *kasbah* of the Udayas. They were joined, in 1018/1610, by Andalusians, who themselves moved into the *medina* of Rabat. The two communities then establish the Republic of Salé, which is in practice independent from all other powers. This republic developed strategies of sea warfare against the Christians. *"The fourth pirate town after Algiers, Tunis and Tripoli, Salé had, after 1050/1641, the most dreaded pirates on the seas"*. The win-

Privateer embarkations, port of Salé, engraving, Rabat General Library.

Historical Introduction

Kasbah of the Udayas, general view, Rabat.

nings are enormous. Precious metals, captives, manufactured goods, diverse products, all the contents of the attacked ships are tipped out into warehouses or depots of Salé. Morocco remained fragmented for 60 years, until 1074/1664, when Mulay Rashid, having triumphed over his brother Mulay Mohamed, undertook to conquer the country and establish the dynasty of *chorfa*s 'Alawites.

City of Salé, engraving, Rabat General Library

The 'Alawites originated from Tafilalet in the south-east of Morocco. Their ancestor, Hassan al-Dakhil, arrived from Yanbô in Arabia in around the 6th-7th/beginning of 13th century. *"His family is immediately surrounded by the respect due to members descended from the Prophet".*
Strengthened by this trump card, by the esteem which the Arab tribes and Berbers bestowed on them due to their noble birth and, without doubt, due to the charisma shown by the first heads of the family, the 'Alawites succeeded in anchoring their religious and spiritual power. The anarchy rampaging through the country throughout the first half of the 11th/17th century offered them the possibility of trying out a political experiment. Although sketched out by Mulay Mohamed, it is Mulay Rashid who activates the process of creating a government and a dynasty. He neutralises the power of practically every local government, and proceeds to extend his author-

ity by centralising the power mainly into his own hands. He also had the foresight of neither restricting himself to the aspirations of the people, nor to the expectations of the elite.

For instance, to conquer the minds and mollify its inhabitants, he placed his capital in the devout and commercial town of Fez. He even built a *madrasa* there: the Cherratin Madrasa. On his death in 1082/1672, *"Morocco has clearly not merely got a chieftain, but has the Emir of believers for a leader. He leaves his successor a well-trained State"*.

Mulay Rashid is succeeded by his half-brother Mulay Isma'il (1082/1672–1139/1727). As soon as he comes to power, he initiates two huge campaigns: to unify the country under his authority, and to construct a capital fit for a king of Morocco which he would situate in Meknès.

By the time of Mulay Isma'il's death, Morocco is both unified and sovereign. However, this status quo, established at the price of heavy fighting to reclaim what had been lost, quickly disappeared with the death of its creator, Mulay Isma'il, since he had made himself the foundation on which he had built his own power structure.

Despite the troubles which scourge the country for more than 30 years, the dynasty remains in place. The whole of the country recognises the authority of the sultan, and his religious prestige remains intact.

These advantageous factors are exploited by Mulay 'Abd Allah (1140/1728–1170/1757) who, despite being deposed three times, succeeds in restoring order. His achievement would be bolstered and sustained by the tenacity, intelligence and wisdom of his son and successor Sidi Mohamed, or Mohamed III (1170/1757–1204/1790).

Being very up-to-date with world affairs of the time, this sultan undertook the task of opening up his country's doors to Europe and to America simultaneously. On the level of diplomacy, he recognised the independence of the United States, maintained amicable relations with George Washington, for whom he could do favours on account of the embassies in Tunis and in Tripoli. On the economic level, he signed treaties based on the principle of reciprocity, which offered merchants essential guarantees, both for themselves and for their goods.

Within Morocco itself, he chose to utilise the resource offered by the Atlantic ports. He thus undertook to develop Anfa, actually Casablanca, and Tangier. He took Mazagan back from the Portuguese (1079/1769). Most importantly, he founded Essauira, which he based on the French town of Saint-Malo, and raised it to be the kingdom's leading port.

The 19th century should therefore have been characterised as a time of rediscovered strength and renewed stability. But internal difficulties arising from a seven-year long drought (1190/1776–1196/1782), followed by a terrible epidemic of the plague (1211/1797–1214/1800) swiftly put an end to the piecemeal reparations, and provoked profound upheaval. Mostly affected was the demography of

Cherratin Madrasa, upper part of the gallery wall, Fez.

Historical Introduction

the land, as it led to the death of more than half of the entire country's population. As a result, Morocco possessed neither the political strength nor the economic and military capacity to confront the 19th century, during which events taking place in its first half would have determining consequences on Morocco's future.

Despite the mighty efforts deployed by the three monarchs who, from 1206/1792 to 1289/1873, succeeded on the throne – Mulay Sliman (1206/1792–1237/1822), Mulay 'Abd al-Rahman (1237/1822–1275/1859) and Sidi Mohamed, or Mohamed IV (1275/1859–1289/1873) –, the problems were too Grand to all be resolved. The threat this time is mainly from abroad.

Indeed, in 1830, French troops occupy Algiers. The era of European Imperialism has begun, and Morocco finds itself in direct confrontation with France.

The Moroccan troops were defeated during the first battle which took place between the two nations, the Battle of Isly, near Oujda (1260/1844). It was their first defeat in two centuries, a result which had far-reaching effects: it revealed Morocco's fragility to Europe which had viewed it as a powerful empire whose frontiers reached the river of Senegal. Thus, in 1859-1860, Spain was able to conquer Tétouan following a battle in which the disorganisation of the Moroccan troops, rather than their courage, was to blame. Morocco faced such high war indemnity payments that, for the first time in her history, she needed a loan from Britain.

Morocco was forced beforehand to sign a detrimental treaty under pressure from the British which was reinforced by France and Spain. Over and above unfavourable commercial and navigational measures, the treaty of 1856 in effect brought an end to the sultan's freedom of action and to his sovereignty in matters of jurisdiction. Morocco abandoned *"her judicial rights at her loss to the Europeans and a sector of their subjects"* whilst recognising the principle of extra territoriality and submitting to a regime of guardianship. Pressure from Europe was even Greater than it would have been due to Morocco's possession of one of the shores on the Strait of Gibraltar, *"a passageway whose value increased after the opening of the Suez canal"*. But the Greatest problem arising from its relations with Europe was that of guardianship.

The substitution of Moroccan authority over its own citizens for that of a foreign one introduced by the guardianship regime became a serious obstacle for all attempts at progress.

The first task for Mulay Hassan I (1873-1894) was thus to try and resolve this situation. But all his attempts were doomed to failure. For, in addition, the International Conference of Madrid in 1880 *"created a dangerous precedent: from now on no*

State of the Kingdom of Fez, 1140/1728, Rabat General Library.

changes could be introduced in Morocco without the agreement of the Powers". Furthermore, although the conference of Algeciras in 1906 recognised the integrity of the Sherifian Empire, Morocco was placed under a kind of International Protectorate in which France appeared to be a major player. The treaty formally confirming the establishment of such a Protectorate was signed on 30th March 1912 in Fez.

This event, which, from the powers' point of view, put an end to decades of political-diplomatic shilly-shallying between them whilst weakening Morocco once and for all, actually ignited the flame of fierce resistance. During the 44 years of foreign presence consequently endured by Morocco, through invasions by France and Spain, this flame was never to be put out.

After having existed as a military state for 22 years (1912–1934), and been witness to acts of heroism (as seen during the War of the Rif and in the resistance put up by the Middle-Atlas, the High-Atlas and from within the Saharan borders surrounding Aït Baamran etc.), Morocco's struggle became a political one. It remained unabatingly political until it obtained its independence in 1956 under the auspices of Sultan Mohamed V (1927-1961), who himself led the campaign for independence, (preferring to be deposed and forced into exile rather than having to keep submitting to and maintaining the Protectorate). On 16th November 1955, Mohamed V and his family undertake a triumphant return to Morocco. The legitimate sovereign reclaims his throne, and Morocco's independence is proclaimed in March 1956.

In everything it undertook, the reigning 'Alawite dynasty was thus the defender of national unity, the guarantor of the consolidation of a Moroccan specificity. The political realm has provided an idea of the extent to which various monarchs have engaged themselves in the fight towards independence and freedom. In terms of civilisation, these monarchs knew how to perpetuate, in form as in spirit, the achievements of earlier times. 'Alawite art is, indeed, an art which demonstrates loyalty to its past, continuously returning to its sources. However, in various forms, it also manifests the exploration of new directions, some of which would even become distinguishing signs of 'Alawite creativity: the taste for grandeur, thematic unity, attaching new ideas to new techniques.

Mohamed V Mausoleum, general view, Rabat.

ANDALUSIAN MOROCCO

Naïma El-Khatib Boujibar, Mohamed Mezzine

The history of al-Andalus has fused with that of Morocco since they have been inextricably linked, at first by the comings and goings of men on missions to convert the Iberian Peninsula to Islam in the $2^{nd}/8^{th}$ century, then by the attempts to evade Christian domination seven centuries later. If the political history which unites the two shores can be deemed turbulent, then it is this turbulent exchange of cultures, people and commerce which brought about the birth of a flourishing art form, the most beautiful examples of which materialised in Morocco. Experts are agreed that the founding of the two Grand sanctuaries in Fez in the middle of the $3^{rd}/9^{th}$ century – the Qarawiyin and Andalusian mosques – marks the true beginnings of Islamic art in Morocco. As their names indicate, the first is the creation of Ifriqiyan immigrants, the second of Cordobans. As such, they both bare the marks of their creators, evidence of which can be found in the liturgical furnishings as well as in the architecture. Even in the following century, when Morocco fell prey to the power struggles in the Maghreb between the Umayyads of Cordoba and the Fatimids of Ifriqiya, architectural and artistic creations still remained under the control of these opposing factions.

Indeed, during the Idrissid period (171/788–363/974), relations between the two shores facing one another across the Strait were dominated by the conflict between the two great dynasties of Islam at the time: the Umayyads of al-Andalus and the Abbassids of Baghdad, and later between the Fatimids of Ifriqiya and of Egypt. The Idrissid dynasty, established in Morocco, found itself playing for time, wilfully adopting the role of arbitrator and intermediary for nearly two centuries.

This period of internal struggle turned out to be beneficial for artistic endeavours undertaken in Morocco. Each dynasty

Andalusian Mosque, courtyard, Fez.

tried to rival the next, endowing the country (mainly through religious buildings) with works of architecture and furnishings whose signature style would come to define Moroccan art, thus giving birth to the first elements of Andalusian art.

This rivalry explains why the Fatimids elevated the two mosques in Fez to the status of *Jami'*, "mosque-cathedrals", from where the Friday prayers were delivered. On his own initiative, the Spanish Caliph, 'Abd al-Rahman II, enlarged the Qarawiyin prayer hall and constructed the minaret. This tower, built with sizable stones which were whitewashed during the time of the Merinids, was decorated with certain details: a band of sculpted panelling, a hemispheric dome, a framing of the entrance door. Although these decorative aspects link it to Ifriqiyan and Eastern traditions, they ensure that it remains as close to the Andalusian style of design. Built on a square structure with a height equal to squared area of its base (a design and a proportion which reflect the towers of the mosques in Cordoba), it was to become the prototype for all further minarets built in Morocco.

Another definitive construction, which was also to become a model for future ones of its kind, also came into being during this time. This was the pulpit of the Andalusian mosque. This liturgical piece of furniture, possessing a fine quality of execution whilst eloquently baring witness to the battle of influence between the Fatimids and the Umayyads, points to the existence of a carpentry workshop in Fez, the first of its kind in Morocco it seems, that was capable of mastering different decorative techniques for wood carving: sculpture, joinery, wood turning and painting. This pulpit, or *minbar*, offered by the vassal of the Fatimids (the Ziride Bulughin) to the mosque of the Andalusian in 369/980 when he seized Fez, was partly destroyed in the name of Muslim orthodoxy. Repaired under the directives of the Umayyad governor in 375/986, it was given a new back onto which motifs entailing oriental inscriptions were engraved.

In the $5^{th}/11^{th}$ century, when the Almoravids come to power, one sees the Eastern Maghreb opening up towards Andalusian influences, and a veritable "Hispanisation" of the architecture, the culture and the army ensues, particularly in Fez and in Marrakesh.

Qarawiyin Mosque, minaret, Fez.

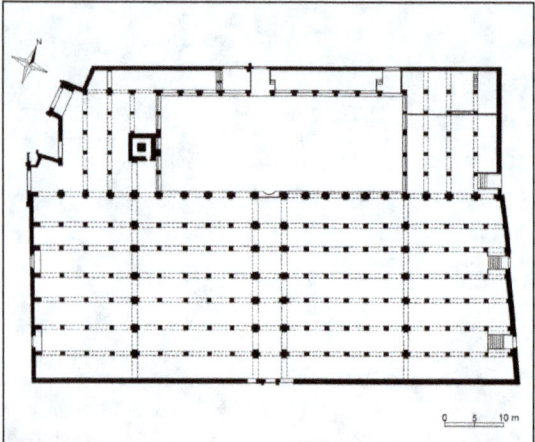

Qarawiyin Mosque, plan of the mosque under 'Ali Ibn Yusuf, Fez.

Qarawiyin Mosque, span of the mihrab, Fez.

If it is true to say that, in the domain of architecture, the Almoravids were neither the initiators nor the first to introduce the art of Andalusian architecture to Morocco, then it must also be said that they largely contributed to its diffusion across all regions. Keen builders, their reign distinguished itself on the foundations of fortresses and sanctuaries. Marrakesh, the capital of their kingdom, was the first to benefit from their patronage. As for Fez, it had a fortress – the Kasbah of Bujlud – built for it, by Yusuf Ibn Tashfin as soon as it was conquered in 461/1069. He ordered for mosques to be constructed in each neighbourhood, and chose to enlarge the Qarawiyin. His son 'Ali, born in *Sebta* (Ceuta) of a Christian slave, continued with his work. Having spent a large part of his life in Spain, he was particularly seduced by the beauty of Andalusian architecture and its decorative arts, and thus introduced these new designs, such as horseshoe arches, rectilinial arches and ribbed domes which Andalusian architects of the time had blended into Cordoba's heritage, into the monuments he went on to erect.

From 528/1134 to 538/1144, the Qarawiyin Mosque is redeveloped: its prayer hall is enlarged by three naves, and a new *mihrab*, preceded by domes covering the central bay, is constructed. This part of the mosque, where Andalusian influence is clear, has been paid particular attention to, as much in terms of architecture as in terms of decoration. The tent-like capitals which top the pillars reflect the composite capitals of eastern Umayyad art, in the sense that they have a vaulted design composed of a quartered concave circle, set above two rows of stylised acanthus leaves. The arcatures which rest on the pillars take on various forms borrowed from the Andalusian repertoire, in which the horseshoe and semicircular arch, the simple arch or the arch softened with foils and panels predominate. Arising as ever from under the same Andalusian influence, sculpted plaster was introduced for the first time to Morocco and to religious monuments. The floral decoration carved into the stucco coating, which frames the arcature of the *mihrab*, is executed to perfection; stems and reeds, combined with single or double, smooth or ribbed palmettes, interlace one another, proving both the virtuosity of the Moroccan artisans and their complete mastery of these imported techniques. Similarly, stucco is utilised to ornament the dome which immediately precedes the *mihrab*, and around which an inscription, sculpted in a flowery Kufic font and mentioning the name of 'Ali Ibn Yusuf, is produced. These decorative elements, enhanced by a variety of colours, evoke the panelling of Arab monuments of the Iberian Peninsula through the delicacy and abundance of their features. The same care was given to woodwork originating from the same source of inspiration. A fitting example is the magnificent cedarwood panel deposited at the Batha Museum in Fez, the decoration of which consists of floral motifs superimposed onto geometric ones, intertwining to create a new pattern on which to feast the eyes.

All artistic creations commissioned by the Almoravid princes thus presented similarities to the art of the Iberian Peninsula. However it is not until the Almohads come to power that one can see the birth of a symbiotic, Morrocan-Andalusian art form.

Due to the religious rigour which they advocated, the Almohads were, on arrival, viewed as being the enemy of all pleasurable arts, having provoked fear in the inhabitants of Fez by whitewashing the rich Andalusian decor of the Qarawiyin's *mihrab* with a thick coat of lime paint. Nevertheless, they wasted no time in becoming the most efficient propagators of Andalusian art within Morocco and the whole of North Africa.

Possessing valuable financial resources, taken from the provinces of their vast empire, which extended from al-Andalus up to the state of Tripoli, they dedicated large amounts of material wealth to the construction of monumental art. Their towns and capitals, Seville, Rabat and Marrakesh, among others, were saturated with important architectural projects, in the middle of which grandiose monuments of vast dimensions were erected: massive clay walls, sizable stone gates, and sanctuaries "expressing both the beauty of al-Andalus and the force of Africa". The new dimensions imposed on monuments would revive, and, in so doing, improve on the artistic designs inherited from al-Andalus. Henceforth, Morocco would be the one to export its new aesthetic concepts to Muslim Spain and the other provinces, and would do so for nearly half a century to come.

Almohad ramparts, Bab Ruah, arcature and frame, Rabat.

Kasbah of the Udayas, door of the kasbah, detail of the architectonic forms, Rabat.

The gates belonging to the solid enclosures surrounding the town of Rabat and the Udaya's Kasbah do not open out onto a direct, straightforward gangway as Andalusian gates do, but open onto a bend – a design which would become a general rule for town gates to come. The large stone bays belonging to their facade support a series of superimposed arches which are framed by a rectangular band, on which an inscription, written in strong, uniform, *kufic* letters, is engraved; writing which privileged the Almohads as much on monuments as it did in the transcription of Holy books. The space in between the frame and the arches is decorated with an abstract floral motif, whose fine lines describe large, smooth palm leaves, from which, at each corner, a smaller palm leaf hollowed out from the soft shadows detaches itself. This type of thick-featured palm leaf, whose contours are of such perfect clarity that the leaf seems supernatural, would become greatly significant within the ornamentation of all Almohad monuments. It would even bring about new styles of architectonics, consoles, arches and capitals, styles which can be admired on the facades of the gates of the Udaya's Kasbah, and which characterise Almohad art having contributed largely to its elegance and beauty.

In terms of their sanctuaries, the Almohads, whilst keeping the basilica T-shape of the mosque of Cordoba, applied their full attention to two perpendicular naves: the nave adjoining the wall of the *qibla* or transept, and the axial nave. Larger than the other naves, they were embellished with decorated cupolas. The minaret, the only part of the religious building visible from the outside, is also paid attention to. The three famous towers built by Prince Ya'qub al-Mansur – the Giralda of Seville, the Kutubiya of Marrakesh and the Tower of Hassan in Rabat – all of which demonstrate remarkable unity, project their soaring silhouettes high above the green-tiled roofs which top the naves of the prayer hall. Although different in size and in build, they seem to have been conceived by the same architect. The decoration which adorns their hierarchically segmented facades echoes motifs of polyfoiled arches or panels and, especially, of intertwining geometric patterns, throughout. This latter motif, which covers the diamond-shaped meshing of other Almohad monuments, such as their gates, became a design classic. Drawing its origin from the interweaving arches of the mosque of Cordoba, it would grow in importance as an element of decoration and would be revived through the introduction of plant features.

The Almohads were also responsible for introducing, for the first time to Morocco, chequered and multicoloured wall tiling, placing the tiles around the surface of the highest minaret, as can be seen on the Kutubiya. This decorative process, already well-known in the *Qal'a* of the Bani Hammad (the Zirid principality of Algeria) would be expounded and then greatly utilised later on, as much within the Nasrid kingdom of Spain as by the Merinid dynasty in Morocco.

When they succeeded the Almohads in reigning over Morocco, the Merinids renewed close links with al-Andalus after relations had been badly affected by the onset of the Christian invasion. This marked the pinnacle of Andalusian art in Morocco.

In terms of art, the Merinids produced works of great accomplishment, more than fulfilling the mould of Hispano-Maghrebic art implanted and affirmed by the Almoravids and the Almohads. A range of very refined styles, of sculpted and multicoloured surface decoration, as well as the receptiveness to, and absorbtion of recent innovations, were the principal traits of the architecture of the time. The overall body of work lies in close proximity to the Andalusian art of the Nasrids.

In keeping with the tradition of artistic patronage initiated by the Almoravids and the Almohads, a tradition which would continue to play a major role in the development of Islamic art in urban Morocco, the Merinids built, within the fortifications of their towns, religious foundations, mosques, *zawiya*s and *madrasa*s, all

The esplanade of the Tower of Hassan, facade which looks onto the Bu Regreg, Rabat.

Chellah, minaret, detail of the skylight covered in multicoloured tiles, Rabat.

Buinaniya Madrasa, courtyard, Fez.

Nejjarin Square, funduq, general view, Fez.

of which contained the full repertoire of Merinid decorative arts.

It was Abu Yusuf, founder of *Fas Jdid*, who inaugurated the construction schedule of *madrasa*s by building the first, followed by Abu Sa'id, who increased their number. But the most intensive period of construction fell under the reign of Abu Hassan, a reign which marked the dynasty's climax, during which every great city in the kingdom was endowed with a *madrasa*. Abu Inan would put an end to the building schedule by constructing the two last *madrasa*s of this era in Fez and in Meknès.

Differing in size, proportion and decor, the *madrasa*s, which acted as hostels and occasionally as schools for students, were built along the same architectural principles: ground and first floor rooms arranged around quite a large patio surrounded by porticoes, the centre of which is occupied by a pool or basin, with a prayer hall opening out onto a small corner of the court. The patio walls, and the walls of the galleries and of certain corridors, are richly decorated with mosaic tiles known as *zellij*. The tops of the walls consist of chiselled plaster which protrudes out over sculpted and painted wood panels, whilst in the prayer hall, ornamentation is concentrated around the *mihrab* and the ceiling. The *madrasa*s, having become creative masterpieces, represented the contemporary taste for excess in the decoration of monuments, as well as every subtle nuance, of Merinid art.

Private residences, as well as *funduq*s and *hammam*s — a few examples, or at least a few museum-conserved pieces, of which remain — were also built during the same period and in the same spirit. The houses, which echo in a more simplified version the architectural and decorative features of the *madrasa*s, also have the lower half of their walls and their floor covered

Andalusian Morocco

Buinaniya Madrasa, mashrabiyya window framed by decoration in sculpted stucco, Meknès.

'Attarin Madrasa, bay opening onto the prayer hall, detail of the stucco openwork, Fez.

in mosaic tiles, and their upper halves adorned with plaster and carved wood. The rooms which open out onto the patio are very long, with an alcove at each end. The houses had, more often than not, an intermediary mezzanine floor; latrines and a fountain were fitted on the ground floor. The urban housing built later on remained loyal to this design, which was similar to that of the Nasrid houses of Granada.

The architectural concept on which *funduq*s or *caravanserai*s were built, serving as lodgings for men, shelters for beasts of burden, and storage space for goods, was similar to that of residential houses. They only differed in that their front gates were large and not angled so as to allow for the access of carts; their portico courtyards took on greater importance, whilst the rooms became smaller. This is how the *funduq* "Corral del Carbón", also in Granada, appeared.

The *hammam*s retain the classic Andalusian layout, adopted since the $5^{th}/11^{th}$ century. The three rooms – cold, lukewarm and hot – and often even the relaxation area, are set out in series.

All of these Merinid creations, in which surface decoration is glorified, seduce the viewer through the confidence of their composition, the delicacy of their colouring, and the finesse of their execution. Whether covered with plaster, wood, or square tiles, all of which would be ornamented, the space designated for decoration was divided into panels, bandwidths and horizontal sections, most of which balanced each other out perfectly, with a different shade of colour for every section, combining to create a marvelously harmonious formation. Several designs, discovered through minor demolition, prioritise the decoration of wood and plaster over materials. The decorative background patterns consist of a network

Kasbah, Museum, ceremonial room, muqarnas dome, Tangier.

Buinaniya Madrasa, pillar, epigraphic frieze in kursif lettering on square tiles, Meknès.

buildings constructed from the Merinid era onwards. The friezes, the sculpted corbels, the lintel porticoes made of cedarwood based on building techniques involving mortice and tenon joints – all these attest to the high standard reached within the carpentry of this period.

The influence on Andalusian wood decoration in $5^{th}/11^{th}$-century Granada, Toledo and Tarifa is clearly visible in its floral design, the vigour in the carving, and the opulence of the composition.

One form of an Eastern geometric design that would find itself replicated onto all supporting columns, wood, plaster or *zellij*, was the polygonal star, the number of corners of which varied. Used alone or inserted in the gaps between floral designs (particularly on plaster panels), it was also utilised to decorate dome structures. The ceilings of the 'Attarin Madrasa of Fez, a jewel in terms of Merinid art, are a fine example of this: they are covered by an interlacing pattern of star-like polygons. Festooned arches as well as embossed or puckered arches took root over foiled arches.

Muqarnas or stalactites made of plaster or wood pervade arches and ceilings in equal measure. Created by stacking a group of seven small prisms, which are chopped when made out of wood and moulded when made out of plaster, they form decorative units of great beauty.

In terms of epigraphic decoration, the Merinid artists, just like the Nasrid artists of Granada, used, above all, cursive, supple and elegant script to decorate the *madrasas*' narrow borders or circular plaster cartouches with Qur'anic verses, prose, or phrases praising the founding princes and their achievements. They also continued to use *kufic* characters when inscribing dedications on monuments, as can be seen on the gate of Chellah in Rabat, but embellished the letters with

of foliage onto which palm leaves, or interlacing geometric and floral patterns, attach themselves, weaving in large and small palm leaves and pine cones into their mesh.

The embroidered cedarwood bestowed a unique value on the religious and civil

palm leaves and flowers to fill the voids in between the upper spaces of the letters' shafts. Furthermore they sometimes used these embellished characters on a smaller scale to inscribe on the turban-like tops of certain capitals such as the ones in the 'Attarin Madrasa of Fez.

Like those in the Alhambra in Granada, the shape of these capitals evolved noticeably from those of previous centuries. In these newer and more simply shaped capitals, whose interior decoration is more minute and more dense, the division between the two superimposed sections is very clear: the lower cylindrical half adopts the curve at the rounded summit which arises from the crown of acanthus leaves, whilst the upper parallelepipedic half is generally square in design, and is decorated with faintly carved floral pattern, at the centre of which is a strip in the shape of a flat turban along which an inscription is sometimes written.

Another innovation introduced by the Merinids and the Nasrids in the $8^{th}/14^{th}$ century was the widespread use of *zellij*, coating the surface of minarets, walls, and columns as well as floors. Although used in their multicoloured inlay work, this technique was not invented by the Merinids, as is testified by the presence of *zellij* in the civil and religious monuments of Fez dating from the end of the $7^{th}/13^{th}$ century, a period which predates the principal constructions of the Alhambra. In artistic terms, the Merinid era thus denotes a time of maturity, during which the decorative styles, which would later become classics, asserted themselves, and in which Moroccan artists (who acquired great skills through working in the field of creative expression) obtained letters patent of nobility for the workshops they established.

The political as well as economic expansion of the Merinids slowed down during

Fragment of mural surfacing in tiled mosaic, geometric decoration, Batha Museum (Inv. No. C2), Fez.

the dynasty's second century in power. However, when, in 897/1492, the last Muslim principality (that of Granada) fell under the battle blows of the Reconquest, the Andalusian Muslims were already well placed to follow the tradition of having to go and find a new homeland. This was thanks to the Merinid court, which, having encouraged families of aristocratic, scholarly or princely backgrounds to come and settle in the Medina of Fez, subsequently opened the doors of the administration, the *madrasa*s and the mosques to them.

After Granada was captured in 879/1492, the emir emigrated with ten ships and more than 1,130 managerial and legal advisers towards Fez. He was accompanied by 2,919 Andalusians from the port of Ghadra and 1,166 from the port of Mankab. Following this, the influx of Andalusians entering Morocco accelerated, and between 932/1526 and 977/1570, nearly 200,000 Moriscos from Valencia, Oliva, Almeria, Cullera, Castille, Palmeira and Alicante settled there. Those chronicling the period that followed differ in their estimation of how many Andalusians immigrated to Morocco, but, viewed together, Moriscos

Qarawiyin Mosque, Sa'adian pavilion, Fez.

Moriscos of Castille in 1017/1609, of Catalonia in 1018/1610, of Murcia in 1023/1614 – came to install themselves in Morocco, in both towns and fields, particularly in the areas between Rabat-Salé, Meknès, Fez, Chefchaouen, Tétouan and Ouezzane (Wazzan). The Hornacheros from the region of Extremadura settled in Rabat, inside the actual Kasbah of the Udayas, and were joined by other Andalusians; they participated against Christian ships in the race for the seas, and set up the Republic of Salé.

Arab chroniclers and stories by Christian voyagers note the presence of these newcomers in all areas of activity and life, in towns as well as in the countryside. They tell of the agricultural techniques, the distribution and painstaking exploitation of water, which is reminiscent of the *huertas* of Valencia, and of the fountains belonging to the various palaces of the Alhambra.

Arts and crafts, composed from or in any form or material – *zellij*, stucco, marble, wood, iron, copper, gold – would carry the mark of the craftsmen that had arrived from Spain. From the $10^{th}/16^{th}$ century up to the present time, the *m'almin* and the wood, plaster and *zellij* craftsmen continued to use artistic formulas inherited from their predecessors within the field of architecture and traditional furniture design. They also borrowed from the Merinids' and the Nasrids' repertoire of Andalusian decorative styles with respect to the art of ornamentation, whilst simultaneously adding new elements which came from the East or were carried over from Mudéjar Spain by Moriscos emigres.

Influenced by the pavilions of the Court of Lions in the Alhambra, the Sa'adian monarchs had embellished the Qarawiyin Mosque by placing two pavilions quite

sources indicate that a figure of around 800,000 Andalusians came to live in Morocco.

It would be true to say that the integration of these loose-fitting immigrants was not always without its difficulties.

The Andalusians founded Tétouan in the $9^{th}/15^{th}$ century, and Chefchaouen in the $10^{th}/16^{th}$ century. Finally, in the $11^{th}/17^{th}$ century, the remaining mix of Andalusians issued with expulsion edicts – the

Andalusian Morocco

Kasbah, Museum, ceremonial room, reconstruction of furniture belonging to a traditional living room, Tangier.

happily side by side in the small corners of the court, a result of the place and time at which they were built.

From the moment they came to power at the end of the 11th/17th century, the 'Alawite sovereigns erected, throughout the kingdom, imposing fortresses, *kasbahs*, religious buildings, mosques and *madrasa*s (of which the most characteristic is the Cherratin Madrasa in Fez), palaces and residences, all of which echoed the Andalusian styles which had taken root in the country. Yet each reign was distinguished by its own particular character.

At Rabat and at Salé, the Moriscos emigres of the 11th/17th century had carried over with them certain features from the Spanish Renaissance, such as elaborate mouldings of raised Roman arches, lavish treatment for gates belonging to residences, and a type of chest made in cedarwood, the front of which, delineated by small twisted columns, was framed by puckered mouldings or embroidery motifs.

Morisco influence is even more evident in the towns situated in the north, such as Tétouan where there is a wealth of Andalusian heritage in the realm of architecture and furniture, and where a style of *zellij* which differed from that in Fez was adopted, remaining until this day a speciality of the town. It involves the cutting and separating of the tiny pieces of ceramic before they are glazed.

The mosques and residences of Fez and of Chefchaouen, built at the beginning of the 11th/18th century, also differentiate themselves by the extreme modesty of their appearance and lack of surface decoration. The oratory minarets, which are of a remarkable simplicity, are merely decorated with a band of bricks and occasionally with a blind arcature; they could be compared to the bell towers of the Mudé-

jar-style churches of Spain. The funeral slabs of the Jebel Dersa, conserved in the Archaeological Museum of Tétouan, can also be attributed to Spanish Renaissance and Baroque Art. Similarly, certain details in the dress of women from Chefchaouen – a large hat, short coat and gaiters – and in the dress of Jewish women in Tétouan

Lebbadi Palace, zellij from Tétouan, detail, Tétouan.

Al-Ansar Mosque, Chefchaouen.

Detail of an Andalusian-style motif on an embroidered curtain from Chefchaouen, Kasbah Museum, Chefchaouen.

A number of aspects – in particular cooking and music – which belonged to daily urban, as well as certain rural, ways of life, remained impregnated with influences inherited from al-Andalus. Moroccan recipes have retained their original names which date back to the $7^{th}/13^{th}$ and $8^{th}/14^{th}$ centuries, such as *mruziya*, a bitter-sweet dish, and *bestela*, a filo-pastry tart filled with chicken or meat. Classical Moroccan music is none other than Andalusian music, or music known as *Gharnati*, from Granada.

It is this element of ebb and flow between the two shores of the Strait, and ultimately that of symbiosis, which composes the study "ANDALUSIAN MOROCCO: A Discovery in Living Art". Encompassing eight itineraries which cover 12 centuries of history, from the $2^{nd}/8^{th}$ century up to the present day, this study reveals the different facets of this reciprocal influence.

If the layout and organisation of the **Royal City** of Meknès (itinerary I) reflects royal Andalusian cities, then **A Day in the Life of a *Taleb* in Fez** (itinerary II) or indeed that **of an Artisan in Fez** (itinerary III) reminds the visitor that a similar organisation ruled over Fez and over Granada during the mediaeval era, at the height of the Moroccan-Andalusian civilisation. As a country of welcome, Morocco knew how to accommodate with complete tolerance both Jews and Muslims who had been chased out of Spain, and Fez in particular accommodated the largest community of Maghrebin Jews where the **Day in the Life of a Jew in Fez** (itinerary IV) was lived out between the workshop and the synagogue. The influence from al-Andalus was even stronger in the north, as is evident in **Chefchaouen, the Holy City of the Rif Mountains** (itinerary V) and **Tétouan, the Patio of a Civilisation** (itinerary VI), a town also and Tangier, as well as in the motifs of embroidery and in the jewels of these towns, are reminiscent of the artistic features manifest in Spain during the $10^{th}/16^{th}$ and $11^{th}/17^{th}$ centuries.

named the daughter of Granada. But it is in following the lead of merchants, craftsmen and princes along the route which connects **The Ports of the Strait** (itinerary VII) and runs along the Moroccan coastline, that one can better understand the attraction which both shores exerted over each other. Finally, it is exclusively at the Bou Regreg site that the whole history of Moroccan and al-Andalus relations comes to a close, by way of **Ebb and Flow, Shine and Eclipse** (itinerary VIII); history which resulted in the north of Morocco becoming the principal region in which this secular inheritance was conserved.

ITINERARY I

The Royal City

Mohamed Mezzine

I.1 MEKNÈS
    I.1.a Dar Jamaï Museum
    I.1.b Great Mosque
    I.1.c Buinaniya Madrasa
    I.1.d Bab al-Mansur al-'Alj
    I.1.e Pavilion of the Ambassadors
    I.1.f Mulay Isma'il Mausoleum
    I.1.g Grain Silos
    I.1.h Basin of the Norias
    I.1.i Bab Berdeïn

I.2 MULAY IDRISS ZERHUN (option)
    I.2.a Mulay Idriss Zerhun Mausoleum

Mulay Isma'il

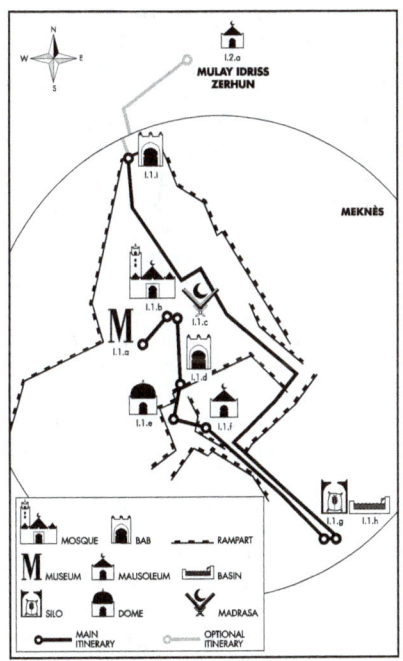

Mulay Isma'il Mausoleum, third courtyard, Meknès.

ITINERARY I   The Royal City

*Bab al-Mansur,
general view, Meknès.*

In Arab-Muslim culture, the location of the "Royal City" which the sovereigns inhabit is primordial. It always occupies a large area, whether located in al-Andalus, the Maghreb or the Mashreq. Often surrounded by ramparts, it encompasses the palaces of the sovereign as well as its amenities, its gardens or *riyad*s, the living quarters of the court and of high dignitaries, the commercial districts and currency-minting workshops.

It is certainly the case that the origin of this spatial plan in general and of the Royal City in particular is not Andalusian; indeed it dates back to the Greeks, the Romans, the Persians, and finally the Muslim dynasties of the Mashreq. But the framework on which cities are planned, particularly in Morocco, owes as much to this direct Eastern influence as to the influence of the Andalusians. One sees this framework as clearly in Granada and in Seville as one does in Fez, in Marrakesh and in Meknès. For all the towns in al-Andalus or in Morocco, and right up until the 11th/17th century,

the predominant framework of town planning was bipolar: the *medina* on one side and the Royal City or *kasbah* on the other.

The Royal City of Meknès, as it was conceived by the 'Alawite Sultan Mulay Ism'ail, is particularly representative of this type of town, which bases itself on the Eastern structuring of space, whilst maintaining the ornate decor and colouring of al-Andalus, and the local Moroccan architecture developed by great princes.

Using a Merinid urban community as his starting point, the 'Alawite Sultan Mulay Isma'il (1082/1672–1139/1727), surrounded by counsellors amongst which were a number of Andalusians, undertook, during the 55 years of his reign, enormous constructions, built primarily of hard-packed clay, which housed thousands of people: workers who had come from all round Morocco, as well as slaves, prisoners of war and Christian captives. There are a number of reports written by foreign chroniclers who witnessed or even participated in the building projects, such as the Frenchman Mouette, kept prisoner from 1670 until 1681, who worked for years on monuments raised by the king, and who published, in 1683, an account of his captivity. According to his account, Mulay Isma'il firstly cleared the Almoravid *kasbah* where he had settled, by tearing down the buildings which were adjacent to him. A clearing appeared which became known as al-Hedim or "of the Debris" due to the amount of material amassed at this spot following the successive demolitions, creating a natural barrier between the *medina* and the *kasbah*. An enclosure was thus erected separating the *kasbah* from the rest of the town: it consisted of a simple interior enclosure which had neither a path nor a bastion, and a separate exterior enclosure, which was 9–12 m. high and was pierced with various gates.

Inside the *kasbah*, a vast quadrilateral area, approximately 500 m. x 1000 m., housed the three palaces which Moulay Ismail had built: the Grand Palace, *Dar al-Kebira*, to the east of the *medina*, and the Imperial Palace, *Dar al-Makhzen*, containing the *Dar al-Madrasa* and the *Dar al-Mehencha* palaces. *Dar al-Kebira*, whose construction began in 1082/1672, was intended to house the royal family and close relatives of the king. An architectural complex covering over 13.5 hectares, set apart from other palaces in the *kasbah*, it was composed of several palaces which together contained a whole body of functions: patios, reception rooms, *hammam*s, kitchens and gardens.

In contrast to this first Isma'ili palace, which was densely built and very urban, the Imperial Palace, *Dar al-Makhzen*, the principal residence of Mulay Isma'il, occupied a space far smaller than the vast expansive area occupied by the gardens, making Meknès, according to the historian Ibn Zidane, *"a town in the countryside and a countryside in the town"*. This part of the *kasbah*, enclosed by high walls, encompassed, within a space of about 60 hectares, two palaces which were separated from each other by a fence forming an impressive passageway: *Dar al-Madrasa* and *Dar al-Mehencha*.

Dome of the Ambassadors, park and rampart, Meknès.

ITINERARY I   *The Royal City*

Conscious to preserve the city from all threats, whether external or climatic, the sultan had immense underground silos and provision sheds installed at 500 m. from the palace, in case of drought or an eventual siege of the city. An artificial tank, known as the Basin of Norias, was placed next to the silos, and was intended to provide water for the city.

Due to the architectural originality, the grandeur and the beauty of both private and public monuments, every traveller was impressed by the enormity of Mulay Isma'il's work, as the description by Father Dominic Buscot, who came to Meknès in 1704 to buy back Christian slaves, testifies: *"On approach, this town seemed to me to be something significant, as much by its sprawl, the quantity of its diverse houses, and the elevation of several mosques as by its pleasant variety of gardens, in which an infinite number of fruit trees of all kinds grew; we see the* Alcassave *or the Palace of the king,* which appeared to finish the town off magnificently towards the north. The grandeur of its enclosure, the building of a number of pavilions covered in varnished tiles with the pointed tips of two or three mosques, giving us a completely different impression than that which we got when we saw them up close... "* Through the richness in their conception and lay-out, the Isma'ili palaces conformed to this sumptuous image of the palace and of Arab dwellings, evoking patios and fountains, leafy shades and alleyways, basins and kiosks. And even if what is left of the city today is only a fraction of what Mulay Isma'il built, the visitor can still dream of past splendours and appreciate this *"architectured nature"* which reflected perfectly the requirements of a Moroccan princely court of the $11^{th}/17^{th}$ century.

Meknès, originally *Meknassa al-zitun*, "Meknès of the olive trees", was born through the settlement of a branch of the Zenets Berber tribe, called the Meknassa, on the riverbanks of the Bufekran *wadi* valley. Attracted by the fertility of the soil and the abundance of water, and having taken advantage of the power struggle which was agitating the north of Morocco following the fall of the Idrissid dynasty, these Berbers established a series of small, non-fortified conglomerates, which centred themselves within gardens.

When the Almoravid Prince Yusuf Ibn Tashfin seized these "garden-towns" in 455/1063, he set up a military garrison or *kasbah* on the site of the ancient *medina*. The Almohads, arriving in Meknès in 544/1150, put themselves in charge of enriching the town with the construction of murals and fountains. The town, or more accurately the four townships which formed it, were modest, and its place on

Grain Silos, interior of the House with Ten Norias, central corridor, Meknès.

Basin of the Norias, enclosure of the ancient silos reinforced with buttresses, Meknès.

the chequer board of Moroccan cities remained significantly limited.
On the Merinids' accession to power in the middle of the $7^{th}/13^{th}$ century, the town, from being a large citadel, became a commercial centre with its own *funduq*, *madrasa*s and mosques. The city thus became the residence of *viziers* – the ministers – while Fez remained the city of princes. During the time of Abu Inan (752/1351–759/1358), several Andalusian families came to settle in Meknès and in its surrounding area. The Cordobans and the Sevillans practised their trades in town, organised markets and influenced arts and crafts with their decorative techniques in wood work and *zellij*. They settled in a new neighbourhood which still retains their name up to this day: the Andalusian quarter. Certain amongst them, especially those who originated from the region of Valencia, located to the surrounding countryside and contributed to the prosperity of an agriculture already wealthy in terms of fruit: quinces, granates, Damascus apples, figs, raisins and olives. The city of Meknès is obliged to the Andalusians for attaining the level of prosperity which the chroniclers of the $9^{th}/15^{th}$ and $10^{th}/16^{th}$ centuries would focus on; a prosperity which had been difficult to maintain during the centuries characterised by hardships, wars and famine which had affected the whole country, particularly the $9^{th}/15^{th}$ century. Leon the African, who had visited the city at the beginning of the $10^{th}/16^{th}$ century, described it as a beautiful, fortified city, well populated, with airy and pleasant streets.
But it was the wish, two centuries later, of the 'Alawite sovereign Mulay Isma'il (1082/1672–1139/1727) to construct a capital worthy of a king of Morocco, which gave Meknès a definitive place in history.
Situated in the heart of one of Morocco's wealthiest regions, the city of Meknès offered the further advantage of being far from both the Mediterranean and Atlantic coasts, and thus held an element favourable

ITINERARY I   *The Royal City*
Meknès

Dar Jamai Museum, exhibition room, Meknès.

prisoners, Mulay Isma'il sought to gain the respect of the Christian princes, since, according to him, foreign relations towards Morocco could only be kept harmonious if the princes of Morocco were considered to be great builders and veritable men of State. A number of Moroccan ambassadors, stationed in France, England and in Spain, reported to the sovereign on the luxuries of the European courts. Deciding to construct palaces capable of rivalling European palaces, he chose to make Meknès the "Moroccan Versailles", employing 55,000 men, whether workers or slaves, Christian and Muslim, to undertake the task, commencing in 1082/1672. At the sultan's death in 1139/1727 (who, having waged battles continuously, had managed to stay in power), the city would come to experience numerous difficulties. As a central authority which was no longer capable of keeping control over the whole country, Meknès suffered several revolts which put a stop to any further developments. And although stability was restored towards the end of the $12^{th}/18^{th}$ century and the beginning of the $13^{th}/19^{th}$ century, Meknès would never recover the role it occupied from 1082/1672 –1139/1727 as the country's political capital.

1.1 MEKNÈS

1.1.a Dar Jamaï Museum

Follow the sign marked Ancienne Médina. *The museum is found on 'place al-Hedim'. There is supervised parking around the square. Entrance fee. Open from 09.00–12.00 and 15.00–18.00.*

Built at the end of the 19th century, under the reign of Sultan Mulay Hassan

to the sultan, who decided to situate his family there, a family estimated (often with exaggeration) as being composed of several wives and concubines, several hundred children, and *"some two hundred leaders and chiefs who followed him twice a day during his walk, and the 4000 Negroes who formed his guard"*.

Conscious of keeping face in front of foreign delegations and embassies who had come to negotiate for the release of their

ITINERARY I *The Royal City*
Meknès

(1873–94), this palace belonged to the Jamaï family, whose members were *viziers* to the monarch.
Having fallen from grace at the death of the latter, the family lost its influential position, and its residences were repossessed by the State. Converted into a military hospital during the Protectorate, a section of the palace was handed over for the study of Fine Arts, and thus, in 1926, was transformed into a museum harbouring collections that testify to the artistic traditions of the city of Meknès: ironwork, weaving, leather work, embroidery, book binding and goldsmithing.

This palace, raised off an expansive surface from the ground, consisted of several annexes and subsidiary buildings. On the ground floor, one came across a mosque, a *riyad*, a *minzah*, a court, a small house, a kitchen and a *hammam*. In addition, the annexes outside the palace contained a *funduq* which was transformed into a carpentry workshop, and a fountain which was recently restored. The entrance to the palace was via a gate which was covered with a protruding porch decorated in green tiles. This entrance was put in rather recently, having replaced the original doorway which was situated under the *sabat* of the *riyad*.

This ancient palace distinguishes itself on the magnificence of its *riyad*; one can admire the harmony between its two starry basins and its rivulet which cuts across a passageway made of *zellij*. It holds two fountains, and a portico consisting of seven arcades which rest on pillars and differ in height, and which link up to the principal dome under which the *vizier* received his guests. The dome, or *Qubba*, with its chiselled wood ceiling, its stained-glass windows and its large wood lintels, is Andalusian in both conception and decoration.

It is possible to rent a carriage for the remainder of the itinerary, having visited the monuments I.1.b and I.1.c. For the energetic walker it is possible to do most of the tour on foot.

I.1.b Great Mosque

When exiting from the museum, take the road on the left called Sidi Amor Bouaouda. Follow this winding road which leads to the mosque. Access restricted to Muslims.

The Great Mosque, situated in the heart of the *medina*, seems to have been built in the Almoravid era during the $5^{th}/11^{th}$ century. Important restorations and enlargements were undertaken by the Almohad Sultan Mohamed al-Nassir (595/199–609/1213). He provided the mosque with water which came from the source of Taguema, situat-

The Great Mosque, span of the mihrab, Meknès.

ITINERARY I *The Royal City*
Meknès

Buinaniya Madrasa, bay opening onto the prayer hall and mashrabiyya panels of the entrance bay, Meknès.

ed 5 km. south of the city. The mosque safeguarded, among other things from that period, a copper chandelier which, together with those from the Qarawiyin Mosque in Fez, represents one of those rare specimens that have survived to the present. The arrival of the Merinids in Meknès during the middle of the 7th/13th century saw the rapid cultural expansion of the city and of the mosque, particularly during the reign of Sultan Abu al-Hassan (731/1331–751/1351), who initiated the construction of the city's three *madrasas* (Buinaniya, al-Qadi and Shuhud). He endowed the mosque with a number of teaching posts, and installed a scientific library following the example of the one in the Qarawiyin in Fez, where the *tolba* came to consult manuscripts.

The action taken by the Merinids did not limit itself to just developing the cultural role of the Great Mosque: they also proceeded to undertake restoration and modification work, especially as the minaret of the mosque had collapsed, killing seven worshippers. Today, the mosque, with its 11 gates, stands on an area of 3,500 sq. m. and is composed of two distinctive parts:

ITINERARY I The Royal City
Meknès

Buinaniya Madrasa, pillar, stucco panelling in a geometric, floral and epigraphic design with kufic characters, Meknès.

– the prayer hall, consisting of nine bays and a *mihrab* adorned with painted and sculpted motifs done to perfection, granted that they were redone at several intervals by the various dynasties. The *anza*, which served as a *mihrab* during the summer months, was pitched along the side of the prayer hall. This *anza* dates from the time of Mulay Isma'il. It is contemporary, with its raised fountains sitting along the side of the *sahn*.
– the inner court, the *sahn*, a square area surrounded by a gallery. The minaret which rises at the corner of the *sahn* is decorated with square, green tiles.

I.1.c Buinaniya Madrasa

The madrasa is at the end of the road which runs along the Great Mosque.
Entrance fee. Open daily from 09.00–12.00 and 15.00–18.00.

One of Merinid Sultan Abu al-Hassan's masterpieces, the *madrasa* was built in 736/1336 as is testified by two inscriptions, one poetic, covering the *mihrab* in the prayer hall, the other a tribute to the sultan, traced along the wood lintels in the patio: "*Power, success and victory bursting forth from our master Abu al-Hassan, emir of the faithful*".
Originally called *al-Jadida*, the new madrasa, other than to differentiate it from the old one set up by Abu Yusuf Ya'qub, was re-baptised by the son of Abu al-Hassan, the sovereign Abu Inan, who restored it and gave it his own name: Buinaniya.
Occupying an area of 315 sq. m., the *madrasa* distinguishes itself even at the point of entry by a wooden door covered in pieces of copper which are exquisitely decorated. A long hallway leads to the *sahn*, around which the main parts of the building base themselves. This courtyard is adorned at its centre with a marble basin in the shape of a shell. The pillars, some of which stand in isolation and some of which are cast into the wall, stretch skywards to the top floor, and are interspersed with wooden lintels. *Mashrabiyya* panels, fixed in between the pillars, served to separate the

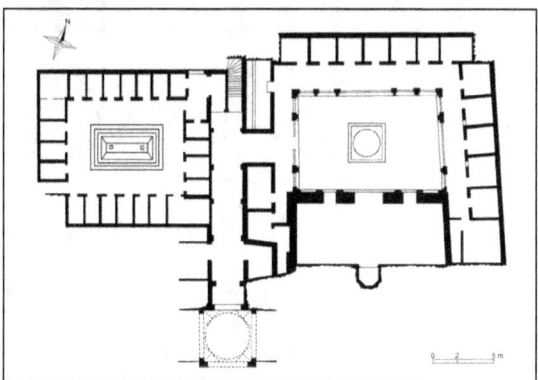

Buinaniya Madrasa, ground-floor plan, Meknès.

73

ITINERARY I   *The Royal City*
Meknès

was endowed with a *mihrab* built into the wall of the *qibla*. This particular *mihrab* is a polygonal niche, furnished on each side with columns which support an arch laid out within a square frame which is covered by an inscription. During Mulay Isma'il's reign, a dome was constructed at the entrance to the *madrasa*. Above all, the Buinaniya of Meknès carries the notable imprint of al-Andalus within all its decorative elements: the interior surfaces of the *madrasa* are richly decorated; the ground is covered with *zellij* tiles composing geometric patterns; similarly, the bases of the walls are decorated with *zellij* tiles up to a height of 1.6 m. These designs are crowned by an epigraphic frieze whose characters are black against a light background. Above, one can see geometric, floral and epigraphic stucco motifs. The upper parts of the interior surfaces are decorated with sculpted wood and panels inscribed with Qur'anic verses, religious sayings, dedications, plant motifs, arabesques and reeds.

Bab al-Mansur, entrance bay, detail of the frame decorated in ceramic, Meknès.

Bab al-Mansur, detail of the bay's frame decorated with interlacing, set, tiled mosaics, Meknès.

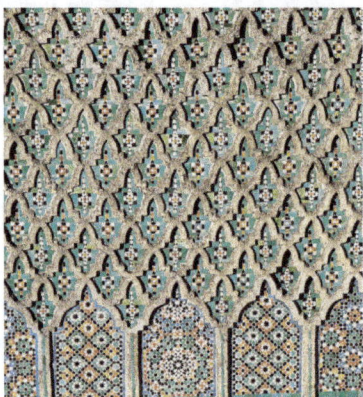

I.1.d Bab al-Mansur al-'Alj

Place al-Hedim. Rebuilt as an exhibition hall, it is situated on the furthest side of the square. Recreated as a watercolour painting on canvas, it was one the subjects highlighting "The Era of Morocco" during four months in Place de la Concorde, Paris.

As the most imposing gate in Meknès, Bab al-Mansur al-'Alj, "The Gate of the Victorious Renegade", is also one of the most original in Morocco. Its construction, as indicated by the large inscription in kursif characters on the upper part of the monument, began at the end of Mulay Isma'il's reign and was completed by his son in 1144/1732.

sahn from the galleries off which the student rooms situated on the ground floor could be reached. Those rooms situated on an upper floor open out onto the courtyard through finely decorated windows. Lessons for young students were taught in the prayer hall, which, being relatively vast,

ITINERARY I   *The Royal City*
Meknès

With an elbow-shaped entrance like most exterior gates of Moroccan towns, the gate opens out onto a bay of 8 m. in height, framed by two square towers which project over some loggias. These two bastions are themselves flanked by two narrower recesses supported by two tall columns of composite capitals.

This gate, remarkable in the proportion and originality of its design, is also astonishing with regards to its elaborate ornamentation, which is dominated by an interlacing pattern. Separated into bandwidths within the framework of the bay and above the dormer arcatures of the two towers, these losange-shaped interlacing patterns, which form a trellis, are encrusted with tiled mosaic, *zellij*, lending a unique charm to this majestic gate. It is recorded that the shafts and capitals of the columns are made from marble exported from Carrara, Italy, something which in itself is quite exceptional. This marble would seem to have originated from the al-Badiya Palace in Marrakesh, which was built by the Sa'adian prince Ahmed al-Mansur al-Dhahbi (985/1578–1011/1603).

The gate had been used in a variety of ways. In the 19th century, Sultan Mulay 'Abd al-Rahman erected a construction to the left when exiting Bab al-Mansur which served as a place for holding reunions between military leaders and other dignatories. The building served as a tribunal for the town *pasha*, who, together with military leaders, lunched there each Friday after prayers. Religious and military ceremonies were also organised to take place in front of this monument. These customs were maintained right up until the the Protectorate was established in 1912.

I.1.e **Pavilion of the Ambassadors**

Return to the car and, after driving past the gate on the right of Bab al-Mansur, follow the sign Mulay Isma'il Mausoleum. There is parking opposite the dome on place Al-Khayyatin. Entrance fee. Open daily from 09.00–12.00 and 15.00–18.00.

Dome of the Ambassadors, exterior view, Meknès.

ITINERARY I *The Royal City*
Meknès

This pavilion, which is still called a dome, is a small building placed next to the first enclosure of the city. Known today as the "Dome of the Tailors", a title which evokes one of its more recent uses, it was nevertheless known for long time as the Dome of the Ambassadors. This designation corresponds to the building's primary function, as Mulay Isma'il had decided to receive foreign ambassadors there who, among other things, had come to bargain to buy back Christian captives.

Built on a large rectangular area of 6 m. x 8.2 m., the building joins onto a square whose sides measure 13.8 m. each. The entrance is covered by an overhanging porch which was added on afterwards. The monumental door is decorated with strips of *zellij* which form a geometric composition, and with friezes of sculpted wood. Here and there within the dome stands a small chamber, whose ceiling is surfaced with green tiles, and whose floor is chequered with *zellij* in a variety of colours, including blue, yellow, white and red.

The interior of the dome, as large as it is harmonious, is made up of 10 arcades which face one another, bearing sculpted plaster motifs which have been partially restored. The pillars which support the arcades are covered in mosaics up to a height of 2 m. The base of the dome's walls are themselves also decorated with mosaic and are crowned by a band of stucco on which is inscribed: *"Power belongs to Allah"*. This building is essentially esteemed for its conical dome whose interior structure is decorated with geometric and floral motifs.

I.1.f Mulay Isma'il Mausoleum

Situated opposite the dome. Non-muslims are also allowed in.

Free entry. Open daily from 08:30–12.00 and 15.30–20.00.

The royal funeral compound of the Kasbah in Meknès is situated south of the *Dar al-Kebira*, in between the first and third enclosure. Its location owes nothing to chance, since Mulay Isma'il chose as his mortuary a sacred place which had been previously sanctified by the tomb of a local saint, Sidi 'Abd al-Rahman al-Majdhub, poet and mystic of the $10^{th}/16^{th}$ century. The sultan Mulay Ahmed al-Dhahbi, son and successor of Mulay Isma'il, ushered in a number of changes. The irregularity demonstrated in the construction, in which certain rooms seem as if they were dug out of the walls, shows that it is made up of an entity which was revised at various stages.

Before going into a detailed description of this immense compound, it is important to give a general overview of this funerary entity. The two *qubba*s which determined the choice of location decided upon by Mulay Isma'il appear to have been joined together, during an earlier period, by a row of the three following elements: patio, funeral hall and Qur'anic lecture hall. It seems that the annexed sections were not part of the original design.

Even if this mausoleum is in no way indebted to those infinitely more complex mausoleums of the East, it can at least be said to be a direct descendant of the Sa'adian tombs of Marrakesh, whose origins are in themselves truly Hispano-Maghrebic. Thus, in the design of the mausoleum, Mulay Isma'il imitated the series of three chambers, one being the square-shaped central room which shelters the prince's tomb, which can be likened to the succession of the three rooms of the Rauda in Granada. Further-

ITINERARY I   *The Royal City*
Meknès

Mausoleum, Mulay Isma'il, courtyard, Meknès.

more, the motif of having a square-shaped room with an ante-chamber seems in this instance to have been directly inspired by Granada's palatial, rather than by its funerary architecture.

The initial design seems to have grouped the row of three rooms to the east together with the outbuildings to the west and to the south, in other words joining the Grand courtyard to two porticoes. Originally, the entrance to this compound was found to the north, facing *Dar al-Kebira*; the actual entrance dates from the time of the Protectorate.

The entrance and the first courtyards

The first compound out onto which the mausoleum's entrance door opens is composed of an entrance hall with three annexes: three courtyards. Whilst this first chamber and the first courtyard are viewed as being used for the purposes of distribution, and the second courtyard is seen as a means of passage, the third courtyard is there to offer a décor and environment suitable for a place in which to rest. The latter differentiates itself through having two porticoes

ITINERARY I *The Royal City*
Meknès

Grain Silos vaulted arcatures, Meknès.

which stand opposite each other, the eastern one facing the western one, with a deep round basin in its centre. A simple and hexagonal *mihrab* was built into the wall of the eastern portico, and a second was embedded into the eastern wall of the courtyard. Two doors along the lengthy sides of this third courtyard are boarded up.

The patio and the funeral halls

The patio, situated in the north-eastern corner of the funeral compound, is a result of rigorous and painstaking labour, which has recently been taken up again, reincorporating the older features. It is distinguished by some marble columns, set out in groups of three, crowned by capitals, of which a certain number are Hispano-Maghrebic in type: a capital which places a cylindrical half with its two rows of leaves in opposition to a heavy prism-shaped half, and with its large décor of palm leaves and palmettes engraved rather than sculpted.
This patio communicates with the other funeral halls through a door built into the

ITINERARY I   *The Royal City*
Meknès

southern and richly decorated wall. It allows access into a sort of ante-chamber which opens out in a big way onto the mortuary via a smooth, horseshoe and slightly pointed bay. The funeral slabs belonging to Mulay Isma'il, to his successor Ahmed al-Dhahbi and to the Sultan 'Abd al-Rahman Ibn Hisham sit in the centre of the hall.

I.1.g **Grain Silos**

Accessible by car. Located on the far north side of the kasbah. Take a left when leaving the mausoleum and go through the Bab al-Rih gate in order to walk alongside the Royal Palace. The silo scheme was in the past known under the name of Dar al-Makhzen. Follow the road to the end, take a right, and proceed straight ahead, going past the main entrance of the Royal Palace (on the right) and walk further still along the camping area from where one can see the silos.
Entrance fee. Open daily from 09.00–12.00 and 15.00–18.00.

A work of Mulay Isma'il's doing, the House with Ten Norias is part of a tripartite compound which consists of a trapezoidal building, a series of parallel barrel vaults whose ceilings have crumbled, the silos, and a trapezoidal basin, the Basin of the Norias. A building with a functional utility, it stands as evidence of Mulay Isma'il's desire to endow his city with infrastructures which would allow him to be prepared for all eventualities, to be armed against possible dangers from abroad, and to fulfil his ambitions through safeguarding his city's imperial status in the same way as Fez and Marrakesh safeguarded theirs.

The House with Ten Norias

Inside this building, a series of cramped rooms surround a central, more spacious chamber of scantly built barrel vaults, and a corridor winds itself around this central massif by lining a system of 15 rooms covered with 12-piece conical vaults. Origi-

Basin of the Norias, general view, Meknès.

ITINERARY I   *The Royal City*
Meknès

Bab Berdeïn, general view, outside entrance, Meknès.

nally, each round room contained a *noria*, that is to say a deep well that reached the phreatic layer by means of a chain of buckets with pointed bases.
The silos were built adjacent to this hydraulic scheme; silos which were too often incorrectly referred to as stables.

The Silos

A series of 22 arcades consisting of 14 arches each, a number of which were later blocked up, are located adjacent to the south-west wall of the building of the Ten Norias. These corridors were incorrectly called stables when they were in fact silos.
Considered to be one of the most beautiful works accomplished by the Sultan Mulay Isma'il, the building was intended to store food products, particularly wheat, as was noted by the historian al-Nassiri in the 19th century: *"Mulay Isma'il also ordered for the construction of a granary to be built inside the kasbah which would be used for provisions, with vaulted corridors for the storage of wheat and other grains, which could hold enough grain to feed every inhabitant of Morocco"*.
The mules which carried the wheat from different regions did not enter via the main gates of the building but crossed over an alleyway which brought them to circular openings pierced into the building's terrace, into which the wheat was tipped. The building, constructed on an area of 182 m. in length and 104 m. in width, contained large rectangular rooms which were in fact underground granaries, even if today all their ceilings have collapsed and there is no longer a trace of "holes in the ceilings" which would have been used there. A central alleyway is maintained in a user-friendly condition as far up as to the back wall. Pillars, which hold up arches whose full arc measures 3 m. diametrically, divide the room into 18 bays and 23

ITINERARY I *The Royal City*
Meknès

naves, originally covered with barrel vaulting. This part of the *kasbah* is particularly impressive today; the picturesque and flowery expansiveness suits this series of hard-packed clay arcades marvelously.

I.1.h Basin of the Norias

Situated at the foot of the building which shelters the silos.

According to the historian Ibn Zidane, Mulay Isma'il *"built inside the kasbah a Grand chamber of water, across which one could sail in a pleasure boat"*. In spite of this description, its functional utility outweighs its element of leisure, since not a single aesthetic preoccupation seems to have prevailed in the construction of the basin.

The basin named the Basin of the Norias, *Sahrij Swani*, is one of the three buildings which constitute the compound known as the House with Ten Norias.

The construction of this hydraulic building fulfilled the population's need for water – the city having been besieged several times by regional tribes – and to provide water to the buildings and work camps of the city, such as the mosques, the bathhouses, the homes, the gardens and the orchards.

This rectangular shaped artificial basin, remarkable in its size of 148.75 m.× 319 m., with a mean depth of 1.20 m., was supplied by ten norias from the neighbouring building, located underneath the subterranean silos; the norias themselves were linked to the basin via channels made out of pottery. Originally, three high crenellated walls would have surrounded the basin. All that is left now is an isolated rampart near the Bani Mhamed neighbourhood in the south-

west, and the base of an enclosure more than 2 m. in thickness.

A Walk in the Medina
It is possible to reach monument I.1.i on foot by crossing the medina. Return to place al-Hedim. Pass the Dar Jamaï museum's vault on the left, and walk towards rue Nejjarin which specialises in the sale of textiles and babouches (oriental slippers). In following the road towards the west, and after having entered rue Sekkarin, one reaches an exit situated within the west wall of the medina which leads to the Mellah. In taking this exit, and in following the alleyway which contours the ramparts from the outside, one comes across a very colourful spice market, followed by a flea market not far from the tanneries of Meknès. In reentering the medina through Bab al-Jdid, take rue al-Hanaya on the left to climb northwards in the direction of the Berdeïn Mosque which is near the Bab Berdeïn.

I.1.i Bab Berdeïn

Located on the far north of the medina. By car, take the circular boulevard, the gate is on your right.

The enclosures of the Isma'ili Kasbah were originally built with 20 fortified gates covered by bastions. Bab Berdeïn, the gate of the pack-saddle makers, situated in the northern part of the city's enclosure, today consists of two gates separated by a courtyard.

The ancient gate, erected by Mulay Isma'il in 1132/1720, stands on the summit of a hill and appears both majestic and slender in between its two towers, hanging over the curtain wall. The decorated section of this gate (which does not lead into

81

ITINERARY I *The Royal City*
Mulay Idriss Zerhun

a bend unlike other gates), a square which measures just over 11 m. on each side, was recently restored. This gate must have held, in the 12th/18th century, and in contrast to today, an important role in Meknès' economy, having been the focus for all commercial as well as diplomatic transactions with the north and thus with foreign lands. One therefore imagines that Mulay Isma'il endowed this entrance to the *medina* with a gate that was worthy of a royal neighbourhood. The new gate, Bab Berdeïn, can be found close by. It opens out onto the mausoleum of Mulay 'Abd Allah Ibn Ahmed, onto the cemetery of the Shuhadas and onto the large cemetery where a number of saints of Meknès such as Shaykh al-Kamal and Sidi al-Harthi were buried.

I.2 MULAY IDRISS ZERHUN (option)

I.2.a Mulay Idriss Zerhun Mausoleum

The village of Mulay Idriss can be found on the Ketrina road, 28km. from Meknès. The mausoleum is located at the centre of the village. Access restricted to Muslims.

A large white village attached to the side of the Zerhun mountain, the mausoleum-town dominates the surrounding plateau and looks over towards the Roman ruins of Volubilis. It is a small town, famous because it holds the mausoleum of the prince who founded the first Muslim Moroccan dynasty. Mulay Idriss Ibn 'Abd Allah, the fifth descendant of the Prophet's son-in-law 'Ali, escaping the wars fought between the Abbassids and the Umayyads in Arabia, came to Morocco, where he was welcomed as the descendant of the Prophet's family. The local Berber prince of Walili, who had rallied himself behind Islam, called upon the tribes to follow the *shorfa* (sg. *Sharif*). But Mulay Idriss' premature death in 176/793, without doubt the result of being poisoned on the orders of the Abbassid Caliph, did not leave him with sufficient time to give his dynasty the structure he would have wanted to give it. Before his death he had married a Berber called Kenza who was to bear him a son posthumously. He was called Idriss the Second and continued the work of his father.

The tomb of Idriss the father, built as a mausoleum with its own dome, became the place of a saint venerated by Moroccans. The monument remained more or less unchanged until the 11th/17th century, when the 'Alawite Sultan Mulay Isma'il gave the order to demolish it and to buy the neighbouring properties in order to add them to the mausoleum. Building works lasted nearly three years, from 1131/1719–1133/1721. Mulay Isma'il ordained it with the Friday prayer, a sign of the importance which was given to the mausoleum and to Mulay Idriss Zerhoun's town.

In 1237/1822, the 'Alawite Sultan Mulay 'Abd al-Rahman took his turn at enlarging and embellishing the mausoleum: he bought the house next to the dome which stood between this monument and the *qaysariya*, and demolished it in order to build an even bigger and more beautiful mosque. The mausoleum of the saint was thus decorated again.

The dome was embellished with gorgeous ceramics by the Grand *m'allem* (an artisan who qualified in ceramics in Meknès) Ibn Makhluf during the reign of the Sultan Sidi Mohamed (1859–1873).

ITINERARY I *The Royal City*
Mulay Idriss Zerhun

Sultan Mohamed V (1927–1961) and his son King Hassan II (1929–1999) initiated the redecoration of the *Darih*, the mausoleum, and once again enlarged the mosque. To this day, Mulay Idriss is the object every year of a large pilgrimage which takes place on the occasion of the saint's *Mussem*. Numerous tribes then come into the mausoleum to pray.

The veil, richly decorated with golden embroidery, which covers up the saint's catafalque, is changed once a year or once every two years amidst a religious ceremony in which the political and religious authorities of the country or of the region participate.

It is a veritable celebration full of song, full of the odour of perfume and of sacrifices, and of the noise of gunfire, during which pilgrims fill the town in a long procession.

Volubilis
5 km. from Mulay Idriss and 31 km. from Meknès lie the most important Roman ruins in Morocco. The site of Volubilis is in fact one of Morocco's cultural highlights. The ancient capital of King Juba II, husband of Cleopatra's and Mark Antony's daughter, it encloses the entire Roman history of Morocco.
Entrance fee. Open daily.

MULAY ISMA'IL

Mohamed Mezzine

Portrait of the Great Sherif Mulay Isma'il, engraving from the 18th century.

A vigorous man, well-built, quite tall but very slender in size, Mulay Isma'il, characterised by *"a long face, more black than white, that is to say decidedly mulatto"* was *"the strongest and most active man of his States"* according to Saint-Olon, the ambassador of Louis XIV to the Sultan. Possessing a strong will which would rise to any challenge – *"If God gave me the kingdom, then no-one can take it away from me"* was a phrase he liked to repeat to himself – as well as having great political insight, Mulay Isma'il intended to forever remain the "primus inter pares". In the affairs of State, as in undertakings of secondary importance, he considered himself to be the first and to set the example. *"Whether in war or in the projects undertaken during peacetime, such as the development of Meknès in which one sees him frequently put his hands to work as if it were his job"*, his effectual presence could never be faulted.

Mulay Isma'il, the second Sultan of the 'Alawite dynasty, spent 24 years of his long 55-year reign pacifying the country, fighting the undefeated and insurgents, and establishing political order. To have done so he needed a strong, permanent and devoted army. He organised one from black conscripts numbering approximately 150,000 men, whom he forced to take oath on the book of *hadiths* of the Imam al-Bukhari, one of the four great traditionalists of Islam; this is where the title '*Abids al-Bukhari*, "Slaves of al-Bukhari", which they were given, derives from. On the other hand, he also needed a presence which would remain permanent throughout the territory. He achieved this through the nationwide construction of fortresses in which he placed heavily armed contingents charged with maintaining order or holding back tribes which had not yet been vanquished.

Towards 1111/1700, the reign of Mulay Isma'il reached its climax. The entirety of Morocco, which includes Mauritania, and Tuat obeyed him. He leads naval battles from which he collects 70 per cent of the captured cargoes' value. Economic contacts with Europe are reestablished and European commercial firms make their presence felt in Tétouan, Salé, Safi and Agadir. Areas on the Atlantic coastline once occupied by Spain were reclaimed. Numerous diplomatic exchanges take place with France and with England. All in all, Morocco's relationships with the

Grand countries of Europe regulated itself and was intensified.

A contemporary of Louis XIV, Mulay Isma'il is considered, by his own contemporaries as by nearly all chroniclers, to be the greatest monarch of the 'Alawite dynasty during its first two centuries of existence. Like Louis XIV, he was set on distinguishing his reign and on leaving behind his indelible mark on the country. He had thus resolved to construct a Royal City, conceived and planned entirely by him: this became the Royal City of Meknès which he raised to the status of a Capital City.

On the Sultan's death (1139/1727) –having held onto power until his death through constantly going to battle– the city would encounter numerous problems. This was because the entire construction created by Mulay Isma'il resided entirely on his person. To take an example: his army, which had been conceived to be the keeper not only of the State's strength but also of its perpetuity, became a dominant destabilising force through its movements and direct interventions in political affairs. For 30 years, practically without fail, the army imposed its rule, nominating and deposing sultans. The result was the ruin of the country: empty of treasure, its economy destroyed, social anarchy, and so on.

Legend, and Moroccan and foreign chronicles have left us with this picture of the Grand Sultan. But only the French chronicles held the correspondence between Louis XIV and Mulay Isma'il in which the latter asks the King of France for the hand in marriage of the Princess of Conti for his brother.

ITINERARY II

A Day in the Life of a Taleb in Fez
Mohamed Mezzine

II.1 FEZ

    II.1.a Batha Museum
    II.1.b Bab al-Guissa
    II.1.c Bab al-Guissa Mosque
    II.1.d Bab al-Guissa Madrasa
    II.1.e Sagha Funduq
    II.1.f 'Attarin Madrasa
    II.1.g Mulay Idriss Mausoleum
    II.1.h Cherratin Madrasa
    II.1.i Qarawiyin Mosque
    II.1.j Mesbahiya Madrasa
    II.1.k Qarawiyin Library

Calligraphy

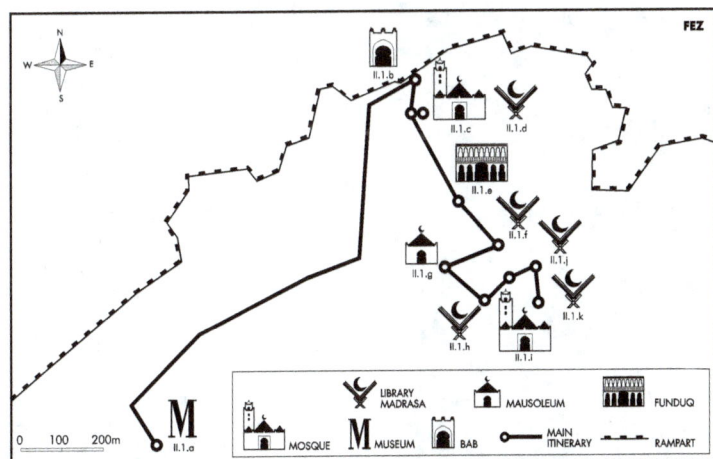

Qarawiyin Mosque, Sa'adian pavilion, ablutions' fountain, Fez.

If the history of Fez, which oversaw the succession of more than seven dynasties over twelve centuries, is fused with the history of Morocco, then the history of its urbanisation is interwoven with its political, cultural, economic and religious history, which one can divide into three major phases:
— the foundation and consolidation of the town from the $3^{rd}/9^{th}$ century to the $7^{th}/13^{th}$ century;
— the height of Merinid power from the $8^{th}/14^{th}$ century to the beginning of the $9^{th}/15^{th}$ century;
— and the renaissance of the town heralded by the arrival of the Sa'adians and the 'Alawites from the $10^{th}/16^{th}$ century to the 20th century.
Since the founding of the town in the $3^{rd}/9^{th}$ century, two distinct nuclei arose, separated by the river *wadi Fas*, still known as *wadi al-Jawahir*, the river of pearls. The city on the left bank, *'adwat al-Qarawiyin*, the seat of Idrissid power, laid out with a *qaysariya* and a mosque (the *al-Achraf* Mosque), quickly took a lead over the right bank of the river, *'adwat al-Andalus*. Enlarged during the $3^{rd}/9^{th}$ and $4^{th}/10^{th}$ centuries by the several thousand Andalusian families expelled from Cordoba who had come to settle on the riverbank to which they were to give their name, the city on the right bank managed to retain a rural character in contrast to that on the left bank, to where some 2000 Kairouanese families had arrived, seeking refuge in Fez.

Each bank-turned-city was surrounded by an enclosure. Despite the grandeur and solidity of the walls, these enclosures opened up to themselves and to the world outside. Fez soon became a very important centre, increasingly attracting the attention of States of the time: the Abbassids of Baghdad, the Fatimids of Egypt and the Umayyads of Spain.

Coveted from tower to tower by the Zenetes, the military chiefs of the Berber principalities of the region, the town experienced a troublesome period which lasted from the end of the $3^{rd}/9^{th}$ century, when the Idrissids fell from power, up to the beginning of the $5^{th}/11^{th}$ century. During this extended period, the town was divided up between the Zenete brothers al-Guissa and al-Futuh, after whom the two great north and south gates are still called.

In reestablishing much needed order, the Almoravids, the new masters of $5^{th}/11^{th}$ century Morocco, rearranged the *medina* by taking down the ramparts which had divided it into two halves. They built bridges, such as the Tarrafin and the Bab Selsla bridges, facilitating the crossing between the two riverbanks. Thus, in 462/1070, the two Idrissid towns transformed themselves into a single city. The new dynasty regulated

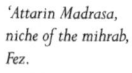
'Attarin Madrasa, niche of the mihrab, Fez.

the flow of the *wadi Fas*, and organised the provision of water and its distribution to the town by building a complex system of dual canals, which allowed for fresh water to be provided simultaneously to mosques, homes and workshops whilst draining their used water.

Continuing on from the work of their predecessors, the Almohads took their turn at demolishing the external ramparts of the town, in an act which was symbolic of the town's power. Furthermore, the following words have been attributed to the Almohad prince 'Abd al-Mumen: "*We have no need to be defended by walls; our ramparts are our swords and our justice*".

The period of prosperity which Fez enjoyed – being, particularly during the $6^{th}/12^{th}$ century, the centre of the Almohad Empire – was signified by great building developments: the reconstruction of the town's ramparts in an Almohad style, and of the Bujlud Kasbah after it was destroyed by the Almohad Sultan 'Abd al-Mumen, as well as the restoration and extension of the *medina*'s two major mosques, al-Qarawiyin and al-Andalus. In the same manner one could total the number of constructions during the period of prince al-Mansur (579/1184–595/1199) at 780 mosques and oratories, 42 ablution halls, 80 fountains, 93 public baths, 467 *funduqs*, 9,082 shops and 29,236 homes. Fez, however, experienced its hour of glory with the accession of the Merinids in the $7^{th}/13^{th}$ century, who made it their political capital. Having rediscovered political stability, the town became the centre of a fervent cultural life and of unprecedented commercial activity, welcoming into their *funduqs* loaded caravans which were coming from or going to western Sudan or al-Andalus. Grand architectural projects were undertaken in which one could witness the achievements of Hispano-Maghrebic art.

The Merinid Sultan, living in cramped conditions in the Almoravid Kasbah of Bujlud, decided in 672/1274 to construct a new city adjoining the *medina*: *Fas-Jdid*, New Fez (Fez Newtown), which was built within several years. Intended to be a symbol of the new dynasty's power and glory, the new town originally held the emblematic name of *al-Madina al-Bayda'*, the white town, in contrast to the town founded by Mulay Idriss whose walls, covered with the markings of time, were already six centuries old. The Merinids kept *Fas-Jdid* for the accommodation of princes and for the residences of important political and military dignitaries of the dynasty, as well as for the housing of the Jewish community which had previously resided in the centre of the *medina* near the Mulay Idriss Mausoleum.

Meanwhile the unique contribution of the Merinid reign affirmed itself in the cre-

Mulay Idriss Mausoleum, screen of entrance in cedarwood, exterior view, Fez.

ation of *madrasa*s, religious foundations which existed both for pedagogic purposes and as new instruments of power. They erected seven *madrasa*s in Fez which were created for the teaching of their own ideology over that of the Almohads, as well as for the formation of civil servants of the judiciary, the administration and of the all-empowering State, through whom the Malekite doctrine could be propagated. Merinid power was supported in its efforts by the al-Andalus who had fled the Christian Reconquest. Scholars, anonymous craftsmen and traders gathered in the Merinid capital and contributed to the reconstruction of the town, its *madrasas* and its mosques, and to the embellishment of its monuments, through the employment of their knowledge and know-how. Mosaic work, *zellij*, woodwork and stucco work, all done in the al-Andalus style, was propagated by artisans who had come from Seville, Toledo and Granada. The great al-Andalus scholars, like Ibn al-Khatib and Ibn Khaldun, contributed through teaching at the *madrasas* and in the Qarawiyin. The last of the Nasrid princes of Granada, Abu 'Abdil, brought his entire fortune from al-Andalus to Fez, where he settled with his entourage.

As the height of Merinid power came to a close, the economic and political problems, which began to plague Morocco during the $9^{th}/15^{th}$ century, did not spare Fez, which only managed to regain its prestige with the accession of the Sa'adians in 956/1549, and the 'Alawites in the $10^{th}/16^{th}$ century. With the Turks, the Spaniards and the Portuguese clamouring at the gates of Morocco, the Sa'adians decided to equip Fez with two bastions, one for the north and one for the south, whose aim it was to control and to protect the town from all external danger. Additionally, the "grand" Sultan Ahmed al-Mansur (985/1578–1011/1603) extended the Qarawiyin, enriched its library, and regulated the flow of the *wadi al-Jawahir*, which ran through the *medina*, by constructing upstream the Abu Tuba dam, at the south-west entrance of the town.

When the 'Alawites came to power, they at first settled in Fez, before proceeding with the conquest of the rest of the country. They pursued, like their predecessors, the restoration and construction of religious, cultural and economic buildings. Economic activities, arts and crafts, and commerce were all based in Fez, as they were during the Merinid period in the $8^{th}/14^{th}$ century, possessing their own centres, *funduqs* and workshops. Professions were regrouped into corporations, *hanta*, which were controlled by a *muhtasib*. The *funduqs* and markets were allocated to different parts of the *medina*: the *'Attarin* Suq, a spice market, the *Chema'in* Suq, a candle market, and the *Nejjarin* Suq were adjoined to the *Sagha*, *Stauiniyin* and *Chema'in funduqs* in the centre of the *medina*, not far from the major trunk roads which cut across it – *Tal'a Lekbira*, the large uphill slope, and *Tal'a Sghira*, the small slope. The neighbourhood markets, which sold all kinds of things, complemented the larger, more specialised markets which set themselves up in the centre of the *medina*. During the $12^{th}/18^{th}$ and $13^{th}/19^{th}$ centuries, Fez once more became a lucrative destination for the traders of Tlemcen, Algiers, Senegal and Europe. *Funduqs* regained their business. Numerous English, French, German, and Spanish consuls and travellers came to visit Fez and to base their representatives there. The treaty establishing the Protectorate was signed in Fez in 1912. General Lyautey, who was in charge of overseeing the Protectorate, put into place a system of administration whose aim it was to safeguard the cultural identity of Fez; religious and cultural buildings were preserved and renovated. He created a new town to the west of *Fas Jdid* and the *medina*, to accommodate the colonials and the town's administration.

Following independence, the town would come to experience a mass exodus of trader families, gone to find their fortunes in Morocco's new big cities: Casablanca and Rabat. In 1981, proclaimed by UNESCO as a world heritage site, the town was to benefit from the attention of intellectuals and patrons. Projects aimed at the protection of architectural heritage would come to life with respect to *madrasa*s, mosques and *funduq*s. The system of teaching particular to the Islamic civilisation was based on a multi-disciplinary approach, which, with the exclusion of theology, considered to be the pillar of all knowledge, consisted of disciplines (termed secular) such as astrology, mathematics or medicine. The literal translation of the Arab word *taleb* (university student) makes this apparent: the word comes from the verb *talaba*, to ask, and thus signifies "the seeker of science". A metropolis of humanities, sciences and arts, Merinid Fez, which lasted from the $7^{th}/13^{th}$ until the $9^{th}/15^{th}$ century, lay at the pinnacle of this teaching system due mostly to the encouragement of sultans, themselves men of science and culture. An event significant to the Merinid period was the introduction to Morocco of *madrasa*s, already widespread in the Machreq since the $6^{th}/12^{th}$ century. Their introduction allowed for the dynasty to establish its power against that of the local brotherhoods, the *zawiya*s. Offering board and lodging as well as the requisite training, this educational system was based on the patronage of the State, coming to the aid of a young *taleb*'s life, a devoted life of abnegation and detachment.

Qarawiyin Mosque, Sa'adian fountain and pavilion, Fez.

These religious colleges, or pious institutions conferred with pedagogic aims, were intended to prepare students for the higher training given at the Qarawiyin. Temple of Knowledge, among the most ancient and most famous in the Muslim world, the mosque provided teaching well before the arrival of the Merinids, having been founded as far back as the $3^{rd}/9^{th}$ century; but it seems to have attained its university status under the Merinids, who organised lessons and programs and oversaw examinations. Frequented by the greatest *'ulama*'s, having come from various towns in Morocco or indeed from Cordoba, Granada and Seville, such as Ibn Khaldun in the $8^{th}/14^{th}$ century, the Qarawiyin contributed to the formation of an intellectual elite who played a leading role in Arab-Islamic civilisation. It should be noted that the urban civilisation of this period was heavily Hispanic in character, as a result of the influence of Andalusian refugees, and of the direct and constant interaction and exchange between Fez and Granada. Writers and artists travelled frequently from one to the other, and the movement of graduates was a common occurrence, involving scholars who had specialised in the sciences known as traditional: philosophy, anatomy, medicine. The cosmopolitan force of attraction that Fez possessed, particularly during the 8th/14th century, drained the land of various populations of young students, who had come from the furthest regions of the Maghreb and beyond in the quest for knowledge. To be accepted into the University of the Qarawiyin was thus the dream of every young *taleb*, at least of the sort of *taleb* one would want to be like, who studiously divides his day between the *madrasa*, the mosque and the university.

Originating from the hills beyond the Rif mountains in the north of the country, the young student would arrive on a market day accompanied by his father with the dream of becoming an *'alim*. Upon entering the gate of Bab al-Guissa, which opens the *medina* up to the north of the country and is the point of entry for those coming from al-Andalus, he would turn up at the Bab al-Guissa Mosque, situated on the side of the gate which shares its name. After having performed his ablutions, he would consecrate himself at morning prayers before heading conscientiously towards the *madrasa* adjoining the mosque. There, he would follow his first lessons given by the the masters from the Qarawiyin or their disciples. Above all it involved demonstrating the ability of memorising the Qur'an and of explaining certain verses, a fundamental ability which every young *taleb* had been trained in beforehand at Qur'anic schools. Indeed, word-for-word memorisation of set texts is the golden rule of classical education: the texts form the basis of the lectures given by the master during the teaching sessions, and are learnt automatically by the student at the same time as his explanations.

As board and lodging was provided for only about 20 students of the Bab al-Guissa *madrasa*, our young *taleb* – who could also have not have admitted to any of the other prestigious "university-residences" of the town, such as the Buinaniya, 'Attarin or Mesbahiya Madrasas, where food and lodging were offered on the condition that one distinguished oneself by one's perseverance with and success in one's studies – would return to his father staying at the local *caravanserai*, the Sagha Funduq, which was built to house all kinds of visitors.

Having gone to eat in one of the various cheap cafes of the 'Attarin neighbourhood, featuring the oldest and most lively suq in town, they would find themselves in one of the alleyways that circle round the sanctuary of Mulay Idriss, founder of the town, where horizontal beams placed here and there just above one's head, forcing unwelcome and dirty animals to turn back and passers-by to bend down their heads, warned each who entered that it was a holy place. The most venerated site in Fez, indeed in Morocco, it gathered together students, *'ulama's* or just simply visitors who had come to meditate close to the catafalque of the patron saint.

Before returning to his lessons, our *taleb* goes to wander in Boutouil Street which stretches alongside the Qarawiyin and is reputed for its booksellers. There, stalls stuffed with manuscripts would open themselves up to the *tolba* (sing. *taleb*) of Fez. From the most rudimentary treaties to the theological writings of the great scholars of Islam, via books on astrology

ITINERARY II A Day in the Life of a Taleb in Fez

Fez

Batha Museum, western gallery, central room of the museum, Fez.

and medicine imported from Marrakesh or al-Andalus – all these were on offer in these cramped, tiny stalls.

Meeting up with his father again, the young *taleb* takes his place in the enormous prayer hall of the Qarawiyin mosque next to a number of students who, with utmost attention, stand respectfully behind their masters. After a solemn prayer lead by the grand *mufti* of Fez, seminars would form, in which each *'alim*, surrounded by his students, and sitting in the place which had been reserved for him on a large, raised chair near a pillar, began his lesson.

Daily life in the "mosque-university" based itself around the culture there which followed the rhythm of the calls of the *adan*, with lessons beginning at dawn, after the prayer ritual. A hundred teaching posts were provided for at the Qarawiyin, where the traditional sciences, jurisprudence, Qur'anic exegesis, and the prophetic tradition, *hadith*, were considered to be as important as language and grammar; but other disciplines were also taught, notably rational sciences such as logic, mathematics, philosophy, medicine and astronomy. Attached to the mosque, the library, built in the $8^{th}/14^{th}$ century, reinforced the cultural infrastructure formed by the Qarawiyin. Having arrived to prepare for the next day's lesson, our young *taleb*, surrounded by copyists working from books bought in al-Andalus or brought back by pilgrims from the Orient, began to dream: one day, he would perhaps become one of the scholars or the Imam of the Qarawiyin.

II.1 **FEZ**

II.1.a **Batha Museum**

Follow the signs for the Syndicat d'Initiative. Passing Place de la Résistance go into the

ITINERARY II   A Day in the Life of a Taleb in Fez

Fez

Batha Museum, riyad, portico in painted wood, detail, Fez.

Avenue du Batha. The main entrance to the museum is in rue Zerktouni on the left.
Entrance fee. Open from 08.30–12.00 and 14.30–18.00. Closed on Tuesdays.

Batha Palace, now a museum, is situated on the intersection of the Idrissid *medina*, *Fas al-Bali*, and the Merinid city, *Fas Jdid*, close to the Boujloud gardens. Construction of the palace, built for the reception and entertainment of distinguished guests, began under the supervision of the 'Alawite Sultan, Mulay al-Hassan, towards the end of the 19th century, and was completed by his successor Mulay 'Abd al-'Aziz. Inhabited at first by domestic staff, it became the seat of the administration. In 1916, this once royal building became the Museum of Folk Art. Made up of two separate buildings, the palace is distinct for its magnificent *riyad*, attesting to its charm and to it being the summer residence of the palace. The galleries along the *riyad* have porticoes which are supported by painted wooden pillars, and are remarkable for the geometric and floral-patterned ornamentation of their ceiling. The eastern courtyards, which before were used as warehouses, and western courtyards of the palace are surfaced with pieces of marble separated by bands of *zellij*.

The gallery along the western courtyard of the museum contains the rooms in which works of Moroccan art are exhibited:

— manuscripts, pottery and ceramic, objects made of copper and silver, rugs and textiles, items in wood, plaster and ancient marble;

— ornamental relics from old houses which have fallen into ruin: decorated doors, sculpted beams, chiselled plaster, precious inlaid woodwork embellished with mother-of-pearl, and finely carved tombstones are all on show in different rooms of the museum;

— windows displaying the variety of jewellery from the region: rings adorned with precious stones, large silver bracelets, finely worked arm bands, necklaces made of small coins, heavy frontal ornaments made of pearl or emerald stones. The pottery, which is decorated with multicoloured tiles, occupies a large room.

Now restored, the museum is also used as a venue for cultural events in Fez.

It is advised to leave one's car in the supervised car park on place du Batha, and to then proceed onto Bab al-Guissa by taxi. The itinerary is done on foot within the medina. *Allow one and a half hours.*

II.1.b Bab al-Guissa

Gate situated north of the medina. *Possibility of entering by car by following the sign Palais Jamai. Supervised parking on the place al-Guissa.*

Opened at the beginning of the 20th century, the Bab al-Guissa is named after an ancient gate built on the old ramparts in the 4th/10th century by prince al-Guissa. With the extension of the town, the Almohads, followed by the Merinids, had to construct new ramparts and thus opened a new gate north of the *medina* which was given the name of its predecessor: al-Guissa.
Restored by the Merinid sultan Abu Yusuf Ya'qub in the 7th/13th century, it was rebuilt after the earthquake of 1147/1735 and the consequential destruction of the *medina*. The embankment, which today lies just outside of the gate, was, according to al-Qadiri, nothing more than the accumulation of material salvaged from the rubble of the destruction.
The gate, made famous by the bird *suq* which stood close by, and by the storytellers who came long ago to tell tales of history and popular legend, reveals a simple architectural décor consisting of several *zellijs* and restored plaster interlace.
Two further gates, standing about 100 m. further down towards the east, today open up this part of the *medina* to the hill where the Merinid tombs are found, and to the numerous *zawiyas* situated nearby.

East of the gate stands the Grand Hotel Palais Jamai, an old palace from the 19th century which belonged to Jamai, a minister of the 'Alawite Sultan Mulay Hassan.

Bab al-Guissa, general view, Fez.

ITINERARY II   *A Day in the Life of a Taleb in Fez*
Fez

Bab al-Guissa Mosque, courtyard and minaret, Fez.

II.1.c **Bab al-Guissa Mosque**

Adjoined to the gate of the same name.

Situated several metres from the Bab al-Guissa, the Bab al-Guissa Mosque is difficult to date. A marble column, from the Merinid period, which sinks into the north-eastern corner of the building, carries the following inscription: *"To our master Abu al-Hassan, emir of the Worshipful"*. Does this refer to the Merinid Sultan Abu al-Hassan? A difficult question to answer, as Ibn Marzuq, who dedicated a work to his master, Sultan Abu al-Hassan, does not cite this mosque in the list detailing the sultan's constructions, writing only that Abu al-Hassan supervised the construction of several mosques in his capital, Fez.

The mosque is, on the other hand, mentioned in the register of *waqf* endowments of 964/1557 which is during the Sa'adian era. It was then extended and restored in the 12th/18th century, when the adjoining *madrasa* was built, during the reign of the 'Alawite Sultan Sidi Mohamed Ibn 'Abd Allah.

The building is distinguished by a huge courtyard enclosing a fountain at its centre, which is surrounded on three sides by a gallery. The prayer hall, which is not very deep, consisting of two transversal naves of five rows each, displays a richly embellished *mihrab*, the niche of the *mihrab* itself being topped by a series of small arches. The "mosque of funerals" or "of the dead", which extends behind the wall of the *qibla*, is composed of two naves which are divided by pointed arches supported by pillars laid out squarely.

This religious institution possessed two teaching posts, and, following the example of the *madrasa*s and numerous mosques in Fez, it participated actively in the spreading of knowledge and culture.

II.1.d **Bab al-Guissa Madrasa**

Adjoining the Bab al-Guissa Mosque. Stairs lead into the building. The madrasa *is occupied by students, but it is possible to visit the courtyard from where the entire building can be seen as a whole. Closed in July and August.*

Linked to the Bab al-Guissa Mosque via a gate built centrally on the northern side, the *madrasa* was erected under the 'Alawite Sultan Mohamed Ibn 'Abd Allah (1170/1757–1204/1790). Like the *madrasa* next to the Mulay 'Abd Allah Mosque in the *Fas Jdid*, it is distinguished by its simplicity and lack of decoration, in contrast to the Cherratin Madrasa built by the 'Alawite Sultan Mulay Rashid (1076/1666–1082/1672).

The Bab al-Guissa Madrasa and Mosque are equal in length, although the *madrasa* is two times less wide than the mosque. Based on the building-layout of Andalusian housing in Granada and Cordoba, the building encloses a courtyard 22 m. in length x 4.8 m. in width. The centre of the courtyard is adorned with a marble basin, and the courtyard is tiled with *zellij*, composed harmoniously, in patterns which display visual equilibrium. In line with the designs of other *madrasa*s, a gallery allows access to the students' rooms.

At the beginning of the 20th century, 40–60 students, or *taleb*s, lived in the *madrasa*, the majority of whom came from the region of the Jbala. Other than the seminars which took place in *madrasa*s, this one in addition offered board and lodging.

Bab al-Guissa Madrasa, courtyard, Fez.

II.1.e Sagha Funduq

Go down rue Brad Ayin, opposite the main door of the Bab al-Guissa Mosque, heading towards place al-Achabine. Having reached al-Achabine, take a right, then a first left, which leads onto the place Sagha in which the funduq is located.

Built in 1122/1711, under the reign of Sultan Mulay Isma'il, the Sagha Funduq is a contemporary of the Nejjarin Funduq. The large door remains the most original feature of the building, even though it is, in terms of size and decoration, reminiscent of that belonging to the Nejjarin Funduq.

On the semicircular arch of the entrance, whose corners are embellished by superimposed tiles, is written the following inscription: *"Praise be to God alone, may God bless Him after whom there will no longer be*

Sagha Funduq, upper galleries, Fez.

ITINERARY II   *A Day in the Life of a Taleb in Fez*

Fez

'Attarin Madrasa, entrance bay of the patio and central basin of the courtyard, Fez.

'Attarin Madrasa, prayer hall, bronze chandelier, Fez.

any prophets. This blessed door was built in 1122".

The upper part of the door is decorated by a series of blind arcatures sculpted in wood, and is shielded by a protective little roof of enamel tiles.

Inside the building, a monumental niche, decorated in stucco and mosaic motifs suggestive of wall fountains, faces the main entrance. Two floors rise up around the patio, in a display of perfect symmetry. The upper parts of the pillars, the arches and the cornices are covered in stucco decoration.

In front of the entrance door of the funduq, a set of stairs leads to a traditional "Moorish" cafe where you can order a glass of mint tea.

II.1.f 'Attarin Madrasa

Take the road on the left which runs along the funduq. At the first intersection, bear left, then turn right immediately. Drive up this narrow road which leads onto rue 'Attarin. Go up rue 'Attarin; the madrasa is located at the far end.
Entrance fee. Open daily from 09.00–12.00 and 14.30–18.00.

The 'Attarin Madrasa, founded in 709/1310–731/1331, situated northwest of the Qarawiyin Mosque, in the street from which it derives its name, is one of the most beautiful Merinid monuments.
Despite the narrowness of the space in which it was built, which forced the architects to alter the classic layout of *madrasa*s by introducing a variant in the position of its oratory, the monument manifests a classical architectural form proper to its buildings.
An angled entrance opens up onto the vestibule, where a staircase leads to 30 small student rooms situated on that floor, and onto a patio, bordered by galleries through which the prayer hall is reached. A bay made of spun wood (*mashrabiyya*) looks onto the courtyard, in which a marble, carved contoured basin, stands. The two, five-bayed galleries are part of the original construction: wooden arches, supported on thick pillars which are covered in mosaic-tiled panelling and chiselled plaster, and lateral arches supported on fragile marble columns which are topped by capitals in a style representative of the 8th/14th century.
The prayer hall, whose entrance door is bordered by panels of *zellij* and whose corners are decorated by a floral motif rarely used during this time, is unique in terms of its wall decoration. The bay of the *mihrab*, recessed into the wall, is framed by a panel of chiselled plaster, and sits under six small openings, four of which hold real, lead-free stained glass windows, a technique rarely seen in Morocco during this time.
In the centre of the hall, a bronze chandelier, dating from the time of the *madrasa*, hangs beneath a wooden dome, and carries an inscription praising the founder of the establishment.
The plaster and tile work, particularly impressive in the delicacy of its execution and in the extravagance of its ornamentation, turn this small building into a masterpiece of Merinid art.

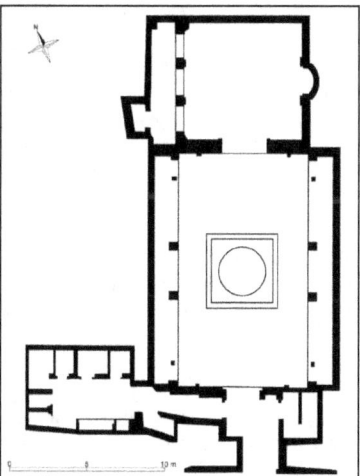

Plan of the 'Attarin Madrasa, Fez.

ITINERARY II A Day in the Life of a Taleb in Fez

Fez

Mulay Idriss Mausoleum, tomb of the saint and niche of the mihrab, Fez.

II.1.g Mulay Idriss Mausoleum

Walk down rue 'Attarin, opposite the main gate of the madrasa. On the left, a zellij door opens up into a jewellers, onto whom one of the mausoleum's doors also opens. Access restricted to Muslims. It is nevertheless possible to appreciate the totality of the monument through the four gates. Walk along the right-hand side of the monument until you reach the fourth gate, the main gate.

The mausoleum of Fez's patron Mulay Idriss, otherwise known as Idriss II or even as Idriss al-Azhar, stands within an urban development called *horm*, "forbidden", which includes:
1. The "House of the Tent", *Dar al-Gaytun*, which was Mulay Idriss' dwelling place during the construction of the town in 192/808.
2. The *al-Achraf* Mosque, "Mosque of the Nobles", where the town's founder prayed.
3. A fountain and a building reserved for ablutions, *Dar al-Wudu'*.

The mausoleum was originally a large and beautiful mosque, the al-Achraf Mosque, erected whilst the town was being constructed, and which risked losing an element of its prestige when the Qarawiyin mosque, to where Friday prayers was transferred, was built in the $4^{th}/10^{th}$ century. The building kept its original design up until 707/1308, when it was rebuilt by Idrissid *shorfa*s, descendants of Idriss II. A century later, part of the mosque was allowed to deteriorate, and one of its walls crumbled down.

In the $9^{th}/15^{th}$ century, a mystical movement spread throughout Morocco which called for the renaissance of religious *Sufi* practices. Numerous saints crisscrossed the country. The most famous of these were buried in mausoleums, and were surrounded by important religious ceremony. At the same time, the Merinid political authorities were on the search for the burial place of Idriss II which ancient texts had positioned to be in the al-Ashraf Mosque. During restoration work to the mosque carried out in 840/1437 under the Merinids, the sarcophagus of Idriss II, believed to have been buried in Volubilis, was discovered, and a convex construction was erected on the site of the discovery to distinguish it from the tombs of other saints.

Since then, a veritable cult established itself around the Mulay Idriss Mausoleum. The veneration accorded to this human being is based on two factors: on his origin, Mulay Idriss being the sixth descendant of the Prophet; and on the basis of his political position, as the son of the founder of the Idrissid dynasty of Morocco, and as founder himself of the town of Fez.

Each dynasty following on from the Merinids engaged itself in the embellishment of this sanctuary, in particular the Sultan Mulay Isma'il (1082/1672–1139/1727), who supervised the construction of a green pyramidal dome, the *qubba*, which hangs over the building. The tomb was covered by a canopy of sculpted wood encrusted with copper and gold, and was then surrounded by several columns made of black-and-white marble. Finally, he also oversaw the construction of a magnificent fountain in the courtyard, and built a tasteful, multicoloured minaret, the highest in the *medina*. All of these works would have been undertaken by volunteers, and the materials would have been donated by the sultans free of charge.

When it came to his turn, the Sultan Mulay 'Abd al-Rahman constructed a new mosque in 1239/1824 which adjoined the dome, as well as restoring the house of al-Gaytun, the previous residence of Mulay Idriss, which brought to light a small, previously closed-off room, and an ablutions stone. The decor was, for the most part, restored by King Mohamed V, after 1956. The vestibule, elaborately but heavily decorated, with its lamps and chandeliers, is closed off by a sort of gigantic folding screen made of red wood of an extraordinary colour. The floor, paved with multicoloured *zellij*, adds – along with the chandeliers and the chiselled, coloured ceiling – to the creation of a mysterious atmosphere, which is particularly strong in the evening, when the smaller lamps hanging from the dome create a garland of golden lights.

A *mashrabiyya* stands to demarcate the whole of this urban compound, (which is thought of as sacred and hence called *horm*); it is made of cedar wood and has a hole at its centre, which is the shaft through which offerings can be made. Fine mosaics decorate its base, next to a fountain which is protected by a small, iron-forged gate. The wall above is decorated with carved plaster, highlighted with remarkable delicacy through the careful use of colour and gold-leaf. The interlacing and rosette motifs, crafted like lace, surpasses, in terms of perfection, the most beautiful decorations of this type found in any *madrasa*. The whole of it, surmounted by panelling, is adorned with a cedar canopy covered in glazed tiles.

II.1.h Cherratin Madrasa

Located in rue Chemaïne, which is named after the candles sold by the stalls in the street. From the mausoleum, take the rue Chemaïne.
Entrance fee. Open daily from 09.00–12.00 and 14.00–17.00.

Built under the 'Alawite dynasty in the 11th/17th century by Sultan Mulay Rashid,

Cherratin Madrasa, copper Dutch door of the entrance gate, Fez.

101

ITINERARY II   *A Day in the Life of a Taleb in Fez*
Fez

Qarawiyin Mosque, aerial view of the courtyard, Fez.

this madrasa should, according to chroniclers, have replaced a more ancient one, the al-Ebridin Madrasa, which housed students who were unscrupulous towards religion. Compared to the Merinid *madrasa*s of the 8th/14th century, the Cherratin Madrasa is sparsely decorated. However it is distinct in terms of its dimensions, and in terms of its large, copper Dutch entrance doors which open out onto a great square courtyard paved with *zellij* whose centre is crowned by a basin. Like the Buinania Madrasa, its layout is simple, consisting of a prayer hall and student accommodation.

The prayer hall is divided from the courtyard, to the right of the entrance, by three large arcades. The rooms of the *tolba* branch off the corridors which surround the great courtyard. On the lefthand side, towards the west, a separate entrance leads to the ablutions hall, outside which, on rue Cherratin, stands a small fountain.
The Cherratin Madrasa is not a "*madrasa* museum", but should be viewed as an example of the transition that took place between the artistic endeavours of the Merinid era and the strictly utilitarian

ITINERARY II   *A Day in the Life of a Taleb in Fez*
Fez

Qarawiyin Mosque, span of the mihrab, Fez.

buildings which were subsequently erected in the 19th and 20th centuries.

II.1.i Qarawiyin Mosque

Located in rue Boutouil. Return towards the 'Attarin Madrasa, and walk around the left-hand side of the madrasa in order to reach the rue Boutouil which runs alongside the mosque. Access restricted to Muslims. Possibility of viewing the complete mosque through the various gates.

One of the most ancient and most prestigious mosques of Morocco and of the Islamic West, the Qarawiyin is also the country's principal university, one of the oldest in the world, frequented ever since the 3rd/9th century by celebrated foreigners like Gerbert d'Aurillac, who became Pope Sylvester II at the end of the 9th century.

Located in the heart of Fez's *medina*, in the old Kairouanese quarter from where it derives its name, the mosque was founded in 242/857 by a noblewoman, Fatima al-Fihri. A small oratory of 100 sq. m. at its inception, holding a prayer hall of four naves parallel to the wall of the *qibla* – a design common to *medinas* – it quickly grew over the centuries both in its proportions and in its prestige, and became, from the 8th/14th century onwards, a vast "mosque-cathedral", able to welcome over 20,000 worshippers to Friday prayers.

A sanctuary of renown, it became the object of care and concern for monarchs across every Moroccan dynasty. In 344/956, the Settefar Zenet Governor, with financial help from the Emir of Cordoba, endowed it with a minaret whose height was equal to four times the side of its base. It is still visible today in its original

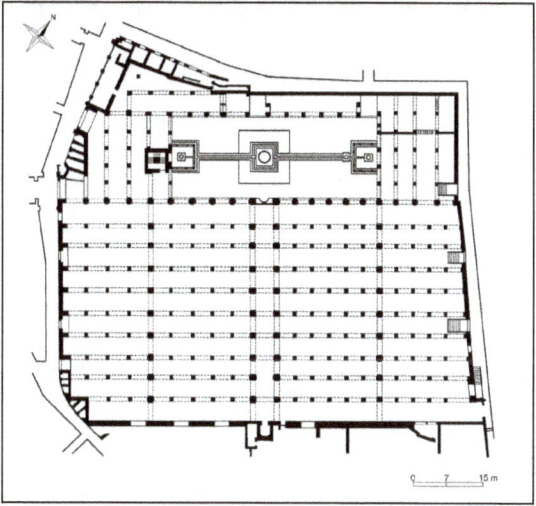

state, having become the minaret to which all common plans diagramming future constructions took as a reference. Its architectural and decorative style dis-

Qarawiyin Mosque, plan of the actual mosque, Fez.

Qarawiyin Mosque, mihrab, Fez.

plays the two parallel artistic influences present in Morocco at the time: the Andalusian influence in the treatment of the platform and in the opening of the bays; and the Ifriqiyan influence from Kairouan, revealed through the presence of a dome at its summit, which replaced the traditional skylight.

In the 6th/12th century the Almoravids extended the prayer hall eastward, and enlarged it by adding lateral naves. They built the courtyard, *sahn*, thus endowing the mosque with the size and structure which is visible today. 'Ali Ibn Yusuf, an Almoravid prince, embellished it further between 528/1134 and 534/1140, by involving Andalusian architects who added six stalactite, or *muquarnas*, and ribbed domes above the axial nave. The carved and painted stucco coating which they are covered in employ the use of stems and foliage in their decorative motifs, as well as single or double palm leaves and acanthus flowers, onto which inscriptions, written in Andalusian *kufic* characters, are incorporated. These decorations, borrowed mostly from the rich repertoire of andalusian-inspired floral patterns, are introduced to Morocco for the first time and subsequently become classic motifs within Moroccan decorative arts.

At the close of the 6th/12th century, the Almohads endowed the courtyard with a marble basin, and installed a bronze chandelier which still illuminates the ribbed dome above the axial nave. Considered to be one of the most luxurious models of its kind, it shows the dexterity of the chisellers and copper engravers of the period which is also evident in the bronze surfacing of the mosque's main doors.

For their part, the Merinids added, during the 8th/14th century, a small room situated in the minaret, whose function it was to shelter astronomical measuring instruments: astrolabes and clocks, one of which calculated the hours of prayer.

The Sa'adians, in the 10th/16th century, oversaw the construction of two symmetrical pavilions in the courtyard, built to shelter the ablution basins. The pavilions recall those of the Court of Lions in the Alhambra of Granada in terms of their design and decoration.

Numerous renovations were undertaken by the 'Alawites, who notably built the famous library which adjoins the mosque.

II.1.j **Mesbahiya Madrasa**

Situated in rue Boutouil which runs alongside the Qarawiyin Mosque, the main door of the madrasa *stands opposite the Bab al-Khassa* gate of the Qarawiyin. Monument undergoing restoration.

Erected by the Merinid Sultan Abu al-Hassan in 746/1346, the *madrasa* carries the name of Mesbah, a jurisconsult who became the first professor to teach there following his inaugural ceremony in 749/1349. Also known as *al-Khassa* Madrasa, "the *madrasa* of the elite", or alternatively as *al-Rkham* Madrasa, "the marble *madrasa*", due to the preponderance of marble within the decoration of the monument, the *madrasa* distinguishes itself from others via its magnificent marble basin, brought over from al-Andalus, as explained by the historian al-Nasiri: *"In short, one finds, in Fez, in Meknès and in the whole of the Maghreb, constructions built by the Merinid sultan Abu al-Hassan (73/133–751/1351). Among the remains in Fez, there is a block of marble from Murcia which weighs 143 quintals. It was disembarked in the port of Larache, then transported by river to Ksar Ketama, now Ksar al-Kabir. From there it was transported on a wooden chariot pulled by tribal peoples and their chiefs to the village of the Ulad Mokharreba on the border of the Sebu. It was carried on this river until the river joined with the* wadi *Fas; then it was carried on carts pulled by men, finally reaching the Sahrij Madrasa in the al-Andalus 'adwat. After several years, the block was transferred from this* madrasa *to that of al-Rkham, which Sultan Abu al-Hassan had built south of the Qarawiyin"*.

One of the largest *madrasas* in Fez, the Mesbahiya Madrasa consists of a ground floor and three upper floors, the third of which is completely destroyed. The original elements of the building reside in the bay which dominates the northern façade of the patio. A unique composition in terms of Merinid religious architecture, at least in Fez, it consists of two twinned arches supported on marble columns. A band of kursif inscription, framing the arches, is surmounted by three arcades of an openwork design, which in earlier times were embellished with plaster interlacing in a floral pattern. This particular bay is flanked by two small blind arcatures, above which is a geometric interlace made of plaster, a diamond-shaped lattice pattern, much admired by Merinid artists.

At the beginning of the century, this *madrasa*, along with the Cherratin Madrasa, accommodated the greatest number of *tolba* who came mainly from Marrakesh and the Dukkala region. The rooms, distributed across the ground floor and upper floors, could house up to 140 students. This *madrasa* could be viewed as an annex to the Qarawiyin, by virtue of its proximity, and thus neither possesses a *mihrab* nor an oratory.

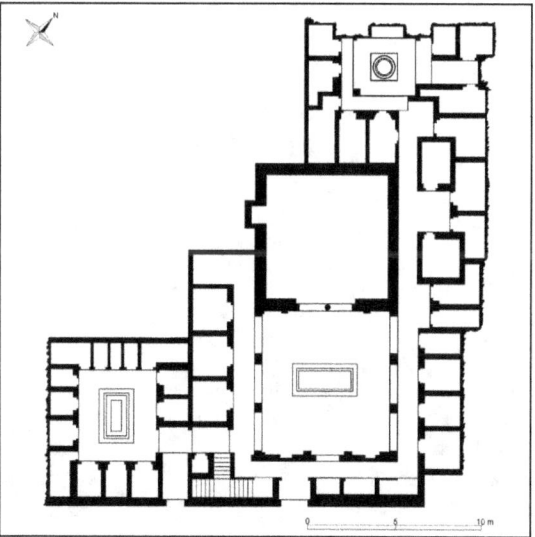

Mesbahiya Madrasa, ground-floor plan, Fez.

ITINERARY II   A Day in the Life of a Taleb in Fez

Fez

The wear and tear of time did not spare the *madrasa*, even though it has retained certain original features – epigraphic, floral and geometric – of the Merinid decor. A restoration and conservation project, financed by King Hassan II, was underway at the beginning of the 1990s.

II.1.k Qarawiyin Library

Situated on the south-eastern corner of the Qarawiyin Mosque, on place Seffarin, (square of the brassworkers). It is possible to visit the lecture hall.

Qarawiyin Library, entrance portal, Fez.

If one considers the building as being recent, since it was constructed in the 20th century, then one should be made aware that the far end of the old library dates from the Merinid period, in the 8th/14th century. Sultan Abu 'Inan (751/1351–759/1358), a man of science and culture, gave the order for a scientific library to be founded, to complete the cultural complex formed by the Qarawiyin. Built in 750/1350, as indicated by a lengthy kursif inscription which can still be seen today at the entrance of the library, it occupied the north-eastern part of the mosque and was endowed at the far end with an important archive. The works it contained heralded from as far as the Maghreb, the Machreq and al-Andalus. The Merinid Sultan Abu Yusuf Ya'qub had recovered 13 loads of Arabic manuscripts from his enemy, King Don Sancho of Spain, from the libraries of Seville, Granada, Cordoba, Malaga and Almeria, which he returned in the first instance to the library belonging to the Seffarin Madrasa, built in 668/1270, before moving them to the library of the Qarawiyin Mosque.

Frequented mainly by students coming from all over the Maghreb, the library was managed by a supervisor, a *qayim*, who administered the library and looked to the preservation of works, which, for reasons of security, could only be consulted *in situ*. Thanks to this rigorous regulation, the library was able to preserve its basic archive, at least during the 8th/14th century.

The Sa'adian Sultan Ahmed al-Mansur ordered for the construction of a new building to be placed south-east of the mosque, which was to house the actual library. It was to be linked to the mosque via a door in the wall of the *qibla*, and was

ITINERARY II   *A Day in the Life of a Taleb in Fez*
Fez

Qarawiyin Library, reading room, Fez.

to be named after its founder: *al-Ahmadiya*. As well as containing the works from the old Merinid library, it was extremely well-stocked and held, in 1021/1613, according to one of the conservationists at the time, more than 32,000 volumes. Mulay Isma'il, the 'Alawite sultan (1082/1672–1139/1727) exchanged Christian captives for original Arabic works which were part of the library resources of Andalusian towns.

However, from the 19th century onwards, the library stock began to dwindle until a single room was all that was required to house all the literary works. In 1940, the building underwent substantial modifications. A large lecture hall, 23 m. in length, was built on the grounds next to the al-Ahmadiya Library. The interest in this building lies in its ceiling which has been glorified by a magnificent dome of painted and sculpted wood. The decorations display a variety of geometric compositions, padded out with floral designs. These motifs, traced onto *zellij*, or engraved into plaster, are living representations that confirm the continuity and the survival of Andalusian-Maghrebic art in Fez. Moreover, the archives of the library today still hold works of Andalusian origin, some of which are rare and unique.

There are several ways of leaving the medina. The quickest is to descend rue des dinandiers (Brassworkers Street) heading in the direction of the Bab Rcif, from where it is possible to take a taxi. For active and fit strollers, it is possible to return to the Batha Museum on foot in 30 minutes. To do this, return towards the 'Attarin Madrasa; from there, walk down rue 'Attarin and go up rue Tal'a Lekbira onto which it runs, in order to exit through Bab Bujlud which is next to the Batha Museum.

CALLIGRAPHY

Mohammed Mezzine

Manuscript belonging to the Sultan Mohamed Ibn 'Abd Allah, end of the 12th/18th century, Rabat Royal Library.

Calligraphy is one of the most important artistic manifestations of the Islamic world. In contrast to Christian artists, who could resort to the figurative in order to express their devotion, Arab Muslim artists used calligraphy, the symbol of Islam, to decorate religious places. Since the start of Islam, the use of Arab script within religious buildings has become a norm. The town of Fez, founded by the Idrissid *shorfa*s from the Machreq, displays a repertoire of ornate and varied inscriptions. Two types of script predominate within the monuments of the town: *kufic* scripture, in which letters are engraved onto a background of ornate arabesques, usually finished off with a floral motif; and cursive scripture, in which supple and svelte letters spread themselves out in a balanced manner. These two types of script occupied a privileged place within historical buildings, although the kursif script – which differs in terms of the materials it uses and the place to which it is allocated – predominates mainly in the writing of manuscripts.

The oldest inscription, dating from the time of the Idrissids in the $3^{rd}/9^{th}$ century, was discovered in the Qarawiyin Mosque. It consists of angular *kufic* characters, lacking in ornamentation, sculpted onto a lintel made of cedar wood, and which can be admired today in the Batha Museum of Fez.

The number of inscriptions would multiply across the centuries; those of the Almoravids have reached us in a well-preserved state. It must be noted that the calligraphers of Fez, who were of Arab-Morisco origin, benefited from the industrial development of paper beginning at the time of the Almohads. The copyists, truly creative calligraphers who worked at a page- or at a daily rate, were already, by the $5^{th}/11^{th}$ century, using paper made in Morocco. At which point Fez alone had 104 paper factories. The amount of factories increased so rapidly with time that, by the mid $7^{th}/13^{th}$ century, their number had reached 400. It was only in the $9^{th}/15^{th}$ century, due to the problems which hit Morocco, affecting Fez in particular, that paper began to be imported from Venice.

Under the Merinids, calligraphy became utterly prestigious; this was due, on the one hand, to the increase in the number of religious buildings like the seven *madrasa*s of Fez, and on the other hand to the massive influx of al-Andalus to whom the Merinid administration had opened its doors. It should be noted that the Merinid Sultans practised calligraphy themselves. Abu al-Hassan and his son Abu Inan, remarkable calligraphers, wrote out pieces from the Qur'an which they placed in a trust for the benefit of the great mosques of Islam.

The Merinid calligraphers often used five types of script in the writing of an inscription:

— the *mujawhar* type: the most frequently used, particularly inside chanceries;
— the *mabsut*: reserved for the writing of the Qu'ran,
— the *musnad* or *zimami* type: reserved for the writing of legal contracts, *adul*s, and of private correspondence;
— the *kufic* type: used mainly in religious buildings.

Calligraphy would find a new lease of life with the Sa'adians, under the reign of Ahmed al-Mansur (985/1578–1011/1603) who initiated a course in calligraphy to be held at the al-Mawassin Mosque in Marrakesh. The Sa'adian calligraphers are distinct for the ornamentation of their manuscripts. They use plant and geometric motifs which relate to the characters in order to design a harmonious image, particularly for the fly leaves. *'Ambar* based ink, orange and rosewater were all prepared fastidiously.

The reproduction of manuscripts would gain great magnitude under the 'Alawites. For instance, the Sultan Mohamed Ibn 'Abd Allah (1170/1757–1204/1790) ordered for 57 camel loads of original works to be sent to Fez, the centre of calligraphy, for them to be rewritten. The 'Alawites calligraphers placed huge importance on the binding and decoration of manuscripts. They diversified the tools of their trade, using different types of gold-nibbed ink pens and crystal ink pots. The *kufic* script was used less and less, for it was judged to be too illegible due to the lushness of its ornamentation, having a tendency to become fused and confused with the plant motifs surrounding it.

Today, calligraphy is a luxurious art which only institutions of great wealth can afford, and this has thus lead to the increased scarcity of the profession.

Manuscript belonging to the Sultan Mohamed Ibn 'Abd Allah, end of the 12th/18th century, Rabat Royal Library.

ITINERARY III

A Day in the Life of an Artisan in Fez

Mohamed Mezzine, Naïma El-Khatib Boujibar

III.1 FEZ

   III.1.a Batha Museum
   III.1.b Bab Ftuh
   III.1.c Andalusian Mosque
   III.1.d Sahrij Madrasa
   III.1.e Chauara Tanneries
   III.1.f Stauniyin Funduq
   III.1.g 'Attarin Suq
   III.1.h Sidi Frej Maristan
   III.1.i Place Nejjarin: Funduq, Fountain and Suq
   III.1.j Buinaniya Madrasa
   III.1.k North Burj, Arms' Museum (option)

Ceramics

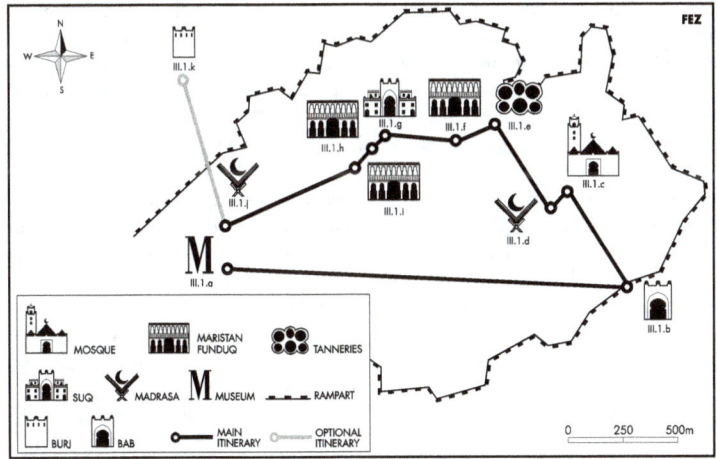

Chauara Tanneries, vats and building annexes, Fez.

ITINERARY III   A Day in the Life of an Artisan in Fez

Fez

Stauniyin Funduq, galleries, Fez.

The city of a thousand and one shops and of countless *suqs*, or markets, where local products were sold next to those from the Far East and West, Fez became, in the 6th/12th century, under the Almohads, an "industrious" town. According to chroniclers at the time, on both sides of the river stood nothing but industrial and craftwork establishments. But having become the political capital under the Merinids, Fez was referred to, in the 8th/14th century, as an economic metropolis. Being at the centre of caravan commerce, Fez – a city which, according to Ibn al-Khatib, "*made fortunes grow*" – attracted the most flourishing of commercial and craft-producing activities. During the time of the sovereigns Abu Inan and Abu al-Hassan, the number of professional guilds was counted at being about 150, grouped together as corporations, *hanta*, and directed by a *muhtassib*. Furthermore, from the Merinid era onwards, the economic topography of Fez starts to base itself around the space occupied by the town, even though a partition along lines of industrial activity has already begun to create itself. The city of the two river banks thus kept the right river bank, the Andalusian river bank, for the purposes of industry, and reserved the left bank, the Qarawiyin side, for the purposes of commerce.

Equipped at an early stage with river canals, the right bank appealed to the major industries of the time: weaving workshops, sawmills, brick yards, potteries, dyers and tanners who themselves were grouped around both sides of the watercourse. On the left bank, a truly commercial city, the *qaysariya*, containing neighbourhood markets, like that of the 'Attarin Suq, coupled with smaller, specialised markets, gathered together the main trade associations. Thus, in a complementary manner, the Andalusian bank restricted itself to the means of production, whilst the Qarawiyin bank charged itself with the distribution and trade of its produce across the town and beyond.

As the centre of commerce for manufactured goods, this part of town included – in addition to all kinds of trade – *funduqs* in which both Jewish and Christian merchants could settle themselves. These establishments, following the example of the *caravanserai*s of Africa or the *khan*s of the Orient, were intended for the lodging of camel and mule drivers as well as of lone or mounted voyagers; the animals were kept in the courtyard, whilst the men sought refuge in rooms on the various floors.

Located near the Qarawiyin and the Mulay Isma'il Mausoleum, the *qaysariya* was compared by Leon the African to a small town surrounded by walls, with its 12 gates, each of which were cordoned

ITINERARY III   *A Day in the Life of an Artisan in Fez*
Fez

off with iron chains to prevent horses and livestock from entering. Divided up into 15 neighbourhoods, according to the description given by the author, each was determined by the type of trade it promoted; it allocated a large space for the sale of leather goods. We should note that ever since the Middle Ages, leather from Fez, *maroquin*, rivalled that of Cordoba and that of Algeria, *bokhari*. The craftsmanship of leather assembled a large number of guilds together: saddlers, *serraj*, slipper makers, *kharraz*, leather craftsmen, *shkayri,* and bookbinders, *seffar*. But being a tanner was considered to be one of the most noble professions.

A descendant of an old family of tanners having come from al-Andalus in the $6^{th}/12^{th}$ century, the artisan, who we propose to follow, whose day is divided between going to the mosque, the sales' room, the workshop or the *funduq*, is a tanner by trade. Dressed in a white *jellaba* and a *selham*, wearing a turban, he mounts his mule at dawn as he always does, once a week, to get near to the Bab Ftuh, where animal-hide merchants, who had arrived during the night, had come to sell their raw materials at auction, not far from the Andalusian Mosque. In these highly colourful markets one came across farmers from the surrounding countryside, like those from the Sais with their fruit and vegetables, miners or their intermediaries from Day offering copper to the highest bidder, or indeed hide salesmen. The skins of sheep and of goat, both of which were the most sought after, were the most expensive; the larger hides of beef, cow and camel, all of which were far cheaper, were sold, after being tanned, to workshops producing harnesses and shoes.

On the other side of the *wadi*, on the Qarawiyin bank, stood four tanneries along the town's river, not far from the *qaysariya*, where dozens of tanners ennobled, under difficult conditions, different kinds of skin. One could follow the process undergone by these skins – from the cleaning vats and the vats of yellow and red colour for soaking the skins in, through to elegant shoe shops and slipper shops – by following the smell, which was said to be a cure for asthma and anxiety. Leaving his workers to their own toil in the *Dar Dbagh Chauara*, the most important tannery in the town, our *m'allem* makes his way towards the Staouniyine Funduq, since, as well as having his own place at the tannery, our artisan has a workshop in the *funduq* set aside for the creation of slippers. In contrast to the funduqs located in the outer neighbourhoods near the great gates of the town, those located at the heart of the *qaysariya*, like the Nejjarin and Stauniyin, served as both

'*Attarin Suq, 'Attarin Street, shops, Fez.*

113

ITINERARY III   *A Day in the Life of an Artisan in Fez*

Fez

Ceramic panel decorated with an interlacing pattern, Batha Museum (C5), Fez.

shopping centres, where cobblers and weavers rubbed shoulders with one another, and as meeting places, since, as is noted by the historian Henri Gaillard, *"the merchants rent out one or more rooms in the funduq, using them as storage space, and they go there for several hours each day to do their stock taking and to chat amongst themselves"*.

III.1 FEZ

III.1.a Batha Museum

Follow the sign Syndicat d'Initiative. Once in the Place de la Resistance, turn down Batha Avenue. The main entrance to the museum is on the street, rue Zerktouni on the left.
Entrance fee. Open from 08.30–12.00 and 14.30–18.00. Closed Tuesdays.

Opened as the Museum of Popular Arts, the Batha Museum consists of a collection of traditional objects, most of which originally came from Fez. Gathered up in the rooms of the west gallery, the different collections aim to show the variety and diversity inherent within Moroccan crafts. The section on Islamic Arts contains elements of architecture such as extremely rare ceramic panels dating from the $8^{th}/14^{th}$ century. Everyday ceramic objects, occupy one of the main rooms of the museum. Large couscous-serving dishes, plates with straight or rounded edges, jugs made to hold and keep water and oil fresh – all these objects, endowed with specific names and functions, were used traditionally by generations in their daily life, and each object reflects the refined taste of the old Moroccan bourgeoisie.

As an old Moroccan tradition, woodwork also occupies a significant place within the museum's collections. The beam made of cedar wood which came from the Qarawiyin Mosque (ref. no.149) dated by its finely chiselled dedicatory inscription to being from 263/877, attests to the existence of one of the first sculpture and wood-painting workshops. Different dynasties would, later on, foster this tradition, but the Merinids would enrich it by introducing cedarwood. This material would come to be relied upon for the crowning of patios within civil or religious buildings, as can be seen in the cornices, the corbels and the platforms or indeed in the friezes which can be seen higher up. One can admire the whole talent of wood craftsmen through looking at the collection of doors which belonged to old bourgeois houses, and which are richly decorated through the jointing and sculpting of wood.

III.1.b Bab Ftuh

Eastern gate of the medina. *Follow the sign Son et Lumière. Supervised parking. The itinerary is done on foot. It is advisable to take a taxi to Bab Ftuh, as one has to cross the* medina *from west to east, and one can leave the* medina *again at several feet from the Batha Museum.*

ITINERARY III   A Day in the Life of an Artisan in Fez
Fez

Literally meaning "The Opening Gate", and known historically as "The Gate of Victory", Bab Ftuh, situated in the southeast of the *medina*, links Fez to the East, providing it with knowledge of the towns and countrysides of the East, of Taza, Oujda, and of north-eastern Africa, of Tlemcen, Tunis, Tripoli and Cairo.

Bab Ftuh was built in the $4^{th}/10^{th}$ century on the site of the ancient gate of Bab al-Qibla which had been erected by Mulay Idriss, the town's founder, and destroyed a few years later.

When, in the $4^{th}/10^{th}$ century, the two brothers, Guissa and Futuh, divided the town of Fez between themselves, one settling on the Qarawiyin river bank, and the other on the Andalusian river bank, they started up a war between them which lasted for several years, from which Prince Futuh emerged victorious. The latter, reigning over the Andalusian river bank, built a gate, which was later to bear his name, and a *kasbah* nearby in which he settled with his court and his army; his brother, who himself reigned over the Qarawiyin, did the same thing in building a gate, Bab al-Guissa, in the north-eastern part of the town.

An immense and complex gate, reaching a height of 15 m., its external facade is constructed of a central archway flanked by two lateral arches. In contrast to the gates which were built later, such as Bab Mahruq and Bab Bujlud, the gate has not been placed at an angle (so that there is no corner to negotiate upon entry), and even though it has undergone a number of restorations, it has still retained its original design. The materials used in its construction are of local origin, the bricks and mortar having been produced in the potters' quarter or in the al-Wajriyyin workshops.

Bab Ftuh, general view, Fez.

ITINERARY III   A Day in the Life of an Artisan in Fez

Fez

A witness of history, this gate saw off troops of the Merinid Sultan Abu Inan, leaving to go and conquer Ifriqiya, with the hope that his army would return victorious, as the gate's name suggests.

> In taking the Bab Ftuh Gate in order to reach the Andalusian Mosque, one comes across the Zawiya (mausoleum) of Sidi 'Ali Bughaleb, with its whitewashed walls and its green-tiled roof. The memory of Sidi 'Ali Bughaleb, who was from al-Andalus but studied in Fez, is still honoured there as it has always been. Dying in 517/1124, he was a scholar and commentator of sacred texts, famous for having been a friend to cats.

III.1.c Andalusian Mosque

The two roads leading from the Bab Ftuh lead to the Andalusian Mosque, the one which steers off gradually to the right is more direct. The main gate of the mosque is located on a little terraced square. Access restricted to Muslims, but one can look into the interior through the different gates.

As soon as the sovereign Idriss II founded the town of Fez in the year 192/808, he called upon a large Muslim Andalusian community to move there. The settlement of these families gave rise to the construction, on the right bank of the *wadi*, of a neighbourhood which came to

Andalusian Mosque, fountain of the northern facade, Fez.

bare their name – the Andalusian Quarter – and of a mosque to celebrate their presence and balance out the Qarawiyin Mosque established on the other side, on the left bank of the river.

Built in the same era as the Qarawiyin Mosque, the Andalusian Mosque was founded by a pious woman called Meryem, sister of Fatima al-Fihri, herself the founder of the Qarawiyin; their father, having come originally from the town of Kairouan settled in Fez, bequeathing a large fortune to his two daughters.

Originally a modest building, *"it was composed,* according to the geographer al-Bakri (4th/10th century), *of seven rows of benches and a small patio planted with walnut and other trees which received an abundant amount of water from a canal called wadi Masmuda"*. Enlarged in the 4th/10th century by the Umayyads of Cordoba, it was given a minaret identical to and as new as that of the Qarawiyin.

The monumental North Gate, which, according to G. Marçais, counts as one of the most impressive achievements of Maghrebic Art, was built between 599/1203–603/1207 by the Almohad Caliph Mohamed al-Nassir, who had a special interest in Fez's *medina*. A monumental gate, preceded by a 14-step staircase dominating the north face, it was embellished with two domes, one of sculpted plaster, the other of cedarwood to which was fixed a talisman, intended to scare birds away to deter them from entering the mosque. This gate exhibits decorative, harmonious compositions done in tile and in wood.

The Almohad Caliph had a basin, a fountain and a pavilion, similar to that in the Qarawiyin, built inside. The Merinids, when their turn came, undertook the restoration work of various ceilings and pillars, as well as the construction of a fountain in the north face of the building. The custom of fixing a white flag to the top of the minaret at prayers during the day, and a lit lantern for prayers at night, began during the reign of the Merinid Sultan Abu Inan.

These various construction projects turned the Andalusian Mosque into the town's second most important religious building, able to welcome up to 4,200 worshippers. A room at the top of the minaret was reserved for the 20 *muezzins* who oversaw the call to prayers night and day. Furthermore, as the town's second most important cultural centre, it was surrounded by two *madrasas* and possessed seven teaching posts and two libraries.

The Andalusian Mosque remains, along with the Qarawiyin, one of a few monuments in Fez through which the traces of different Moroccan dynasties can be traced.

Andalusian Mosque, north portal, frame of the entrance bay in sculpted-plaster and cedarwood canopy, Fez.

ITINERARY III *A Day in the Life of an Artisan in Fez*

Fez

Sahrij Madrasa, courtyard with view onto the entrance bay of the prayer hall and the basin, Fez.

III.1.d Sahrij Madrasa

On the street, rue Yasmina. Take rue Jama' al-Andalus which runs along the right side of the mosque, then take the stairs on the left which lead to the mosque's fourth gate. The madrasa is in rue Yasmina.
Open daily from 09.00–12.00 and 14.00–18.00. The building is occupied by students.

Situated in the Andalusian Quarter, this *madrasa* was erected in 721/1321 by the Merinid Prince Abu al-Hassan, who spent considerable amounts on the project, exceeding 10,000 dinars. He appointed a *fqih* and some scholars as teachers, and accommodated *tolba*s of religious sciences and readers of the Qur'an to whom he granted maintenance, salaries and clothes. The design of the *madrasa* is simple. Composed of a basin, *sahrij*, after which the *madrasa* is named, the courtyard is lined by galleries along its east and west sides which lead to the student rooms.
A large bay opens up onto the prayer hall where the *mihrab* is placed at the centre of the *qibla* wall, in line with the door of the main entrance. The foundation tablet, engraved onto a marble slab, is embedded in the west wall of this room.

The interior facades of the patio still retain many of their ornaments, and one can admire the geometric composition of mosaic tiles which covers the floor as well as the bases of walls and pillars. The sculptures on plaster and on wood are in themselves perfect. Restored at various intervals, especially during the Saadian era, the monument benefited from rehabilitation projects by the Beaux-Arts service under the Protectorate between 1917 and 1924. Through its construction techniques and its elements of decoration, this *madrasa* is proof of the skilfulness with which the artisans and *m'allems* were graced.

III.1.e **Chauara Tanneries**

Retrace your steps back to the Andalusian Mosque. Descend the street opposite the main gate; pass the Lemti fountain, go down the left of the whole street of the same name. Walk down in the direction of the Rcif Gate. Once at this door, take rue Khrchfiyin, the street on the right (facing the gate which leads to Place Rcif). Pass the bridge, go up rue Seffarin leading to the square of the same name where the Qarawiyin Library is situated, then take rue Mechatin, the street, on the right, which is named after the combs which are made there. At the end of this street, veer left, then take a left again onto the street where the mausoleum of the saint Mulay Ahmed Scalli can be found. Pass a fountain on the left, take the street on the right which descends towards the tanneries. From the bazaar, one can see the entire view of the tanneries for the cost of a penny.

Literally meaning the "House of Tanning", Dar Dbagh Chauara is the most imposing

Chauara Tanneries, general view, Fez.

ITINERARY III *A Day in the Life of an Artisan in Fez*

Fez

of the four tanneries which exist in Fez today.

Although Leon the African made allusion to the tanneries of Fez without citing their names, Mármol de Carvajal mentioned the Chauara Tannery in the 16th century. Built on a vast area, the tanneries, provided with water which partly came from a source near the *wadi* Fas, are composed of numerous brick ditches in which the hides of sheep, cattle and goats are treated. They themselves are surrounded by buildings which house the workshops in which the hides were treated. The tanners, 400 in all, descend into the ditches of various colours, and wash and scrub the hides.

The working methods date back from a secular tradition described in kind by Maurice de Perigny, who wrote in 1916: "*One puts the hides in water to soak for a while in order to remove the fur, then one plunges them into ditches filled with lime, leaving them there for twenty days. One then places them in special vats, lined inside by brick walls, 1.25 m. deep, narrowing at the bottom, in which one mixes pigeon droppings with water which the workers then knead with their feet. The hides stay in there for two or three days, then are washed and rolled in damp bran to remove the lime which they by now are impregnated with. At the end of three or four days one tramples them under a layer of water with one's feet, and one then soaks them in a liquid paste made of dried figs with the aim of making them soft and shiny. One leaves them there, again for twenty days, but on the seventh day one starts salting them, which should make them gain solidity without removing their suppleness. It is a very delicate operation which the master-tanner himself takes charge of, throwing rock salt onto the hides which have been stretched vertically in front of him in small but ever increasing doses. One then proceeds onto the tanning which occurs in special containers filled with grains from Tafilalet called* takaut, *which have been pounded and mixed with a little oil. The hides are stirred continuously for two or three days, after which they are left to dry. They are spread across flat slabs of stone and are beaten to be softened; they are then washed again and scraped on the inside with a piece of porcelain*". These vats form one of the most picturesque landscapes within Fez's *medina*. The buildings and vats are endowments, *habus*, owned by the Qarawiyin, the use and enjoyment of which are purchased by the individual tanners: one or more rooms together with a certain number of vats are accorded to each tanner.

Considered to be a source of wealth, the tanneries, or *Dar Dbagh,* were also known as *Dar Dhahab,* "House of Gold". The tanners, who thus occupied a desirable position in society, were grouped into corporations directed by an *amin* in line with other trade associations.

Stauniyin Funduq, shop and galleries, Fez.

The *Dar Dbagh* Chauara remains to this day a living force of leather craftsmanship in Fez.

III.1.f Stauniyin Funduq

Located in rue Butuil, opposite the Qarawiyin Mosque. Retrace your steps by walking up towards the street on which Mulay Ahmed Scalli's mausoleum is located. From there, take the road which goes up in steps and adjoins the fountain. Walk up this street, called rue Derb Tuil, "long Street" which has alternating open and closed passageways until you reach rue Ab Khaiss. In walking up this very commercial street which specialises in the sale of textiles, one comes across the 'Attarin Madrasa. Walk round it on the left to reach the Qarawiyin Mosque. The funduq, *in which certain artisans are established, can be found opposite one the gates of the mosque.*
Entry free. Open daily from 09.00–13.00 and 15.30–19.00.

Intended for the shelter of animals and goods, the Stauniyin Mosque, frequented mostly by merchants from Tétouan from whom it derives its name, is one of the oldest commercial centres of Fez. Situated on the east of the Qarawiyin Mosque, it is a contemporary of the 'Attarin Madrasa, built in the $8^{th}/14^{th}$ century.
Its layout, similar to the Nasrid *funduqs* of Granada, consists of a rectangular area over two floors. Shops and storage space are positioned around a courtyard on the ground floor. Small rooms lit through skylights are spread across each floor; each floor also possesses a gallery which is hidden by *mashrabiyya* wood panels.
Out of the whole building it is the hallway which stands out due to its remarkable decoration. The Stauniyin Funduq is covered by a carved wooden ceiling, enlivened by geometric and floral decoration, and holds an inscription engraved in *kufic* characters which are embellished with floral motifs.
The lavishness of this ceiling was the reason for which the *funduq* was classified as a historic monument in November 1925.

'Attarin Suq, shop, Fez.

III.1.g 'Attarin Suq

Located in rue 'Attarin. Retrace your steps back to the 'Attarin Madrasa. Turn onto the street

ITINERARY III A Day in the Life of an Artisan in Fez

Fez

Sidi Frej Maristan, interior, Fez.

of the same name, a shopping street facing the main gate of the madrasa.

As well as *funduqs*, Fez possessed markets, *suqs*, whose reputation extended far beyond the town walls. The *qaysariya*, a term signifying a commercial neighbourhood, which was situated at the heart of the Qarawiyin Quarter, with its numerous *suqs* and shops, is one of the oldest of its kind, offering goods imported from Europe and the East ever since the Middle Ages.

Destroyed at first by a great fire in 724/1324, and then by floods in 725/1325, the *qaysariya*, with its thousands of terraced houses, was then rebuilt. The 'Attarin Suq, one of the most reputable in the *qaysariya*, occupies the length of a long street which links up to the Merinid *madrasa* of the same name, at *Bab al-Faraj*. Complemented by trade on adjacent streets and places, this market extends over more than 600 m. and was equipped with a large gate at each end, whose *"guardians"*, wrote Leon the African, *"do their rounds at night, with dogs, with weapons, holding up lanterns in their hands. They were paid by the traders themselves".*

The *suq*, according to Leon the African, consisted of 150 stalls, which grew in number to 170 a few years later according to the Portuguese historian Mármol de Carvajal (16th century). Originally specialising in the sale of medicinal products and groceries, medicinal stalls stood shoulder to shoulder with hardware stalls which were distinct for the opulence of their ornamentation. Doctors themselves made up the medicinal preparations, and then sent them to specialised stalls where staff would dispense them under medical supervision.

In the 10th/16th century, the *suq*, through the importance it had gained in terms of the geographical area it fulfilled, through the number of important shops it represented and through the abundance of specialised products it sold, was unrivalled. Even if the *suq* of today has lost a little of its identity through the growth of product variety, one can still find some traditional hardware sellers who are living examples of this market, typical of its kind.

III.1.h Sidi Frej Maristan

Located in rue 'Attarin. About 100 m. from the 'Attarin Madrasa on the left one can find the old hospital which has now been taken over by various stalls. It opens out onto Place Frej.

The Merinid Sultan Abu Yusuf Ya'qub was responsible, at the end of the 7th/13th century, for the construction of *maristans* in the town of Fez. There were several of these institutions in Fez, which were intended for the care of mental illness, where each was cared for and provided with medication. But the Sidi Frej *Maristan*, literally "the Lord who delivers", remains the most famous, continuing to serve, well into the 20th century.

Frequented by celebrated Andalusian doctors like Abu Bakr al-Qurayshi, who was from Malaga, this hospital was managed by Leon the African, who worked as an agent of the administration of the *maristan* in the 10th/16th century.

Destroyed in the 20th century, it was replaced by a *funduq* which was, among other things, set aside for trade, and where to this day traditional cosmetic and pharmaceutical products are sold.

III.1.i Place Nejjarin: Funduq, Fountain and Suq

Leaving Place Sidi Frej, take a left onto the group of narrow and very busy shopping streets. By constantly taking and keeping to the right, one will stumble across Place Nejjarin.
The suq *is closed on Friday afternoons. The* funduq *houses a Woodwork Museum.*

Situated strategically in the heart of the *medina*, in *Place Nejjarin*, the place of the Carpenters, named after the *suq* adjoining it, it links Bab Bujlud to the commercial and cultural core of the *medina* (Mulay Idriss, Qarawiyin). The *funduq*, the *suq* and the fountain, an architectural and urban scheme known as the "Nejjarine Complex", rises up around the square.
Built at the beginning of the 12th/18th century, the *funduq* was built for the storage of precious merchandise belonging

Nejjarin Square, funduq entrance door and fountain, Fez.

to the men of the *makhzen* and to wealthy merchants. It seems that this monument held this role until the advent of the French Protectorate, when it had its function altered, becoming a police station in charge of the surveillance and repression of nationalists.

This *funduq* is distinct for its portal which displays compositional unity: a horseshoe arch supported by two pillars of plain brick, paralleled by another polyfoiled arch made of sculpted plaster; bands run across above the arch, displaying either an inscription or a succession of carved plaster or wood arches. The interior, analogous to all other *funduq* interiors, was restored in 1998 and was converted into a Museum of Woodwork.

The fountain next to the *funduq* is a principal component of this architectural development. It was built a century after the *funduq*, and in terms of its structure and decoration, it is reminiscent of the

ITINERARY III   A Day in the Life of an Artisan in Fez

Fez

Nejjarin Square, funduq, galleries, Fez.

funduq's portal. The basin, rectangular in cross-section, is covered in panels of *zellij* patterned geometrically. Its mid-section is dominated by a horseshoe blind arch, decorated with tiled mosaic rosette motifs. This bay is highlighted by a panelled arch which is framed in a rectangle of chiselled plaster panels. Lateral pillars, surfaced with *zellij* and sculpted plaster, support a wooden lintel on which an inscription in kursif lettering is engraved. The lintel is surmounted by wooden consoles which support a sculpted and painted canopy, which hangs over slightly and is covered in green-glazed roof tiles.

As regards the *suq*, it dates from the Merinid era. A centre of production for wood products, from timber to mobile objects, it stands within a rectangular area, and is traversed by an alley full of stalls and workshops, which are more boringly built in brick and have plain cedarwood doors. Woodwork, wood being a very prized material in Morocco, comes from an ancient tradition, as is made evident by the preacher's pulpit from the Andalusian Mosque dating from the $3^{rd}/9^{th}$ century, exhibited in the Batha museum.

The friezes, sculpted corbels, the raised lintel porticoes made of cedarwood based on mortice and tenon joint-building techniques – they all attest to the high level attained in the field of woodworking during the Merinid era.

III.1.j Buinaniya Madrasa

Situated in the Tal'a Lekbira, 15 minutes from Place Nejjarin. Take the covered passageway to the right of the fountain. Passing the stairs, go up the street on the left, rue Al-Hajel, for about 700 m. Then up the Tal'a Sghira "little hill". At the top of the road, take the covered passageway on the right (Derb Tariana) which runs alongside the madrasa.
Entrance fee. Open from 09.00–12.30 and 14.30–18.00; Fridays from 09.00–11:30.

Named after its founder Abu Inan, the Buinaniya Madrasa, built in 751/1351 and completed in 757/1356, comprises in fact of a group of buildings which include: a mosque, whose *minbar* is today displayed in the Batha museum in Fez; two classrooms facing each other; a large ablutions hall, *dar al-wudu'*, as well as an annexed building, known as the House of Clocks, which stands in front of the *madrasa*'s main gate. In line with other religious monuments of Fez, the Buinaniya Madrasa was endowed with a number of important *habus* gifts whose revenues were intended for the payment of professors and administrators, for the feeding of *tolba*s and for the maintenance of the building's upkeep and preservation. The most immense *madrasa* built by the Merinids, it is described by Ibn Battuta – who called it the Madrasa *al-Kabira*, the Great Madrasa – as the most beautiful creation of the Sultan Abu Inan: "*Amongst the most beautiful actions of our master Abu Inan, may God help him, we cite the following: the construction of a large college on the site known as 'castle', very close to the citadel of Fez, it has no equal in the entire world embodying as it does grandeur, beauty and splendour.*"

Whilst the whole world is agreed in his recognition of the *madrasa* as one of the most beautiful realisations of the Merinid Dynasty, numerous legends abound as to the reason of its foundation. Alfred Bel reports that "*Abu Inan, having often sinned in his conduct towards his father, had much to be forgiven for. He gathered the scholars of the age and asked them how he could atone for his mistakes and earn Allah's forgiveness. They counselled him to choose a site situated high up in the town, which was thus used as a rubbish tip, on which to build a house dedicated to prayer and religious sciences. He therefore*

Buinaniya Madrasa, north-west facade, Fez.

ITINERARY III   A Day in the Life of an Artisan in Fez

Fez

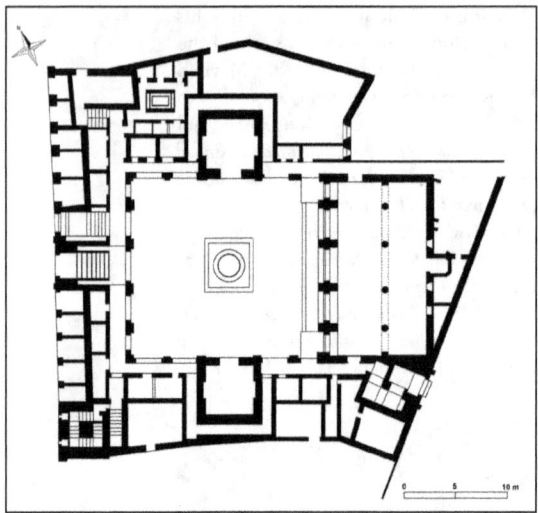

Buinaniya Madrasa, ground-floor plan, Fez.

did this, and the conscience of Abu Inan was purified in the same way as the chosen site was by the foundation of this establishment".

A spectacular architectural creation, the Buinaniya was meant to eclipse all other *madrasa*s. This is what was said to the sultan when he was presented with the list of expenses which he then hastened to throw into the *wadi* after having come to realise the considerable sums spent: *"What is beautiful is not costly, however large the sum"*.

The *madrasa* underwent several restorations, in particular during the 11th/17th century after the earthquake which affected the town. Under the reign of the 'Alawite Sultan Mulay Sliman (1206/1792–1237/1822), entire walls were rebuilt. In the 20th century, the restorations concentrated mostly on the plaster, wood and *zellij* decorations.

On the north side of the *madrasa*, two adjacent doors open out onto the street, *rue Tal'a Lekbira*; on the south side also, a third door opens onto *rue Tal'a Sghira*. All three doors offer access to a hallway which leads to a patio, entirely paved in marble and containing at its centre a basin, which today one can only see the remains of, which then leads to a study room.

The Lamtiyyin *wadi*, a branch of the river of Fez, crosses the south side of the patio, separating it from the mosque. Two small bridges, thrown across the *wadi* here and there, allow one to reach and enter the mosque. The layout of this latter is based on a rectangular design. Its north face opens widely onto the patio through five large bays. The mosque is divided into two rows of benches which run parallel to the south wall. The archway which separates them is composed of five arches resting on six columns of yellowing white marble. The *mihrab*, recessed into the centre of the south wall, is elaborately decorated. The minaret, square in shape, rises up from the north-west corner.

Exit the medina *via Bab Bujlud, near the Batha Museum.*

III.1.k North Burj, Arms' Museum (option)

Situated outside the medina. *Take the Boulevard of the northern ring road, the Arms' Museum is indicated by an arrow.*
Open from 09.00–12 and 15.00–18.00. Closed Tuesday.

The north Burj or bastion, facing its counterpart the south Burj, stands at the summit of one of the hills which lies north of the *medina*, close to the cemetery which houses many of the Merinid sultans tombs.

Built, according to town chroniclers, on the site of an ancient *burj*, at the time of the Sa'adian Sultan Ahmed al-Mansur (985/1578–1011/1603), this military building aimed to protect the town from all outside attack, as well as to control and survey the Fassi population, often in revolt against the Sa'adian princes. The *burj* underwent important modifications during the run of the last few centuries, but, with a lack of available documentation, it is very difficult to date them. A huge clay construction, this building, of a sensible square-plan design, actually houses the museum of Arms. Canons from the Sa'adian era form part of the museum's rich collection. However, it is the swords of different origins and historical periods which constitute the most important collection of arms on show here. The museum's important collection explains the evolution of arms production in Morocco: from lightweight, more traditional weapons like swords and spears, to relatively heavy ones like canons.

CERAMICS

Naïma El-Khatib Boujibar

Large plate with multicoloured "epi" decoration, Batha Museum (Inv. No. 45 777), Fez.

Composing what is formerly known as the "Fired Arts", the ceramic arts were focused on the creation of tiles, porcelain, and other glazed ware. An old tradition of Morocco's, it is also one of the most respected, transforming a ceramicist into an artist.

Two kinds of ceramic coexisted across various periods: one was rural pottery, painted with plant extract colours; the other was a traditional enamel ceramic shaped into specific forms with specific decorations, which set them apart from the tiles made in other Islamic countries. Strongly based in the Rif mountains, rural pottery, simple and essentially consisting of daily utensils, derives its origin from the Phoenicians and Romans, as is commonly referred to as Berber pottery.

In contrast, enamel ceramics, imported from Spain and from the Machreq, developed in a finer and more meticulous manner in towns.

This latter kind of ceramic was made in turn in the workshops of the towns of Fez, Meknès, Salé and Safi. But it is in Fez, artistic town *par excellence*, where the industry flourished most, and it is from Fez that the potters who settled in Meknès, and later in Safi, in the $12^{th}/18^{th}$ century, came from. As creations of artisans who worked within a corporation under the supervision of a *m'allem*, the ceramics were neither signed nor dated. From washing utensils to perfume bottles, these objects, characterised by the elegance of their form, the delicacy of their decoration and the harmony of their colours, attest to the perfect mastery reached by artisans of ceramics across the whole chain of production. To start with, the basic material, clay, undergoes various stages of grinding, kneading and fermentation before being cut into more malleable pieces and thrown upon the wheel. Fashioned on the wheel, the object, after being dried in the fresh air, was placed in an oven for a first firing. Before being decorated, the object, having already been fired once, was plunged into a bath of white enamel, created by mixing enamel oxide, lead and siliceous sand. On this sun-dried lump of clay, the potter, using a paintbrush of mules' hair, traced decora-

Soup tureen with interlacing pattern, Batha Museum (Inv. No. 45 954), Fez.

tive motifs taken from the classical repertoire of Morocco-Andalusian architectural art and furniture: floral-type ornamentation designed as palm or palmettes; or even that of a geometric-type in the form of a diamond-shaped maze, of a curvilinear interlace or polygonal stars. In line with other traditional art forms, the decorator forbid himself of all natural figurative subjects, with the exceptions of a motif of sailing boats (taken from an image which adorned Iznik Turkish plates from the 11th/17th century) and of rare naive representations of birds.

After having sketched the outlines of the motifs on the plate or the vase – in blue if the objects were to be only blue in colour and in brown if they were to be decorated in various colours – the artisan then applied the colours, prepared as a mixture of water, powdered minerals and siliceous white sand.

The traditional palette of a Moroccan ceramicist consisted of four colours: brown, green, yellow and blue. The first three were obtained through the oxidation of iron and manganese to create brown, of copper to create green and of alluvium to create yellow. As for blue, which was ranked as the colour of first choice within the ceramics of Fez, it was obtained through oxidising cobalt, an imported mineral which cannot be found pure in its natural state. The nuance of the tint, after having been fired, depends on its purity, on how well it has been purified, which explains the differences in the tones of blue, which in turn enables the plates to be approximately dated accordingly: lightly washed out pale grey-blue would have signified a date prior to the middle of the 13th/19th century, whilst a clear purplish blue, obtained through industrial procedures of purification, points to a more recent time.

Small plate with multicoloured "millepattes" decoration, Batha Museum.

Fragment of wall covering in mosaic tiles with a geometric design, Batha Museum (Inv. No. C1).

ITINERARY IV

A Day in the Life of a Jew in Fez

Mohamed Mezzine

IV.1 FEZ
        IV.1.a Cemetery and Synagogue Museum
        IV.1.b Mellah
        IV.1.c The House of Maimonides
        IV.1.d Funduq Lihudi Quarter

IV.2 SEFROU (option)

Maimonides

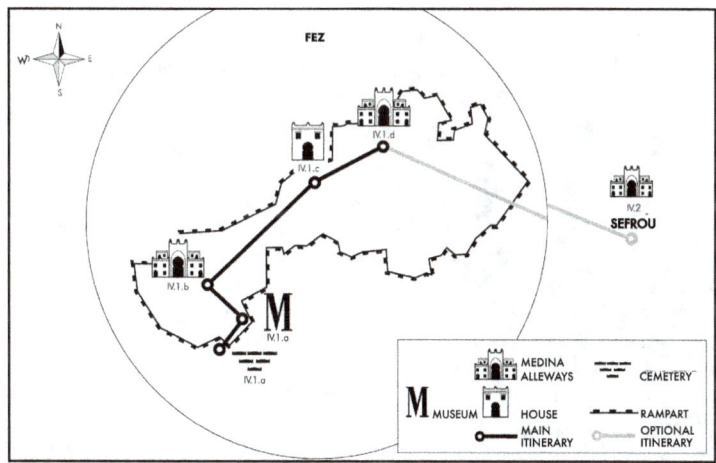

Jewish Cemetery, whitewashed tombs, Fez.

Housing the oldest and largest Jewish community in Morocco, *"Fas"*, wrote the 5th/11th century historian al-Bakri, *"is the centre of Jewish commercial activity, and it is from where they depart on their voyages to other lands"*.

Indeed, ever since its formation, the Idrissid capital housed a particularly active minority of Jews who took advantage of the freedom afforded to cults, and of the security afforded to their person and their belongings. This community was composed of the descendants of native Jews, the *toshabim*s, who lived in Morocco prior to the arrival of Islam, and of Jewish emigres who had fled from Cordoba and from Kairouan. The community grew in importance with the arrival, in successive waves, of refugees from the Iberian Peninsula, and benefited by a significant amount in 794/1391–1392 when Jews, fleeing the bloody repressions unleashed against them in Castille and in Aragon, moved to Fez. A century later, the expulsion edict sealed by the Catholic kings in 897/1492, after the fall of Granada, instigated the rush of thousands of Jews and Andalusian Muslims towards Fez. In 854/1451, the number of Jews in Fez was evaluated at being higher than 4,000 in a town which held a population of 50,000 Muslims, and, in 1545, their number came close to 10,000, according to the voyager Mármol de Carvajal.

Ever since the foundation of the town, the Jewish community had settled *"in quite a large quarter which stretched from Aghlen out to Hisn Sadun"* which was called *Derb Lihudi*, at the heart of the *medina*. In exchange for the protection offered to them by the sultan, they were forced to observe certain requirements such as the payment of an annual tax to the State's Treasury, the *jizya*, an annual tax which already at the time of the Idrissids was levelled at 30,000 gold dinars. This community assured its own cultural growth partly thanks to the prosperity it generated, ever since the Middle Ages, through its dynamism within crafts and widespread commerce.

Towards the middle of the 9th/15th century, the Merinids moved the Jewish community to *Fas Jdid*, close to their palace. This transfer, from an old neighbourhood situated on the bank of the Qarawiyin, to a new and distinct quarter situated near the seat of government, was not without its ruptures, even though their new placement close to the sultan's palace offered supplementary guarantees regarding their security as a result. It is noted that the Merinids, to secure their power in Fez, which they had made their capital, ensured that they had the support of the Jewish community. Indeed, powerful through their craft-making, commercial and financial activities, the Jews of Fez had maintained a tight relationship to

Synagogue Museum, exhibition room, Fez.

their European religious brothers; useful contacts for all kinds of diplomatic reasons which the Merinid Sultans could exploit. From that time on, the fate of the community would be closely tied to the fate of the royal dynasty, and *"certain amongst them would know of the fascinating routine of these Jews at the royal court, whose ascension was as fast as lightning"*.

The new Jewish Quarter was named Mellah, after the saline soil on which it was built, *al-Mallah* in Arabic. This would become a generic term for the reference of a Jewish Quarter in all and every Moroccan town. The new quarter, with its synagogues, its cemetery, its shops and workshops, developed rapidly, offering the Jewish community the possibility for great cohesiveness. Concentrated on craft-making and commerce, economic life depended largely on relations and exchanges with the *medina*; links between them were rarely broken, as a number of those living in the Mellah kept their shops in the *medina* and commuted there for the needs of their business. Grouped into corporations similar to their Muslim counterparts, the Jewish artisans were active in all sectors of production, but they exercised a monopoly within the gold industry. *"The majority of goldsmiths are Jews who work in the Fas Jdid and bring their creations into the old town to sell them"*, wrote Leon the African. *"A market near the hardware sellers was assigned to them there. In the old town, one cannot work with either gold or silver ... as it is said that to sell objects in gold or silver at a price which is higher than that paid for their weight is usury. But the sovereigns give the Jews permission to do so"*.

The witness account given to us by Leon the African in the $10^{th}/16^{th}$ century could be applied to the $9^{th}/15^{th}$ century. Outside the realms of goldsmithing, money stamping and craft-making in general, the

Mellah, Bab Mellah, Fez.

Jews worked in agriculture, playing a substantial role in the grain trade between Morocco and Europe.

In a general way, the Jewish community of Fez was able to enjoy a long period of tranquillity, a height of peace which corresponded with the arrival of the Merinids in Fez. Thus, during a period of political quiet, life at the heart of the Mellah was carried out between the undertaking of daily prayers in one of a number of synagogues, and economic activity, conducted to the rhythm of the comings and goings between the Mellah and the old *medina*.

IV.1 FEZ

IV.1.a Cemetery and Synagogue Museum

Follow the sign indicating Palais Royal. Park the car on the Place du Palais (square next to

ITINERARY IV   *A Day in the Life of a Jew in Fez*

Fez

Jewish Cemetery, whitewashed tombs and view onto the housing in the Mellah, Fez.

the palace). Enter the Mellah Quarter via the Bab al-Mellah. Before taking the main road in the Mellah, take the road on the right which descends to where the cemetery is located. The museum stands within the cemetery's enclosure. Open from 08:30–12.00 and 14.30–18.00. Closed Saturdays.

The cemetery of the Jewish community in Fez was one of the most important institutions of the community and was managed by the *Hebra qadicha*, the congregation in charge of the burial of the dead, who were also in charge of fire fighting.
In fact, the Jewish community of Fez did have, according to ancient texts, three cemeteries. The first, not a single trace of which remains today, was situated outside the Bab al-Guissa and was abandoned, in the 7th/13th century, at the time when the Merinids had begun the construction of the *Fas Jdid*. The second, situated to the west of the Mellah, established itself on a plot of land offered by a Merinid princess in 869/1465. The third, still in use today, is located in the extension of the second, south of the Mellah. A number of people who played a major role in the town of Fez are buried there.
This cemetery is distinct for its tombs, which have vaulted rooftops and are whitewashed.
At the far end of the cemetery stands an ancient synagogue, which today houses a museum. The walls of the prayer hall are decorated with mosaics and chiselled plaster in the purest Andalusian tradition.

ITINERARY IV   *A Day in the Life of a Jew in Fez*
Fez

It is preferable to do the itinerary on foot. Allow two hours. This offers the chance to get a complete picture of the medina *of Fez, which is composed of two distinct parts,* Fas Jdid *and* Fas al-Bali. *For this itinerary, go straight to the cemetery by taxi.*

IV.1.b **Mellah**

One can stroll in the Mellah without fear of getting lost. The main street runs alongside the Royal Palace.

The date of when the Jewish community settled in the *Fas Jdid*, in the quarter near the Royal Palace, is very often contested, but the Mellah as we know it today only had its boundaries defined in the $9^{th}/15^{th}$ century. The actual, physical boundaries in fact date from the time of the 'Alawite Sultan Mulay Lyazid. The spatial constraints obliged the inhabitants, whose numbers were growing, to build upwards rather than outwards, usually constructing two floors, and to reduce the width of alleyways.

Delineated today in the north and northwest by the ramparts of the Royal Palace, in the south by the Jewish cemetery, in the east by the commercial and residential quarters, and in the west by the old Jewish cemetery,

Mellah, housing in the main street, Fez.

ITINERARY IV   *A Day in the Life of a Jew in Fez*
Fez

the Mellah was, during the 9th/15th and 10th/16th centuries, much larger and was divided into two extensive neighbourhoods. The first, situated in the northern part of the Mellah on the surroundings of the Bulakhsissat, housed the rich Jewish merchants, most of whom had been expelled from Spain. Accustomed to a refined way of life from their days in the Iberian Peninsula, these Jewish immigrants from al-Andalus handed down, from generation to generation, the Andalusian legacy as is made apparent by their houses. Their dwellings were luxurious, decorated in *zellij*, like those belonging to the rich living in the *medina*. The second neighbourhood, in the southeast of the Grande Rue (the Main Street), and thus less airy, housed the *toshabim*s, the native Jews. It housed workshops, small shops and poorer housing.

A dozen synagogues religiously framed the Mellah. The largest was situated in the northern sector of the neighbourhood, the only area that was provided with drinking water ever since the 9th/15th century, whilst other synagogues were spread across the neighbourhood.

Whilst the Mellah offered the Jewish community the benefit of uniting their talents in the craftsmanship of gold and in the production of precious items, other activities, such as textile production, also featured. A local tradition in the working of silk had already existed in Fez since the Middle Ages, but was refined with the arrival of Sephardic Jews from al-Andalus. Two sorts of workshops were involved in the silk industry: those in charge of its production, and those in charge of the preparation of textiles for Jewish or Muslim religious ceremonies, or indeed of ceremonial dresses for the Royal Palace. The Mellah was also reputed for its shoe workshops. A guild incorporated numerous cobblers from the Mellah. The basic material was bought in the *medina*, but certain Jewish artisans prepared the hides themselves, which they then used or exported out of Fez.

The Mellah of today still harbours a large amount of these commercial and craft-making activities. Stalls are to be found not only in the main street, which itself was built after the fire which ravaged the Mellah in 1912, but exist in the little streets which surround this main one. It remains the centre for the production and commercialisation of objects fashioned in gold.

IV.1.c The House Maimonides

From the Mellah, head towards the Kasbah of Flowers otherwise known as the Old Almoravid Kasbah. From there, walk along the palace gardens in the direction of the Bab Bujlud in order to reach rue Tal'a Lekbira. Maimonides' House is situated on this street close to the

Mellah, housing in the main street, Fez.

Buinaniya Madrasa. The entrance gate is on the alley facing the madrasa. *It is a private house, but visitors are welcome.*

Situated, according to oral tradition, on the *Tal'a Lekbira*, facing the main gate of the Buinaniya Madrasa, the residence lived in by the philosopher and doctor Moshe Ibn Maimun, known as Maimonides, stood on the actual site of the building which holds the famous hydraulic clock, built in 758/1357 as part of the *madrasa*. The interior of the neighbouring building had been transformed; after being decorated, it had become annexed to the *madrasa*.

Moshe Ibn Maimun, an Andalusian emigrant, came to settle in Fez for two and a half years with his family, around the mid-$6^{th}/12^{th}$ century.

It was there that he composed his famous *Epistle on persecution, "Iggered Hachemad"*, around 560/1165. Evoking his emigration from Cordoba, he advocated, for the Jews persecuted by the Spanish Inquisition, to *"leave these places for those where one is able to practise ... the Torah without constraint nor fear"*, or better still, to opt for a sort of *marranos, a certain tolerance, whilst waiting for better days to come"*.

The house became a place of pilgrimage for the Jews of Fez ever since the time of the Merinids. It remained so for a long time, as Jewish women who hoped to become mothers would pay visit to the spirit of Maimonides. The site is still a sacred one for the Jewish community of today, and there are many who, when visiting Fez, still undertake to do the pilgrimage.

IV.1.d Funduq Lihudi Quarter

There are several possibilities for getting to Derb Lihudi. From Maimonides' House (this one takes 45 minutes): descend rue Tal'a Lekbira towards the 'Attarin Madrasa. From there, go towards the Sagha Funduq (take rue Ab Khiss on the left, then the first left followed by an immediate right). Arriving in Place 'Attarin, make your way to Place al-Achabine. From there, take the main road. At 200 m. on your left is the quarter in which the Lihudi funduq *is situated, signposted by a plaque. Down below lies the ancient* funduq.

It is also possible to reach the Bab al-Guissa by car which one can leave in the car park. From there, descend rue Brad Ayin until you come across Place al-Achabine to then reach Derb Lihudi.

Maimonides' House, Fez.

Located right on the Qarawiyin river bank, the Derb Lihudi in fact maps out a neighbourhood composed of three commercial alleyways with housing. Creating a junction between the Sagha Suq and other commercial quarters, the *Derb Lihu-*

ITINERARY IV *A Day in the Life of a Jew in Fez*
Sefrou

Derb Lihudi, ancient funduq, Fez.

di housed the Jewish Quarter of Fez, from the time the town was founded up until the 9th/15th century.

The name of this *funduq* is derived from an ancient *caravanserai* which today no longer exists. The quarter was frequented by goldsmiths, by silversmiths and by each and every Jew who had a workshop or shop there.

Near Bab al-Guissa, and not far from the *qaysariya*, it remained a repeatedly frequented market even after it was abandoned by the Jewish community in 840/1437, when the Mulay Idriss Mausoleum was built and when the *horm*, the sacred space surrounding the mausoleum, was defined.

Jewish merchants and artisans still visited it until the beginning of the 20th century, the ties between this neighbourhood and that of the Mellah have never been broken except during times of difficulty.

The plan on which the neighbourhood was based, and the architecture of its houses, reproduced the model on which Muslim palaces and residential housing was based.

Exit the medina via the Bab al-Guissa (10 minutes from the Derb Lihudi), from where it is possible to take a taxi.

IV.2 SEFROU (option)

Situated 28 km. from Fez, on the traditional route for the transportation of dates. Leave Fez via the Immouzer road. Once in Sefrou, park in the car park outside the ramparts of the medina.

The town of Sefrou was founded well before Fez in the 1st/7th century, close to the prehistoric site of Bhalil, on the first foothills of the Middle Atlas. Built on both banks of the *wadi* Aggai, it was surrounded by gardens and orchards which it turned into a summer resort, following the example of the neighbouring towns of Ifrane or Immouzer.

One of the first residential centres, dating from before the arrival of the Muslim conquerors, it was originally composed of three townships or *qsur*, divided along the *wadi*: the *qsur al-Fuqaniyyin*, "high town", the *qsur al-Wastaniyyin*, "mid-town", and the *qsur al-Tahtaniyyin*, "low town". These three separate entities grouped themselves together to defend themselves more effectively against the attacks of nearby tribes.

The Jewish community occupied a specific place within the town, having settled in the centre ever since it came into existence. This geographic positioning would have a dual impact on the community.

ITINERARY IV A Day in the Life of a Jew in Fez
Sefrou

The Sefriouris were under constant attack from neighbouring mountain people, but as the Mellah was surrounded by Muslim Quarters, the Jews were better protected and better guarded. On the other hand, due its place at the heart of the *medina*, the Mellah could not grow and extend itself outwardly due to the lack of vacant space. Housing ,therefore, grew in height. The community thus became a victim of its own means of protection and survival. The distinguishing mark of the Mellah, the crucial height of its houses in comparison to those in other parts of the city, attracted the attention of the 'Alawite Sultan Mulay Hassan (1873–1894) during his visit to Sefrou. He began to dream of building a new Mellah to house the growing number of Jews, but the project never saw the light of day in consequence to the sultan's death. The housing in the Mellah, in line with all those of the town, were built in brick or in stone. The terraces were made of cedar joists covered in planks of the same kind; cedarwood from the Atlas forests close by.

Every Christian and Muslim traveller who visited the town was united in their description of it as a quiet and peaceful city, far from the great battles which shook the neighbouring town of Fez. Charles de Foucault estimated that *"Damnat and Sefrou are the two places in Morocco in which the Jews are the most happy"*.

Major players within the town's economy, the Jews of Sefrou enjoyed administrative autonomy, managing their own affairs, even though they were reliant on the *qa'id* in terms of politics and the law, and on the *muhtassib* in terms of crafts and commerce. Three Israelite institutions thus busied themselves with the daily affairs of the inhabitants of the Mellah.

The Jewish community of Sefrou did not stop growing in numbers from when the town was founded. In 1880, their population in the Mellah was counted at 1,000. On the eve of the Protectorate, this number had increased to 3,000, which was over a third of the town's total population, and was the largest concentration of Jews in Morocco. Their number would have increased to over 4,000 in 1951 had a large part of the community not left, in a period of massive immigration, for Palestine, Western Europe and North America. In 1960, the Jewish community was estimated at numbering 3,138 persons, whereas in 1971 this number had dropped to 222. Today, only Jewish women married to Muslims, or pilgrims who come regularly to Sefrou, remember this communitarian past.

MAIMONIDES

Mohamed Mezzine

Rabbenu Moshe Ibn Maimun, called Abu Imran al-Fasi, but also known as Maimonides as he referred to himself during his stay in Fez, was born in Cordoba around 529/1135. Tradition links his genealogy to the Royal House of David.

The historian of Moroccan Judaism, Haim Zafrani, describes him as *"the pilgrim of the Jewish-Islamic intellectual world"* during a time in which Western Islamic civilisation achieved a cultural symbiosis between the various ethnicities and religions of the Western Mediterranean basin.

A son of a Rabbi, Maimonides attended schools and universities in Cordoba, which at the time was a town rich in culture where many scholars of Judaism and of Islam lived. He learnt Arabic and Hebrew, which enabled him to study both Jewish and Arabic thought simultaneously. Many Jewish and Muslim intellectuals left the town of Cordoba when it fell under the armies of the Reconquest and as the Inquisition developed. Maimonides thus emigrated to the Maghrebic coast and, settled in Fez for more than two years, remaining anonymous.

He attended the Qarawiyin under the name of Abu Imran al-Fasi, and even, according to historical tradition, taught there. His research thus focused on two objects of triumphant monotheism: Judaism and Islam. He studied the treaty of the great Islamic theologian al-Ghazali, and the writings of his contemporary, the philosopher Ibn Rushd (Averroës). Maimonides composed his famous *Epistle on Persecution* around 560/1165, providing Judaism with a theology and an ethical and moral code which was as important as the works by al-Ghazali and Averroës.

Leaving Fez during the reign of the Almohads, he travelled across towards Egypt, where he became, in Cairo, the physician of the great Salah al-Din al-Ayyubi, a hero of Islam during the time of the Crusades. Maimonides left, as his legacy, great works in the fields of philosophy, medicine and law. Within his work, the interaction between Hebrew and Arabic and between Jewish and Muslim philosophy is ever present. This interaction represents the symbolic parallel within the life of a great figure of Judaism.

The legendary man began his life anew, for richer or poorer, thus provoking numerous controversy over the importance and depth of his work. However, today, Maimonides is viewed as being one of the symbols of Hebraic culture.

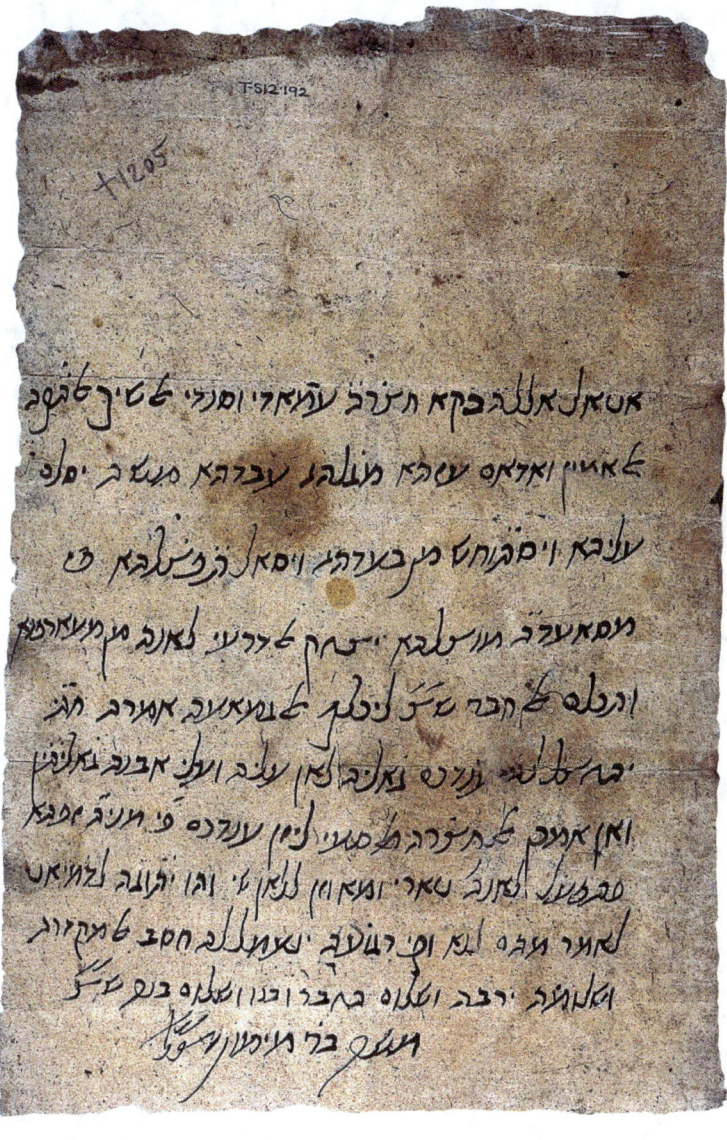

אנא סאל אללה בקא תורך עמאדי וסעדי שיך שמוע
צֿאמין ואדאם עלוה מן הו עבדהא מצאחב יקצי
עלוה ויסתרתא מן בעדהו ויסאל גיאצֿהם פי
מסעתעבד מרסלהם יצחק לידרע לענה מן מעאדרהם
והנסל אל הבר שג'י לנטע צסמאעה אמרהם תי
ינ̇עלל לי געיב נעלא דאין עלוה ועלי אבנה נאלפן
וצן צמרם צחצרת מצסעו לאין ערבה פי מען ונצא
סבנעל לענך סארי יצאון לצאן טי וגי יקוה לצאין
לאמר מרה לנא וק' תסלעה יסמעלה חסב ומקדור
ואלנאכר ירבד יסלום נתבד ובנו יסלום ננפ שנגי
משה בר מימון ציו

*Letter by Maimonides,
written a short while
after his arrival in
Egypt in 566/1171,
University
of Cambridge.*

ITINERARY V

Chefchaouen: The Holy City of the Rif Mountains

Naïma El-Khatib Boujibar

V.1 CHEFCHAOUEN
    V.1.a Kasbah
    V.1.b Uta Hammam Square: Fountain
    V.1.c Great Mosque
    V.1.d Rayssuniya Zawiya
    V.1.e Suiqa Quarter: Streets and Houses
    V.1.f Weavers' Workshop
    V.1.g 'Ayn Suiqa Fountain
    V.1.h Funduq
    V.1.i Andalusian Quarter
    V.1.j Bab al-Ansar: Walls and Tower
    V.1.k Ras al-Ma' Source
    V.1.l Essabanin Quarter: Mill, Bridge, Bakery

Saida El-Horra, Princess of Chefchaouen

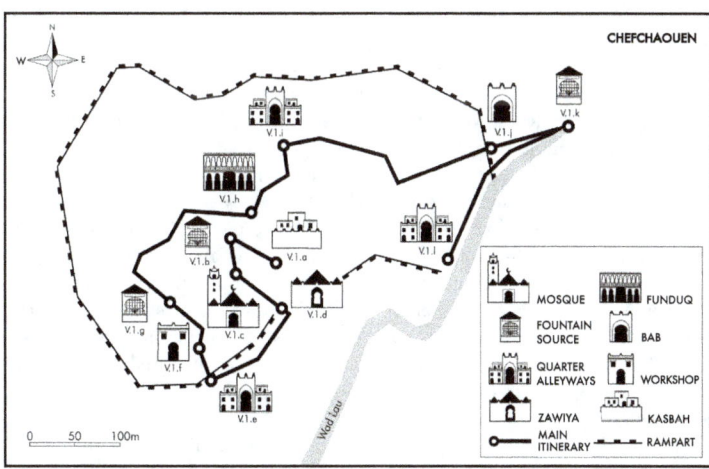

View of the medina seen from the kasbah, Chefchaouen.

ITINERARY V   *Chefchaouen: The Holy City of the Rif Mountains*

Kasbah, enclosure, circumventing path, Chefchaouen.

The small city of Chefchaouen, jewel of the north, is situated in a remarkably well chosen site, strategically as well as from the picturesque point of view. Standing up against a ridge of the Rif mountain range which serves to protect it, it slots itself between two summits which are covered in a dense forest of pine trees and cork-oaks. Abundant amounts of water from a pure and limpid source, Ras al-Ma', gushing from the mountain hillside, running smoothly down the undulating sides of the small valley, transform the surrounding valley into a multitude of gardens and lush orchards. Founded by a family of Idrissid *shorfa* (sg. *Sharif*), descendants of the Prophet Muhammad, this city, blessed by God who had offered it so much bountiful nature, was considered by the neighbouring populations to be a Holy Town, in second place to the town of Mulay Idriss Zerhun.

The respect which the northern tribes devoted to it was so great that the troops of the Rif's hero, Mohamed Ibn 'Abdelkrim al-Khattabi, took their shoes off prior to entering the city, in deference to this sacred space. Consequently very few non-Muslim visitors were admitted to the heart of the city before 1925. Charles de Foucauld, who had the privilege of visiting Chefchaouen in 1882, wrote:
"This town, sunk deep into the fold of the mountain, reveals itself only at the last moment ... One reaches the rocky walls which crown it and walks along them painfully, feeling like one is at the centre of a maze made up of enormous blocks of granite into which deep caves are dug. All of a sudden, the labyrinth ends, the rock turns at an angle: a hundred metres further on, one side of the rock stands out against peaked mountains; from the other side, bordered by ever-green gardens, appears the town ... the sight of which was magical; with its old donjon, feudal in appearance, its houses covered in tiles, its meandering brooks which run in all directions, one would think one was facing a quiet village on the Rhin as opposed to one of the most fanatical towns of the Rif. Chefchaouen, whose population includes a large number of shorfa, is in fact renowned for its intolerance. It is a spacious town. The sheer vertical wall of rock which crowns the Jabal Mezedjel *rises up behind it; from in front, superb gardens spill out across the mountain side, covering a huge area of land".*
Chefchaouen owes its sacred status to its proximity to the tomb of the great Saint Mulay 'Abd al-Salam Ibn Mshish, which is located about 50 km. north-west. Described as the "mystical pole of the West", his mausoleum in Jabal Alem is a place of pilgrimage visited frequently by Moroccans, and, until the first decades of the 20th century, each pilgrim had to reach it via Chefchaouen. This Idrissid

sherif from the Beni 'Arus tribe was an eminent scholar of the end of the $6^{th}/12^{th}$ century. Considered to have introduced *Sufism* to Morocco, he passed his teachings onto his student, the great mystic Eshadhili, who was venerated in Tunisia and in Egypt, and who was also an Idrissid *sherif* from a tribe neighbouring Chefchaouen, the Akhmes tribe.

This explains the religious atmosphere dominating this region, which had been Islamicised since the arrival of the Arabs and which endowed Morocco with many eminent scholars of religious science. These *'ulama' (sg. 'alim)*, who had come to settle in the town right after it was founded, turned Chefchaouen into a radiating cultural and religious centre which attracted the students, religious men and scholars of the region and beyond. It is therefore of no surprise to find, in a town with such little space, a number of significant places of cult worship and prayer: eight mosques, one or two per neighbourhood, nine *zawiyas*, representing the country's leading brotherhoods, and many marabouts, such as the town's founder Mulay 'Ali Ibn Rashid, who was particularly venerated by the surrounding populations.

However, this piety did not prevent its inhabitants from enjoying the gentle way of life and charm which characterises this beautiful city. This beauty is a result of how best the builders were able to work with the morphology of the sloping terrain, in order to erect a town which does fall in line with traditional urban design of Moroccan *medinas*, but which inarguably has its own style inspired by Andalusian Islamic architecture.

In fact the different building developments, rising in tiered steps along paved, narrow and twisted alleyways, radiate out from the initial core of the *kasbah*, which itself is situated on an esplanade. Covered passageways, *sabat*, shade alleys interrupted here and there by open spaces or squares endowed with sculpted fountains or verdant trees.

The austere walls of dwellings and religious monuments – which were whitewashed with lime and had their bases tinted in blue indigo, as was practised in Muslim al-Andalus – were topped with sloping roofs covered in red tiles. Great care was taken in the decoration of the entrances of homes and cultural monuments, entrances which were preceded by vaulted canopies.

The architecture of the houses also feature local characteristics which differentiate them from the traditional houses of other *medinas* in Morocco. An open space, the *qa'da*, is adjoined to the patio, and is sometimes furnished with a wooden

Great Mosque, general view, Chefchaouen.

ITINERARY V — Chefchaouen: The Holy City of the Rif Mountains

bench. Instead of the flat terraces of other Moroccan towns, the original roofs are double sloping, covered in red tiles, underneath which there are lofts, *berchla*, used in the past for the drying of fruit. Small wire-mesh fenced windows break-up, with their awnings, the monotony of the dazzling white of the walls, whilst allowing air and light into the interior rooms of the house. In addition to this, whilst taking well into consideration the Mediaeval residences of the *medina*, there still existed there certain means of arts and crafts production, such as water mills and weavers' workshops, which one can now only come across in certain rural areas. These various elements, both architectural and decorative, confer onto the *medina* of Chefchaouen a certain cachet of authenticity and an undeniable charm which never fails to impress the visitor.

The Suiqa Quarter, angled entrance to a house, Chefchaouen.

Chefchaouen, a Berber name which means "two horns", signifying the two mountain summits which tower above it, was founded in the $9^{th}/15^{th}$ century by a warrior monk from the Akhmes tribe (from the region of Chefchaouen), Mulay 'Ali Ibn Rashid, to serve as a defensive front against external attack. Facing a weak central power, incapable of thwarting the Portuguese occupation of the northern coastal towns, this descendant of the Idrissids, who had undergone his military training in Granada, returned to his country to take up arms and defend his homeland against foreign expansionist threats. At the capture of Tangier and of Asilah in 875/1471, he built a military base, the *kasbah*, which would go on to become the heart of the actual *medina*, bringing with him soldiers from his region and other defenders of the faith, *mujahidins*, along with their families. This initial urban embryo took no time in growing to become a small city covering a surface area of four hectares, surrounding itself with an enclosure reinforced with towers and broken up by gates, certain sections of which remain today. Mulay 'Ali Ibn Rashid endowed the city with a mosque, with the Great Mosque we see today, *Jama' al-Kebir*, and with bath houses which gave their name to the Uta Hammam Square. This citadel, well protected and in possession of a fertile hinterland, rich in sources of water, attracted Andalusian refugees (as well as those from the region) early on, who came to populate the first neighbourhood of the town, called Suiqa. Several years later, after the recapture of Granada in 897/1492, they would be strengthened by a new contingent of refugees from al-Andalus, who settled in the eastern part of town, outside the first enclosure, forming a neighbourhood which would come to be known as *Rif al-Andalus*.

Chefchaouen thus became the county-town of an independent principality lasting from 875/1471 to 967/1560, strong in both the military sense and politically, which the central power had to come to terms with. It extended its political and cultural influence not only over the mountainous region and neighbouring towns close by (Tétouan and Targa), but as far as the Atlantic north coast.

Its perpetual military onslaughts against the towns of Tangier and Asilah, conducted by the son of Mulay 'Ali, Prince Mulay Brahim, although failing to liberate the occupied towns, did nonetheless succeed in halting the Portuguese advance inland, thus crowning the Ibn Rashid family in glory. These military operations earned Mulay Brahim the name of brave warrior and fine strategist, given to him by Portuguese chroniclers who, whilst being on the enemy side, did not stop eulogising him. The operations equally caught the eye of the Wattasid Sultan Mulay Ahmed who, whilst making him his brother-in-law, conferred military commandments and delicate diplomatic missions onto him, and named him Governor of towns such as Meknès, Salé and the province of Tadla. His sister, Saida El-Horra, played an equally important role in the region, as she governed, for a number of years, the town of Tétouan.

During this period of independence which lasted 89 years, the urban plan of the town grew larger, organising itself politically and developing itself economically and culturally. Numerous scholars frequented its mosques in order to give lessons there and to discuss with Chefchaouenese colleagues the theological questions that preoccupied the *'ulama'*

The Essabanin Quarter, building housing the bakery, Chefchaouen.

of the time. The town placed equal value on the technical and artistic knowledge belonging to its inhabitants of Andalusian origin, who conveyed both their *savoir-faire* in arts and crafts and their refined culture through their way of living. Public and private buildings were thus constructed on an Andalusian model, hydraulic water networks were installed, silk- and wool-weaving workshops were opened, as well as the wainscoting workshops which the town is still famed for. At the accession of the Sa'adian Sultan Mulay 'Abd Allah al-Ghalib Bil-lah – who strengthened the power of the central government against the desires for independence of towns and regions – the last of the Rashid Princes, Mulay Ahmed, was dethroned, and the town thus lost its political autonomy. However it continued just as strongly to exercise its religious and cultural influence across the region.

ITINERARY V   *Chefchaouen: The Holy City of the Rif Mountains*

Chefchaouen

Kasbah, eleventh tower, view from the inside, Chefchaouen.

At the beginning of the 20th century, it became once again, during the War of the Rif, a locus of resistance to all outside onslaught. Occupied by the Spanish in 1926, it re-became Moroccan in 1956. In fact, whilst having extended and developed beyond its own walls, the town managed to preserve its *medina* and conserve its ancestral architectural, musical, and arts and crafts heritage, which endows it with a gentle and appreciable quality of life.

V.I **CHEFCHAOUEN**

V.1.a **Kasbah**

The itinerary is done on foot. Once in Chefchaouen, head towards the old medina or follow the sign indicating Crédit Agricole. Leave the car in Place al-Makhzen, at the top of the Boulevard Hassan II. Semi-public parking, belonging to the Hotel Parador. Kasbah and Museum, one and the same building, can be found on the main square Uta Hammam.
Open from Saturday to Thursday from 09.00–13.00 and 15.00–18.30; open Fridays from 09.00–12.00 and 15.00–18.00.

At the start of the 11th/17th century, the town received its final wave of Andalusian refugees, the Moriscos, Muslims and Jews who came to populate this part of the neighbourhood called Suiqa. From that time on, the little life of Chefchaouen's *medina* lived itself out within the walls of its enclosure. New arrivals from the Rif, the *Jbala*s, occupied the Essabanin and Anzar quarters. Mosques and *zawiya*s were erected there.

Situated in the western corner of the *medina*, the beginnings of which it represents, the *kasbah* was the first building erected by the city's founder, Mulay 'Ali Ibn Rashid (875/1471–876/1472), for him to use as a military base camp, a fortified residence and as a seat of command. His design consists of a more or less uniform rectangle, 7 m. in length from east to west, and 5 m. in width from north to south.

The Enclosure

The *kasbah* is surrounded by a thick wall built in clay which is lined along its inside edge by a path. Ten bastions, of which three were successfully recast, stand side by side at unequal distances from one another. These ten bastions, as well as the enclosure, fall within the tradition of Andalusian architecture in terms of their layout and mode of construction.

Entry into the *kasbah* was accessed via two gates, one of which, situated on the eastern side, looked onto the *suq*, whilst the other, on the western side, opened up onto the mosque. These entrances are in fact closed. The gate opening out onto the *suq* is low and narrow, and is based on an angled design. Massive semi-columns made of brick, which cling to the exterior facade of this door, are the remains of an old drawbridge system which was installed beforehand. The gate which opens onto the Great Mosque is actually being used as a temporary exhibition space, and is curiously placed in terms of its position in a corner tower. The actual entrance to the *kasbah* is an opening in the central tower on the north-west side, created in the 1930s.

The Tower

One tower, the eleventh, which rises up from the western side of the little courtyard, separates itself from the group. Built at a later date – to look like it is from the time of Mulay Mohamed, the last son of Mulay 'Ali Ibn Rashid – at the beginning of the $10^{th}/16^{th}$ century, it cuts into a part of the wall to insert itself in there. Square in the design of its base, it differentiates itself from the other towers in terms of its construction materials, its structure and its use. Its walls are in fact built of rubble stone, reinforced at its corners by sizable slabs of stone. It divides upwards into three sections. At ground level, an octagonal central pillar divides the space of the room in four, each part covered by a brick dome. On the first floor, a small pillar supports a longitudinal beam which divides the room into two rectangular parts. The third level consists of a mirador from where the whole of the *medina* can be seen with the naked eye. A parapet, gently protruding over a brick dripstone, protects the latter's terrace. The walls at higher levels are peppered with a series of brick windows. These window bays, composed of raised horseshoe arches, which enliven the facades of this tower through adding to its proportions, structure and construction, encourage the comparison of this building to the "tower-houses" of Granada.

The Kasbah Museum

The *kasbah*'s space is in fact mostly occupied by a garden with wells and basins,

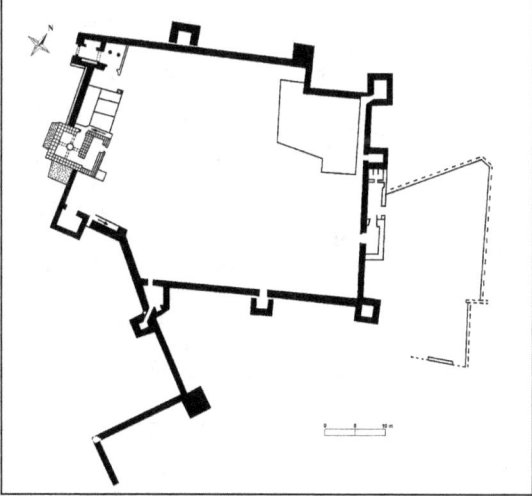

Kasbah, plan of the entire building, Chefchaouen.

Chefchaouen

Uta Hamman Square; fountain, general view, Chefchaouen.

and by a residence in its north-east corner which has been transformed into a museum and centre for Andalusian studies.

Water tanks were discovered in between the residence and the eastern wall, which can be dated to be of the same time as the first residential buildings of the *kasbah*.

The actual residence dates from the end of the 11th/17th century, from the time of Mulay Isma'il, and would have been erected by the Governor 'Ali Errifi. It is exemplary of the classic form of traditional Moroccan houses, with a patio ground floor and a gallery on an upper floor. The museum is located on the ground floor. It brings together certain archaeological and ethnographical objects which relate to the town of Chefchaouen and its surrounding region, including: a multicoloured wooden door knocker, decorated with interlacing polygonals, which comes from the Governor's old house; Andalusian musical instruments (*rebab*, a lute); painted wooden palanquins and boxes; red and white fabrics, *futa*; and embroidery, incorporating stylised flowers set within hexagons and diamond-shapes, which can be compared to the Andalusian embroidery of Granada and to the Mudejar rugs of the 9th/15th and 10th/16th centuries.

V.1.b Uta Hammam Square: Fountain

Uta Hammam Square, covering an area of 3000 sq. m., is both the *medina*'s largest square and its core: all main arteries depart from and converge towards it. It was built by Mulay Mohamed in the 10th/16th century, at the same time as the public baths, *hammam*, which are situated in the north-west corner and from which the square derives its name.

Originally a commercial and trading square, it hosted a market twice a week where the town locals and regional peasants would rub shoulders, the former buying farm products, the latter buying products fabricated by the town. Being a central square, it accessed all the main buildings of the town: the Great Mosque, shops, the *caravanserai* and the *kasbah*, the seat of power.

Today the place has a more modern look: the ground is paved in a mosaic of stones and pebbles, there are verdant trees and cafes.

The fountain was placed at the centre of the square to provide water for visitors and to the local residents. Displaying four sides adorned with simple arcatures, it was covered by a simple dome, and completely whitewashed. In its final appearance, its original structure was cast over with a larger, parallelepipedic frame, two sides of which were decorated with conches, and the whole piece was crowned by a green tile pavilion, topped by an iron rod forged into the shape of a crescent moon.

V.1.c Great Mosque

Uta Hammam Square. Access restricted to Muslims.

The Grand Mosque, *Jama' al-Kebir*, stands high on Uta Hammam Square in the west of the *kasbah*, and was founded by Mulay Mohamed in the $10^{th}/16^{th}$ century. Occupying an area of about 130 sq. m., this trapezoidal-shaped compound has all the annexes which come with a religious institution of such importance: a minaret, a fountain, an ablution hall, a courtyard, and a *madrasa*. The prayer hall takes up the central body of this compound; it stretches across eight naves parallel to the wall of the *qibla*, which was intersected by six rows of seating bays. The archways of the naves and the bays, composed of pointed horseshoe arches supported on pillars, lack ornamentation, and the ceilings are painted a uniform colour. The modesty and minimalism of the prayer hall is a feature of oratories in Chefchaouen. The only parts of this compound which are decorated are its external features, the entrance doors, and the minaret. The minaret, which rises up asymmetrically in relation to the facade, extends two and a half times over and above the height of the prayer hall's red tiled roof. Its octagonal structure puts it in close relation to the minarets of mosques in Tétouan and Tangier founded by Mulay Isma'il's Governor 'Ali Errifi, and can thus be dated from the end of the $11^{th}/17^{th}$ century. Each of its eight faces, divided into three parts, is ornamented with sculpted arcatures, both simple or polyfoiled, the higher ones of which are enriched by square panels of ceramic *zellij*. The edges of the facades, in plain brick, are highlighted with ochre paint. The ochre cuts across the colour of the whitewash with which the top of the minaret and its lantern, as well as the walls of the mosque, are covered.

Great Mosque, entrance door and minaret, Chefchaouen.

Chefchaouen

The lack of homogeneity from which the architecture of this monument suffers is evidence of the different transformations undergone by this building during its 400 years in existence. Founded in the $10^{th}/17^{th}$ century, it was enlarged for the first time in the $11^{th}/18^{th}$ century and equipped with a minaret. Restored in the 19th century, it was extended once again with various additions in the 20th century, one addition being the portal of the main entrance.

V.1.d Rayssuniya Zawiya

Take the street which runs between the mosque and the kasbah, *which leads to a small square where the* zawiya *is situated. This monument cannot be visited, but all that is interesting about the building is located on the outside of its door.*

Zawiya Rayssuniya, entrance door, Chefchaouen.

The Rayssuniya Zawiya is situated in the south of the *kasbah*, and opens onto Belhacen Square. According to local chroniclers, it was the first *zawiya* to have seen the light of day in Chefchaouen's *medina*. According to an oral tradition, this *zawiya* was founded by the famous princess Saida El-Horra, who is buried there. The building originally occupied an area of about 130 sq. m. In recent years, an additional floor unfortunately replaced the traditional red-tiled roof. The ground floor contains a prayer room with a *mihrab*, a further room, storage space and an ablutions room, *meda*.

The building is entered via an angled passage way. The portal of this building is its only ornamented feature. The bay of the entrance, a pointed horseshoe arch, is topped by a half conch: it is protected by a prominent sculpted canopy which is covered in a green-tiled roof. The canopy, supported by a series of corbels cut out as *muquarnas*, is terminated at each side with a pilaster rising from the ground, which are decorated with little blind skylights.

V.1.e Suiqa Quarter: Streets and Houses

The Suiqa Quarter begins on your right, across from the door of the zawiya. *The stairs on your left spill onto the Avenue Hassan II, leading to the car park. Cul-de-sacs (no through roads) can be recognised as such in that the ground has been whitewashed.*

The Souika Quarter was one of the first neighbourhoods of the town to be established, and was populated as early as the $9^{th}/15^{th}$ century. Surrounded in the past by a clay enclosure, certain remains of which can be seen at Derb Essour, it was entered into via several gates in the north, the west and the south. Two of these gates are still well preserved: the Bab al-Harmun in the south, and Bab al-Hammar in the south-east.

The neighbourhood owes its name, literally meaning "small market / little *suq*", to the commercial area which still exists today, the *qaysariya*, which was built up at the end of the 9th / 15th century. This space was in earlier times encircled and closed off by gates, one of which is composed of a festooned, sculpted archway. The *qaysariya* actually consists of many tiny shops, each one of which is glued to the next, forming rows along each side of the narrow little alleyways. The shops each have a wooden Dutch door as their only opening, and in the olden days specialised uniquely in the sale of local wool and linen textiles.

The oldest and most beautiful houses of the *medina* can be found within this maze of streets. Certain residences belonging to important families group together in *derb*s or cul-de-sacs. The entrances to *derb*s are sometimes covered with *sabat*s in order to extend the surface areas of the floors above. The gates which close them off have been crafted with great care. Their height and their variety of ornamentation were the signs which distinguished them as family gates. The gates of bourgeois houses are similar, in terms of their height and decoration, to the gates of religious buildings, mosques and *zawiya*s, whilst the gates of houses belonging to people of more modest means are smaller and display a far less elaborate decor. However, every single door and wall, whether belonging to a rich house or poor one, is daubed in whitewash, and is one of the characteristics of Chefchaouen's *medina*.

V.1.f **Weavers' Workshop**

At the far end of rue Ben Dibane (a very commercial street which leads off from the Suiqa Quarter's main road).

The town of Chefchaouen is renowned in the north both for its wool textiles, which the Rif people use to make their *jellaba*, and for its red- and-white striped fabrics, made of cotton and linen, which the *jbala*

Suiqa Quarter, house, entrance door, Chefchaouen.

ITINERARY V   *Chefchaouen: The Holy City of the Rif Mountains*

Chefchaouen

Weavers' workshop, outside view of the monument, Chefchaouen.

'Ayn Suiqa Fountain, general view, Chefchaouen.

of these textiles. They number about 100, and are mainly to be found between the Suiqa Quarter and the Andalusian Quarter, each one displaying the same architectural style.

This particular one, covering a rectangular area of about 8 m. in length and 2.5 m. in width, and shielded by a dual-sloped roof of red tiles, sits a little further back from its neighbouring buildings. A wooden floor divides the space into two levels. The floor above can be reached via an outside staircase, levered to the outside wall. Each room contains two softly gliding work looms, worked on by two artisans. Light enters the rooms through the door, and there is ventilation thanks to small skylight windows built into the wall.

The walls are made of rubble stones held together with lime mortar, whilst the corners and the level bases of doors and skylights are reinforced with brick.

V.1.g 'Ayn Suiqa Fountain

To be found in the Suiqa Quarter: follow the main road which is recognisable for the presence of numerous bazaars. The fountain is on the left-hand side, in a recess.

This fountain, still in service, sheltered by a porch, must be amongst the first to have been built in the neighbourhood. Its architecture is of the same style as other fountains which have been built onto facades. The basin is a semicircular arc, and the wall is decorated with concentric polyfoiled and festooned arcatures. Certain details however – such as the small blind windows situated above the framing of the arcatures, whose inner surfaces have been painted blue to create an illu-

women wear around their shoulders and waists. There are a plenty of weavers' workshops, which exist for the fabrication

sion of an empty sky, and the decorative use of wall tiling – distinguish it from others. This particular use of multicolour in the surface decoration, which puts this fountain at odds with the usual restraint exercised in the decoration of local fountains, seems to have been a result of a recent repair and of an unfortunate imitation of beautiful *zellij* mosaics.

V.1.h Funduq

Situated on the intersection of Place Uta Hammam and rue al-Andalus. The funduq *can be found in a recess on the left-hand side. Open every day.*

Situated on the north-west corner of Uta Hammam Square, it is the town's largest *funduq*, Chefchaouen having possessed four. Well-preserved, it is alone in continuing to fulfil the functions for which it was originally intended, which was to lodge passing visitors, together with their horses or mules, and their goods. Covering an area of about 596 sq. m., it holds over 50 rooms, spread across the ground and first floors, as well as lumber rooms, storage rooms and latrines.

Through a portico, the small rooms on the ground floor open out onto a huge pebbled courtyard, and those on the first floor open out onto a gallery. Semicircular arches held up by columns support the covered alleyways. Restoration and repair works have been visibly carried out on the colonnades of the interior portico, and on the upper galleries. Pilasters have in fact replaced certain columns in the right wing, and certain bays in the upper gallery have been walled up, most definitely in order to make the rooms larger. The pilasters on the left side of the upper gallery also look like they have undergone some repair work.

This compound, which is distinct for its stripped down style and its simplicity, is in certain respects reminiscent of the Mudejar style brought over by the Andalusians. The only part which is decorated is the outside of the entrance. Treated with care, as are all the doors of public buildings in Chefchaouen, it is fitted with a canopy held up on each side by well-anchored columns and held up at its centre by a multitude of small corbels. Its entrance bay is formed in the shape of a pointed horseshoe arch, mounted by a festooned arcature.

Funduq, outside entrance, Chefchaouen.

ITINERARY V   Chefchaouen: The Holy City of the Rif Mountains
Chefchaouen

Andalusian Quarter, Andalusian Street, Chefchaouen.

V.1.i **Andalusian Quarter**

Take the uphill road – rue al-Andalus – which branches of at Place Uta Hammam.

The Rif Andalusian Quarter, built to house the second wave of Andalusian refugees who came after 897/1492, was erected outside the town's initial enclosure. Its general lay-out, whilst being similar to that of the Suiqa Quarter in terms of size and aesthetic, displays several differences forced upon it by the sharp decline of the land. The interiors of houses were, in the majority of cases, built across two or three levels, in the same way as the interiors of houses that have two entrances, which allow entry into the house via the first or via the second floor. The streets, over which the supporting walls lean, are crowded with staircases and rocks which are used as buttresses.

In addition, the appearance of the gates of the houses is well looked after; the doors, made of wood, and the stucco used in the portals, are treated with care.

V.1.j Bab al-Ansar: Walls and Tower

All ascending roads lead to the northern extremity of the Andalusian Quarter, where Bab al-Ansar Gate can be found.

The Bab al-Ansar, which opens onto the neighbourhood of the same name, demarcates the north-western point of the town's enclosure. This enclosure, which is not homogeneous as a whole, reflects the various stages of the town's history. Indeed, the neighbourhoods which were built here and there following the arrival of emigres and local countrymen, forced the enclosure to expand in response to the need for protection. However, there was little awareness as to how the sections of these walls to which the neighbourhoods would link up, were constructed. This is why this section of the enclosure, which should have linked up to the Lamkadem Gate in the south, looks nothing like the rampart in the Suiqa Quarter, neither in terms of material structure nor in terms of width. In addition, its restoration can more accurately be termed as renovation. The watchtower, which is joined to the wall and opens onto an angled passageway is, equally, a recent creation. Erected on the site of an ancient tower, its construction was modelled on the Bab 'Ayn Watchtower, which is suggestive of the covered towers of Granada.

Bab al-Ansar, tower of the enclosure and gate, Chefchaouen.

ITINERARY V   Chefchaouen: The Holy City of the Rif Mountains

Chefchaouen

Ras al-Ma' Source, rubblework enclosure, Chefchaouen.

V.1.k Ras al-Ma' Source

Go past the gate, Bab al-Ansar, continuing along the street which will take you to the spring.

The Ras al-Ma' is located above the *medina*, outside the ramparts. A mountain source, it was at the origin of the foundation of Chefchaouen's *medina*. It provided the town with water, filled fountains, worked mills and watered orchards and gardens. The site from which the source springs, which could still have been seen a few years ago, is now in fact covered by a stone enclosure.

V.1.l Essabanin Quarter: Mill, Bridge, Oven

Take the stairs beyond the source which lead to the tar-surfaced road; 500 m. further down, some steps on the right lead to the Essabanin Quarter. The bridge is situated below on the left, close to the building which houses the oven. Several mills are placed along the water's flow. The oven and the mill are open every day. There is no visiting timetable.

Mill

The mill is located on the left bank of the river, linked to the right bank via a bridge. Its architecture comprises a very simple structure. A main room, rectangular in shape, is divided into two floors: a ground floor, on which the mill is located, and a basement which houses the machinery. The lateral walls of both floors are punctured with bays which allow for the channels to pass through. The mill is activated by a helical axis which turns under the effect of the water's driving force.

It is difficult to put an exact date on this building, and the same goes for the other three mills which still function, and which were also built above the Ras al-Ma' source. The only thing that can be claimed as certain is that we owe the placement of an ingenious hydraulic system to the Andalusian refugees; installed at the time of the town's foundation, it enabled fountains and mills to be endowed with a carefully monitored resource of water. Legend attributes the installation to a certain Sidi Bubker al-Hadad, an engineer in his profession which dealt with the organisation of these resources.

Bridge

This charming little creation, covered in greenery, is Chefchaouen's only bridge. Situated at the exit of the Lamkadem Gate, it links the right bank of the Essabanin Quarter to the left bank, facilitating the journey to the mills. Solid, imposing walls serve to support the extended arch which reaches across the river. The base of the walls is reinforced by buttresses with cut-off corners to counteract the effects of erosion, in line with bridge construction techniques of the Andalusian period.

The date of when the bridge was created is unknown; but if one judges it against the chronology of the *medina*'s urbanisation, and takes into account the mode of construction, then one can approximately place it, at the very latest, in the beginning of the $13^{th}/19^{th}$ century, at the point when the *medina* was at its expansive climax.

Essabanin Quarter, traditional mill, millstone, Chefchaouen.

ITINERARY V   *Chefchaouen: The Holy City of the Rif Mountains*

Chefchaouen

Essabanin Quarter, bridge, Chefchaouen.

Its design is simple. A rectangular room of small dimensions with a low ceiling, it is covered by a dual-sloping red-tiled roof from which rises a chimney which, as is the law of this town, contains the hearth and a platform on which the clients' baking trays are placed. A space is kept for the storage of firewood.

The walls are made of clay with brick planes, which are also used in the levelling of the door. Skylights pierce them open, to assure that there is ventilation, and a door acts as a means of access and of light.

Bakery

Situated on the square of the Essabanin Quarter, it is one of 15 active bakeries currently working in Chefchaouen. Like the others, it is located at the neighbourhood's crossroads in order to better serve the households which continue to knead their own bread at home, and which thus need the bakery's equipment in order to bake it.

Mountain hikes

The Rif Mountains, which border the Mediterranean coastline, rarely rise above a height of 1800 m., even though they are the highest mountains in the north of the country. They are the most watered mountains of the country, and offer a magnificent landscape to the hill walker. The hills around Chefchaouen thus provide a good excuse for the exploration of the surrounding region. Several excursions are possible, all requiring the presence of a guide. The Culture and Hiking Association propose a variety of hikes, some taking up one day, others lasting four, with the possibility of lodging with an inhabitant of the Rif and of renting mules. The most impressive excursions are those of two and three days which lead you respectively to Lake Ackshuch and to the National Park of Talasmetan, Morocco's only fir plantation, as well as to the "Bridge of God", a local geological landmark, one of Nature's rock sculptures. More ambitious would be to go on a four-day hike which would take you up to the sea after having reached the summit of Jebel Tazut. For information, contact the Culture and Hiking Association located at the Casa Hassan guesthouse.

Tel: 09 98 61 53, Fax: 09 98 81 96.

SAIDA EL-HORRA, PRINCESS OF CHEFCHAOUEN

Naïma El-Khatib Boujibar

Cited many a time in the writings of Portuguese and Spanish chroniclers under the name of "Noble Lady" or "Pure Lady", Saida El-Horra, Princess of Chefchaouen, is without doubt one of the most significant figures of the $9^{th}/15^{th}$ century leading into the first half of the $10^{th}/16^{th}$ century. Daughter of Mulay 'Ali Ibn Rashid, the founder of Chefchaouen, and of a Morisco mother who came from Vejer de la Frontera, she was born in 900/1495. Able to speak both Arabic and Castillian to fluent perfection, gifted with exceptional intelligence and an authoritarian temperament, she was particularly prepared to play the political role which destiny had thrown at her: to govern alone, for 17 years, a town and its surrounding region.

Married at a young age to the Governor of Tétouan, al-Mandri II, the nephew of Tétouan's creator al-Mandri I, she had to replace her absent husband on many occasions. On each occasion she demonstrated her great talent for the command of power; this enabled her to succeed her husband once he died in 924/1518, albeit that she was a woman in a Muslim country.

Nominated time and time again by her brother to be Town Prefect, then Regional Governor, followed by the Governor of Tétouan once he himself assumed the position of Grand *Vizier* of Fez under the Wattassid Sultan, she ended up reigning completely independently from 934/1528 to 945/1539, the date of her brother's death. During her time in power, she carried out the fortification of the town, and worked towards economic development by building shipyards at the mouth of the Martil River. Strengthened by her navy, she had the audacity to throw herself into sea battle, joining forces with Khayr al-Din, the famous privateer from Algiers, otherwise known as Barbarossa.

These military onslaughts which she lead against the coasts of Spain and Portugal enabled her to protect her territory and increase her sources of revenue through negotiating a high price for the release of Christian captives.

Her prestige and power made the central government of Fez fearful and respectful of her whilst they tried, not without difficulty, to maintain their authority over the whole of Morocco. In addition, to increase his power in his struggle against the mounting force of the Sa'adians, the Wattasid King Mulay Ahmed asked for her hand in marriage in 947/1541. However, for the nuptial celebrations, Saida El-Horra demanded that the sovereign himself should travel to Tétouan, contrary to tradition which decreed that it should be the bride who should move to the home town of her husband. Furthermore, without resigning her role as companion, she continued to administer the town of Tétouan, but did so in the name of the King. Stirred up by her half-brother's desire to take Tétouan from her, she was defeated in 948/1542 by the army he raised in allying himself with the Sa'adians, enemies of the Wattasid Sultan. Expelled from the town, having had all her possessions confiscated, she disappeared from history. No written source, which is worthy of being trusted, exists to enlighten us on the last days of her life. Only certain oral traditions speak of her having sought refuge in Chefchaouen, her town of birth. There, she would have founded a *zawiya*, the Rayssuniya, where she would come to be buried; others believe she fled to Ksar al-Kebir, where she died.

Whatever may have become of this exceptional woman, described by some as an intelligent but belligerous woman, and by others as a true saint, she remains a legendary figure who sparks up the collective consciousness of the inhabitants of Chefchaouen.

ITINERARY VI

Tétouan: The Patio of a Civilisation
Mhammad Benaboud

VI.I TÉTOUAN
- VI.1.a School of Traditional Arts and Crafts
- VI.1.b Bab Okla
- VI.1.c Lebbadi Palace
- VI.1.d Great Mosque
- VI.1.e Mtamar Silo
- VI.1.f Tanneries
- VI.1.g Sidi 'Ali Baraka Zawiya
- VI.1.h Rue al-Mokadem
- VI.1.i Lukash Madrasa
- VI.1.j Sidi al-Mandri Kasbah
- VI.1.k Erzini Mosque
- VI.1.l Ethnographic Museum

Andalusian Music

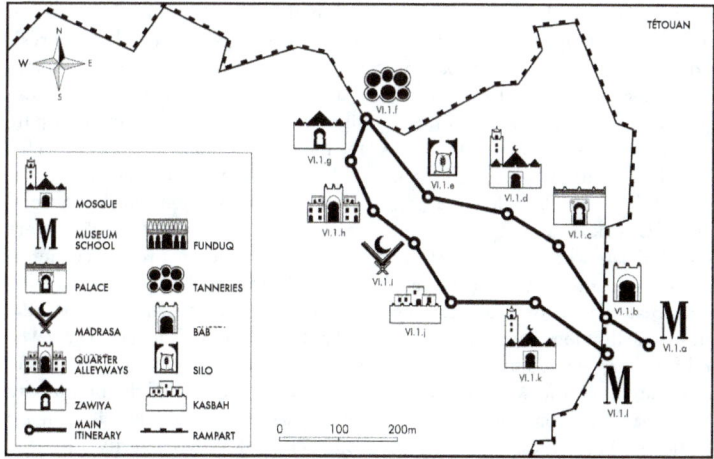

Tétouan, medina, covered alleyway.

ITINERARY VI — Tétouan: The Patio of a Civilisation

Tétouan, general view of the medina.

Tétouan, the "white dove" of Arab poets, was also known as "the daughter of Granada". Open to the outside and yet at the time inward looking and withdrawn, it is the Andalusian patio of Morocco; furthermore, it managed to preserve this vibrant civilisation by conserving a plurality of cultural elements, transforming and developing them across the centuries. The fall of the kingdom of Granada marked the renaissance of the town of Tétouan. Its reconstruction, undertaken in the $9^{th}/15^{th}$ century by Sidi al-Mandri, a native of Granada, in joint forces with the first Mudejars who were fleeing from the Christian Reconquest, turned it into a town created in order to welcome Andalusian civilisation. Protected by the natural frontiers formed by two mountains, situated on the Mediterranean coast, Tétouan's location offered a strategic position to these exiles, who had little if no rest in pushing back the threat of Christian menace.

The town was developed, as well as rebuilt by them. Taking advantage of the central power vacuum which defined Morocco at the time, they supervised their own administration, creating a city in the image of those they had had to leave. Erected in a climate of fight, Tétouan is distinct for its military architecture, the Andalusian character of which is evident. The walls of the town's enclosure, which was designed by Sidi al-Mandri, tall in height, and thick, and the regularity displayed by its towers, are amongst the best examples of this. There are still a few remains of the Mandarite town of the $9^{th}/15^{th}$ and $10^{th}/16^{th}$ centuries, including: the outside walls and three bastions of the Sidi al-Mandri Kasbah; and the Erzini Mosque, which is unique for the simplicity and small size of its minaret, built at a time when the surrounding houses hardly rose above it. Other examples of the architecture of this period are few and far between; the actual plan of the streets, with its cul-de-sacs, its small gardens or indeed its covered passages, its *sabat*, situated in the residential quarter (known as the al-Mtamar Quarter at the time, where subterranean silos were built), evoke without dispute the Morisco town that was Tétouan in the $10^{th}/16^{th}$ century. Leatherwork, for which the town was renowned, datesfrom this time, when the tanneries were grouped into the north-west corner of the original town plan.

Originally a fortress, intended for the protection of the Andalusian emigres who founded it, the town of Tétouan nonetheless reflects the will of the builders to develop a sophisticated urban life bringing together comfort and security.

With the arrival of a new, massive wave of refugees, following the expulsion decree of 1017/1609 ordered by Philip III, the town expanded, gaining in importance. Some 10,000 Moriscos settled in Tétouan, growing in number to between 22,000 and 26,000 by the middle of the 11th/17th century. The town's area quadrupled, reaching the size of the fortified town it is today. Extending far beyond the fortifications established by al-Mandri, it was surrounded by a new enclosure in the 12th/18th century.

Across the 11th/17th and 12th/18th centuries, monuments were subject to Morisco influence, the hallmarks of which are modesty and the absence of surface decoration, as can been seen in the design of houses and mosques. Recognisable by their minarets, whose simple decoration consists of lines of bricks and a couple of blind arches, the interior of the mosques often have semi-circular arcades, not in the horseshoe shape that became prevalent in traditional North African architecture since the Almoravids. In terms of religious architecture, the Lukash Madrasa, built in the 12th/18th century, is the only remaining *madrasa* to be seen.

In the 19th century, the town continued to grow, and one could witness the emergence of a number of palaces, including the Dar Lebbadi. Whilst its style is Andalusian, its construction is based on modern techniques which were brought over from Europe. Iron pillars replaced the wooden ones which characterised the houses of the 12th/18th century.

The Tétouanese art of living bore the trademark of an Andalusian inheritance even more strongly than its architecture. Cookery, music, or indeed even Tétouanese jewellery and embroidery were impregnated with their Andalusian origin.

The tanneries, vats and walls, Tétouan.

Nasrid and Mudejar motifs disappeared out of Tétouanese embroidery, which can be admired today in the Ethnographic Museum of Bab Okla.

However, the conservation of traditional Tétouanese art owes much to Mariano Bertuchi, an exceptional painter and important curator of Moroccan art, who founded the Ethnographic Museum and the School of Traditional Arts and Crafts, two real gems aimed at the conservation of Tétouan's Andalusian art.

Whilst retaining its historic links with other regions of Morocco, Tétouan experienced its own specific and autonomous historical development during the period from the 11th/17th to the 12th/18th centuries. It is only from the 19th century onwards that Tétouan's history entwines itself with that of Morocco's.

A pinnacle of splendour and decadence, Tétouan's history began during the

Roman period with the foundation of Tamuda, a town on the river Martil, 2 km. away from Tétouan itself. The site on which Tétouan is based is mentioned by the Andalusian geographer Abu 'Ubayd al-Bakri in sources dating from the $5^{th}/11^{th}$ century. European sources cite it as the first Moroccan port to hold commercial relations with Catalan merchants, who through their conquest of Almeria had extended their influence over the Mediterranean. But it is not until the Almohad era of the $6^{th}/12^{th}$ century that Tétouan begins to feature in Moroccan sources. Destroyed during the $9^{th}/15^{th}$ century by the Portuguese, who occupied the majority of the Moroccan ports at the time, Tétouan then vanished from history.

At the end of the $9^{th}/15^{th}$ century, the Granadan Sidi al-Mandri, who died in 916/1511, brought Tétouan back to life, just like a phoenix rising from the ashes. Armed with a handful of Granadan exiles, there was no respite for this military leader in his campaign to push back Iberian military advances; an advance which posed more of a threat than the majority of coastal towns occupied by the Spanish and Portuguese, whose main activities were linked to slave trading.

Whilst the name of Sidi al-Mandri has today become the town's symbol, his descendants have continued to play an important role in this part of the country. In fact, Saida El-Horra, who governed the towns of Tétouan and Chefchaouen during the $10^{th}/16^{th}$ century, was the wife of 'Ali al-Mandri's grandson and the daughter of Chefchaouen's ruler, Mulay 'Ali Ibn Rashid. The reign of this liberal woman (943/1537–948/1542) marks a unique stage in the history of these two towns.

Others played a distinguishing role in defending the town against the Spanish invaders. From the $9^{th}/15^{th}$ to the $12^{th}/18^{th}$ century, the privateers of Tétouan contributed in pushing back the military menace. Only their ships, due to them being small in size contrary to the huge battleships, could seek refuge in the town's port situated on the mouth of the Rio Martil's estuary.

Another name succeeded that of al-Mandri's: the name of Naqsis. This family, of Andalusian origin, who reigned over Tétouan for nearly a century (1005/1597–1082/1672), provided the town with a true economic boom. Due to the fact that most Moroccan ports were occupied by the Spanish, Tétouan was, during the $11^{th}/17^{th}$ and $12^{th}/18^{th}$ centuries, the main Moroccan port through which European commerce travelled. The Jewish community of Tétouan played a significant role in this. A solid network

Zawiya Sidi 'Ali Baraka, general view, Tétouan.

of correspondents around the Mediterranean (be them parents, allies or associates) enabled the development of commercial exchange with Spain, Italy and England. Ships navigated between Tétouan, Gibraltar, Marseilles, Algiers, and so on. Professor Jean-Louis Miege describes the splendour of Tétouan thus: *"In this fashion a sort of a veritable city-state appeared, which was Moroccan in its measurements and specificities, and yet slightly reminiscent of Florence during its grand era or of Venice at the time of the Doges".*

The growth of commercial trade and of shared interests demanded the establishment of institutional relations. In 1038/1629, France opened a consulate in Tétouan, and was followed by other countries, which thus turned the town into the diplomatic capital of Morocco during the 12th/18th century.

Ever since the reign of Sultan Mulay Isma'il, the 'Alawite Sultans dominated the political life of Tétouan in that they nominated the town's Governors. Although the Errifis in general held good relations with the central power, their regionalist tendencies began progressively to manifest themselves, leading to confrontation with the central power in the 12th/18th century. This autonomist and regionalist tradition was lost with the nominations of more powerful Governors like 'Ali and his sons Ahmed Errifi, Omar Lukash and Abdelkader Achache.

The 19th century, a century of decadence for Morocco as a whole due to the penetration of the European economy, is a particularly dark period in the history of Tétouan. The plagues of 1214/1800 and 1233/1818, the famine of 1240/1825, and the Hispanic-Moroccan war of 1859–1862 resulting in the Spanish occupation of the town for a whole two years, all weakened the town considerably. In exchange for their

Ethnographic Museum, Andalusian Garden, Tétouan.

Tétouan, plan of the town, extensions of the town walls in the 11th/17th and 12th/18th centuries.

ITINERARY VI   Tétouan: The Patio of a Civilisation

Tétouan

School of Traditional Arts and Crafts, exhibition room, Tétouan.

departure, the Spanish demanded a very high price in compensation, thus leaving behind an economy in ruins.

In the 20th century, Tétouan, as the capital of the Spanish Protectorate in north Morocco, experienced a new political, economic and artistic boom. The modern neighbourhood of Tétouan, with its streets and buildings, squares and markets, built next to the old *medina*, is an accurate reflection of the style of colonial architecture.

VI.I TÉTOUAN

VI.1.a School of Traditional Arts and Crafts

On entering the town, follow the sign Ancienne Médina. Drive down Avenue Hassan II, *then drive alongside the ramparts of the old medina. Park the car, as the rest of the itinerary is done on foot. Supervised parking. Entrance fee. Open weekdays from 08.30–12.00 and 14.30–17.30. Closed Saturdays and Sundays.*

Opened in 1916, the School of Arts and Crafts was a unique establishment of its kind in the entire Arab world. Intended for the conservation and passing on of Arab-Andalusian national heritage, it is today the best guarantor for the conservation of the knowledge brought over by the Moriscos ever since the beginning of the $11^{th}/17^{th}$ century, during the time of their exodus. The works of the artisans who were members of the school bare witness to this knowledge, and are exhibited as such at the heart of the school as well as in a number of Spanish museums. It should be noted that the school took part in various ornamentation and decoration projects, such as those involving the Moroccan Pavilion at the Hispanic-American Exposition in Seville in 1928–1929, or indeed of the 'Caliphal' Palace and seat of certain government administrations in Tétouan.

Situated at Bab Okla, the building which houses the school is in itself an example of Arab-Andalusian architecture. The school constitutes a precious piece of architectural heritage, irrespective of whether one attributes this to its architectonic elements or to its ornamentation, an example of which is the majestic dome of its exhibition hall. The three main buildings, bordered by a garden, contain respectively an exhibition hall, and two lateral wings off which 14 workshops branch out, and to which a number of students come today to gain a secular education. These workshops teach a combination of the main techniques involved in crafts: decorative paintwork on wood; the modelling, sculpting and inlaying of wood; ceramics and *zellij*; the sculpting of plaster; copper engraving; the making of traditional lamps; artistic iron work; leather-gilding; goldsmithing; weaving and embroidery.

VI.1.b Bab Okla

Opposite the School of Arts and Crafts.

Bab Okla, one of seven *medina* gates, is situated on the east of the enclosure. Built around the middle of the 10th/16th century, it was probably restored in the middle of the 12th/18th century, when the last

Bab Okla, general view, Tétouan.

ITINERARY VI   *Tétouan: The Patio of a Civilisation*

Tétouan

Lebbadi Palace, patio, Tétouan.

reconstruction of the *medina* walls took place. It was known for a long time as the "Gate of the Sea" because in the past it was through this gate that one found the path leading to the village of Martil on the Mediterranean.

For the farmers wishing to sell their goods in town, it offered a direct route to one of the *medina*'s most commercial streets, allowing them thus to enter with their mules, who refreshed themselves at the nearest fountain, without disturbing the privacy or peace of the town's inhabitants. The entrance of this parallelepipedic gate is straightforward, as opposed to being elbow-shaped as was the tradition for Mediaeval gates. Its proportions are enormous: 3 m. wide, 4 m. high, and 2.5 m. thick.

Inside the recess of the gate, a bench, which sits beneath an interlacing vault, was constructed for a guard. A room, a *mesria*, was built above the opening of the gate to house a guardian whose principal duties were as follows: to stock the gunpowder used to load the canons in the fortress next to the gate; to open and close the gate at sunrise and sunset.

VI.1.c **Lebbadi Palace**

Walk up the main street, rue al-Genoui (opposite the Bab Okla). The old palace, today a restaurant and hall which can be used on certain occasions to host parties, can be found in the recess on the right.

Open from 09.00–16.00. It is possible to visit without having a drink or a meal, but it is closed to the public when hired out for a private party.

When walking up this street, notice the presence, on various different doors, of wrought iron symbols which indicate the geographical origins of the occupants: the pomegranate thus demonstrates the Andalusian origin of the inhabitants.

This old residence from the 19th century, which belonged to the town's *pasha*, is one of the most beautiful buildings of the time, and moreover is one of the best preserved. Built on sloping ground and set in an area measuring 25 m. at each side, the palace possesses two entrances. The main, elbow-shaped entrance, opens out onto a street further down, and the second entrance, opening onto the landing of a staircase, leads out onto a street which is further up. The ground floor was kept aside for receptions, for the welcoming of visitors and for family reunions. The central patio, measuring 8 m. at each side, bordered by a portico of pointed or semicircular arches, leads to several different rooms. Open, doorless rooms known as *maq'ads* can be found on two of its four sides; the other rooms on those sides serve as bedrooms. Within each of these bedrooms there is a space built specifically for a bed, which is separated from the rest of the room by an arch. Finally, on the third side of the patio, a space opens up to a fountain, leading onto the kitchen and bathrooms.

The ornamental decor –*zellij* on the columns, geometric patterns and floral decorations on the arcades, plaques of painted wood on the ceiling– is particularly accentuated in the ground-floor rooms. Furthermore, the presence of water predominates: a second fountain, in a room next to the patio, has been added to the main one at the centre of the patio – fountains in which one can admire the art of Arabic calligraphy as well as the decorative features mentioned above.

In the kitchen, a small water reservoir has been linked to the terrace via a traditional ceramic canal system built to catch rainwater.

As for the rooms on the mezzanine level, they were mainly used for storage; those on the upper level were closed bedrooms,

Great Mosque, door opening onto the patio, Tétouan.

covering the length of the building. This latter space was essentially used at night, and thus is sparsely decorated.

VI.1.d Great Mosque

Continue walking upwards by taking a left at each crossroads; the mosque is situated in the al-Balad Quarter, in the rue de la Grande Mosquée (Street of the Great Mosque). Access restricted to Muslims.

Built under the order of Sultan Mulay Sliman in 1222/1808, close to *Mellah al-Bali*, the old Jewish Quarter, it necessitated the displacement of the members of the Jewish community who had settled in what had been the gardens of the Sultan's palace. This monument of worship was on the one hand a site for Friday prayers and preaching, and on the other, a site for theological teaching.

Perfectly integrated into the surrounding environment, this mosque, the largest in the *medina* (35 m. long on its east side and 45 m. long on its north side) opens onto a large prayer hall. A spacious patio at the back leads onto the *mihrab*, and onto three U-shaped passageways. Two gates, facing southwards and westwards respectively, open onto the patio. A third, more discreet entrance, facing northwards, opens onto a more narrow street. The overbearing structure of the building is composed of columns, erected every 5 m., which in turn support the pointed arches on which the two pieces of wood – which form the roof trussing and are covered in red tiles – rest. The minaret displays a décor of continuous brickwork as well as a three-dimensional geometric tracery made of lime mortar, the crevices of which are surfaced in *zellij*.

Walk around the mosque, and ascend rue Sloquia Si Saidi. At the second crossing, there are two options: on one side, Bab Sfli, still called Bab Gief, the gate through which the Jewish community carried its dead. And on the other, Bab As-Saida or Sidi Saida, where the patron saint of Tétouan is buried.

VI.1.e Mtamar Silo

Descend the street which faces the main gate of the Great Mosque, take a right at the first crossing, and you should find yourself on rue Mtamar: the silos once existed beneath your feet. This monument cannot be visited, as all that remains of it today are its gates, located at the far end of the street, marking the entrance to the silos.

One of the particular things about Tétouan is that it is built on limestone soil

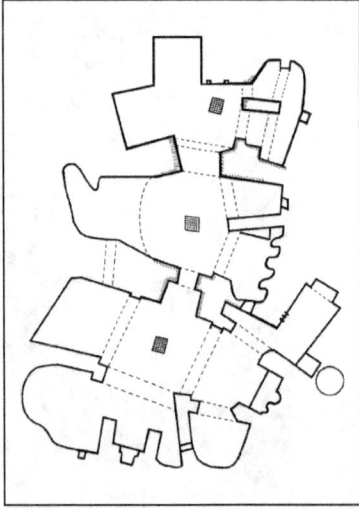

Mtamar Silo, original plan, Tétouan.

ITINERARY VI   *Tétouan: The Patio of a Civilisation*
Tétouan

The tanneries, general view, Tétouan.

which consists of a veritable network of cavities and underground corridors, crossing the town from east to west. Silos were built into these cavities in the 10th/16th century, the period during which Tétouan's *medina* was rebuilt. These dungeons or caves were essentially used to house the 30,000 slaves and Christian captives who helped build the town, and were still utilised in the 11th/17th and 12th/18th centuries.

This subterranean prison, situated close to the Sidi al-Mandri Kasbah, contained three main sections into which light filtered into the sealed manholes through iron grills. The prisoners slid down into them using a rope, and guards could watch over them through the manholes. Smaller polygonal and sinuous compartments were juxtaposed into the three main sections, and were each separated by vaults and supporting arches. A church was also fitted, where Franciscan priests conducted religious services for the Christian prisoners. Towards the end of the 12th/18th century, the Sultan Mulay

ITINERARY VI   Tétouan: The Patio of a Civilisation

Tétouan

Zawiya Sidi 'Ali Baraka, entrance door, Tétouan.

Sliman gave the order for the release of all prisoners, and the silos were closed down. Since then they have remained unused.

VI.1.f **Tanneries**

From rue Mtamar, take rue Marestan on the right. Take a right at the second crossing, then a left, leading onto rue Siarrin, the street of the jewellers. Walk along this street in the direction of rue Kharrazin, in the clog-making quarter, where one can see a number of stalls in which artisans craft leather in order to make slippers. At the exit of this neighbourhood, on the right, is the neighbourhood of the tanneries, Dar Dbagh. *Open daily from 08.00–19.00.*

Established in the north of the *medina* since the 10th/16th century and linked to its enclosure, the tanneries assure the durability of an unchanging tradition within Moroccan crafts. Taking the form of an L-shape, this space under the open sky has two means of access. The first, opening onto the craft quarter, facilitates deliveries to nearby workshops; the second opens onto the Bab al-Kebir, enabling farmers to bring the basic materials directly to the tanners. The tanneries are composed of circular vats built in visible brick, and of square vats and basins dug out of the limestone ground. The whole system is linked to a network of canals which allowed for the transport of water from its natural source. The treated leather was, more often than not, goat skin and occasionally sheep skin. The process of treatment was as follows:
— the first phase, which can take several months, consists of salting (salinisation) and stocking;
— the second phase is 'de-salting' (desalinisation) and treating the hides with powdered lime to clean them, which takes about 15 days;
— the third phase is to place the hides in quicklime so that they harden (again 15 days);
— the fourth phase consists of 'de-liming' the hides with pigeon excrement for the duration of two days, followed by cleaning with flour;
— the fifth is tanning the hides in a liquid whose composition is based on powdered bark (4 days);
— the sixth is the drying, smoothing down and sanding down of the hides (4 days).

As a general rule, the artisans dry the leather out in the cemetery next to the enclosure wall, outside the *medina*.

VI.1.g Sidi 'Ali Baraka Zawiya

At the exit of the tanneries neighbourhood, take rue Suq al-Foqui, which leads to the square of the same name, on which one can find the Sidi 'Ali Baraka Zawiya, in the recess on the right. Access restricted to Muslims.

This *zawiya*, dating from the beginning of the $12^{th}/18^{th}$ century, contains the mausoleum of the great scholar and writer Sidi 'Ali Baraka. The monument is distinct for the ornamentation of its main entrance, which some attribute to a "metropolitan" influence, probably derived from the court of Meknès. A row of concentric decorations, cuspid in shape, surmount the pointed, horseshoe archway of the gate, which is flanked by cabled columns. The springer of the arch is itself also made of brick.

VI.1.h Rue al-Mokadem

Rue Al-Mokadem branches off Suq al-Foqui Square.

Named after a Tétouanese warrior chief, al-Moladem Abu al-'Abbas Ahmed Ibn 'Aissa Naqsis, al-Mokadem Street, which links Suq al-Foqui Square to Gharsa al-Kebira Square, was opened in the $11^{th}/17^{th}$ century. 130 m. in length, this street, the most commercial one in the *medina*, is lined with buildings which rise above 10 m. The interplay of the various sizes of its buildings, the variety of its lights, the whiteness of its walls and the paving of its ground turn this street, together with its numerous ramifications, into an area which defines the urban specificity of Tétouan.

Al-Mokadem street, Tétouan.

ITINERARY VI   Tétouan: The Patio of a Civilisation

Tétouan

VI.1.i Lukash Madrasa

Descend rue al-Mokadem; on the left there is an intersection with rue Gharsa al-Kebira, which leads to Ghauaza Square, named after a walnut tree, the symbol of the square on which one can find the Lukash Madrasa. The monument is closed to the public.

Intended as lodgings for students who came to study in Tétouan for their secondary education, the *madrasa* was built in 1171/1758 under the orders of Sultan Sidi Mohamed Ibn 'Abd Allah and *qa'id* 'Umar Lukash. Whether fact or fiction, it is said that the students refused to move into the charitable foundation until it had been proved to them that the Lukash family had amassed its fortune honestly and without corruption.

The students were housed on the ground and first floors, in 54 little rooms covering 6 sq. m. in surface area, surrounded by two interior courtyards. On the first floor, gangways overlooking the central patio lead to a second set of rooms. A library reserved for the students was constructed on the terrace.

The ornamental decor was minimal and low-key: the ground was tiled with *mzehri*, the columns were surfaced with *zellij*, and, in the guardroom, gangways were open, smaller ones of which were pierced in the form of a *mrachat*.

VI.1.j Sidi al-Mandri Kasbah

Walk around Place Ghauza, always taking a right. This leads you to rue Lussar, which takes you to the passageway of the kasbah. A part of the enclosure wall still remains to this day. Take the stairs on the right which lead to the old pathway of the guard.

This Mediaeval monument was rebuilt in the 9th/15th century by Sidi al-Mandri

Lukash Madrasa, general view of the building, Tétouan.

from Granada. This warrior, who made his name in the army of Ibn al-Ahmar, employed Christians, captured during his campaigns against Ceuta, to build this monumental *kasbah*. The centre of government and of the military, the *kasbah* is situated in the south-west of the primary enclosure of the town. Only the external walls and bastions remain of the original fortress.

The south-west facade of the *kasbah*, the best preserved side, has three forts which are linked to one another by a covered passageway. Alcoves, hollowed out of the thick gates, sheltered the sentinels. The gates, of vaults made out of brick, are similar to those of the *kasbah* in Granada.

A mosque, rebuilt in the $11^{th}/17^{th}$ and $12^{th}/18^{th}$ centuries rose up inside the building. The dwellings of Sidi al-Mandri were not far from the mosque. Nothing but the *hammam* of this modest living space remains, which was the private bath attached to the house, consisting of two domes surmounted by fan-vaulting.

VI.1.k Erzini Mosque

Going past the kasbah, *one is led onto Suq al-Hut. Turn left onto rue Kazdarin, then right onto rue Ahmed Torrès. Descend rue al-Barrid to reach the Gate of Saquia Fukia, take a left onto rue Sebahi, followed by rue Sala. Take an immediate left into the arcade, Derb Es-Safar; the Erzini Mosque is located in the alley. Access restricted to Muslims.*

Built in the oldest part of town, this mosque is the last remaining piece of evidence of its time. It was constructed, it seems, in 999/1591, by one of the Andalusian families who had settled in Tétouan towards the end of the $9^{th}/15^{th}$ century. The minaret seems to have kept its original decoration. Only a geometric design, made of lime mortar, onto which *zellij* motifs are engraved, stands out in relief. The architectural feature which is true to this period is essentially the simplicity and miniature size of brick minarets.

Kasbah Sidi al-Mandri, upper part of the building, Tétouan.

ITINERARY VI   Tétouan: The Patio of a Civilisation

Tétouan

The interior of the mosque does not differ from conventional mosque interiors.

If one walks back up rue Ahmed Torrès in the opposite direction, one reaches Bab Ruah, a gate which joins the old town to the new one. To the left of Bab Ruah, a smaller gate leads to the Mellah, the old Jewish Quarter of Tétouan.

Erzini Mosque, minaret, Tétouan.

VI.1.1 Ethnographic Museum

Located on rue Sqala. Take a right onto rue Sefar, and descend until you reach Bab Okla. Having arrived at Bab Okla, turn onto rue Sqala; the museum can be found in a recess 20 m. to your left.
Open daily from 08.00–12.00 and 14.:30–18.00. Closed Sundays.

Established in 1928, the Museum was moved to the Bab Okla Fortress in 1948. This fortress, built around 1245/1830 by Sultan Mulay 'Abd al-Rahman Ibn Hisham, assured the town's protection, and, through its geographical positioning, was utilsed to control the flow of the River Martil, reaching as far as the mouth of the river. Today the building has been handed over to the Tétouanese branch of the Conservation of Cultural National Heritage: costumes, furniture and traditional arts are thus brought together at the heart of the museum.

Built on an incline, the museum encloses an interior garden, a design which subscribes to the traditional Andalusian palaces of the time, featuring a basin and *zellij*-covered fountain at its centre, under a wooden canopy covered in red tiles. A covered passageway looks over onto the garden, and canons placed through slits top the walls.

The main building opens onto an exhibition hall dedicated to rural life: a traditional kitchen has been reconstructed in the adjoining room.

Upstairs, four rooms offer the visitor an insight into Téouanese interiors, and these are as follows: a reception room of a traditional house, a room displaying the dowry of a bride, a room displaying costumes, and a room of musical instruments.

ITINERARY VI   Tétouan: The Patio of a Civilisation
Tétouan

Ethnographic Museum, exhibition room, traditional Tétouanese living room, Tétouan.

Martil and Cabo Negro
8 km. east of Tétouan, the small town of Martil, which a long time ago was the Port of Tétouan, was once a hideout for pirates. Today a seaside resort, Martil has a proper beach and a number of seafront cafes. Further north along the coast, Cabo Negro, a fashionable seaside resort which can be seen from Martil's beach, juts out into the Mediterranean.

ANDALUSIAN MUSIC

Mhammad Benaboud

Rebab, Andalusian musical instrument, the upper half of which is encrusted with inlaid ivory set in a floral motif, Ethnographic Museum (268), Tétouan.

The arrival of the Arabs onto Andalusian soil gave birth to a cultural phenomenon without precedent, leaving an imprint on architecture as well as on intellectual and artistic endeavours. The introduction of Arab music into al-Andalus through its very first conquerors, gave rise to an explosion of musical activity beginning at the inauguration of the Umayyad state, which was enriched by various creative strands stemming from the different ethnic groups present in Andalusia. 'Ali Ibn Nafi, also known as Ziryab, who was the uncontested virtuoso of Arabic music, was one of the pillars of Arabic music in the East during the reign of the Abbasid Caliph Harun al-Rashid (148/766–193/809). On his arrival in al-Andalus, Ziryab founded the first Arabic school for the teaching of music and song in Cordoba, where he established an original method of teaching based on the principle of progressive apprenticeship, linking poetic text strictly to melodic structure. From then on, other virtuosos continued to add to this musical heritage, which today constitutes one of the most brilliant aspects of what is termed Arab-Andalusian civilisation.

Morocco's contribution to the development of Andalusian music was intensified by the arrival of a massive wave of emigres, following the fall of the Andalusian cities. The symbiosis between the different genres of musical practice and these new musical imports gave birth to a style of composition and interpretation which was utterly unique; evidence of its influence can be found in Andalusian music, which to this day remains strongly impregnated by it.

Andalusian musical heritage is composed of a number of musical works which are gathered together to form larger compositions known as *nuba*. These involve two main elements: preludes and *mizan*s or bars. Each *mizan* has a set of vocal pieces called *sana'a*, which divide themselves into three large sections which are differentiated mainly by their different rhythmical interpretations.

The lyrics that are sung are taken from the rich repertoire of Arabic poetry. It is this clever combination of the human voice with instruments, as well as a certain degree of improvisation, which gives this music its complete originality. The traditional Andalusian orchestra, in which the group of players and singers place themselves in a semi-circular formation, consists of string and percussion instruments. There are three string instruments: the lute, the oldest instrument of Arabic music; the *rebab*, which came to al-Andalus along with the arrival of the first conquerors (and which is more than likely the ancestor of the viol); and the violin, imported into Morocco during the final influx of Moriscos. Three percussion instruments complete the orchestra: the handheld *taussid*, the *tarr* and the *derbuka*, all of which are the main instruments of percussion.

Andalusian music constitutes a national heritage and a cultural inheritance which Tétouan, as well as other Moroccan towns such as Chefchaouen and Fez, helped to conserve. As popular amongst Muslim Moroccans as it is amongst certain sectors of the Jewish Moroccan community, Andalusian music is still very much alive thanks to certain groups, both male and female, within the town's population. It occupies an important place within the various aspects of Tétouanese social life and culture. Joyful and secular during family festivities, spiritual and sombre during religious ceremonies: its roles and magnitudes change according to circumstance and occasion, whilst keeping to its overall unity and authenticity, thus becoming an integral part of Moroccan cultural identity.

ITINERARY VII

The Ports of the Strait

Naïma El-Khatib Boujibar

First day

VII.1 TÉTOUAN
VII.1.a Archaeological Museum

VII.2 BELYUNESH
VII.2.a Tower and Residential Area

VII.3 KSAR ES-SEGHIR
VII.3.a Gate of the Sea and Enclosure

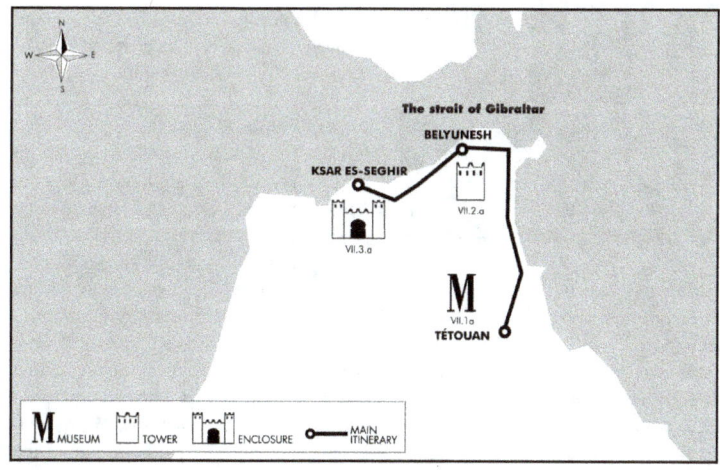

Belyunesh, the Hauz mountain range and view onto the Straits of Gibraltar.

ITINERARY VII   *The Ports of the Strait*

Enclosure, general view, Ksar Es-Seghir.

Kasbah, ramparts, Tangier.

The ports are in a privileged position, in terms of political and cultural relations between Morocco and the Iberian Peninsula, as they are located at the coastal tip of north Morocco, between Tangier and Ceuta, at a point which seems to want to join up to Spain. The stretch of sea filling the Strait which was compared to a river, as opposed to being viewed as an obstacle, and, since the earliest times of history, was always an easy means of communication between Morocco, Europe and other Mediterranean countries. It is through this coastal zone that Morocco came into contact with Punic, Roman, Byzantine, and Visigothic civilisations (as did Spain), and through which the Roman province of Mauretania Tingitania, the capital which was Tangiers, was linked, at the end of the Roman Empire, to the diocese of Spain. Equally, the Muslim Conquest began with the conquest of this zone. In fact, Musa Ibn Nusayr first seized Ceuta and Tangier before penetrating inland; and it is in this northern coastal threshold where the kingdom of the legendary Count Julian, who provided Musa with the necessary information on Morocco and Spain, was situated. Furthermore it was from this region, from the Ghomaran and Rifian populations who had embraced Islam right from the start, that Musa's lieutenant, Tariq Ibn Ziyad, from whom the

ITINERARY VII   The Ports of the Strait

name Gibraltar derives – *Jabal Tariq*, "Mount Tariq" – recruited the contingents who were thrown into the assault against the Iberian Peninsula.

Arab geographers who have described this region noted its wealth of water and fertile soils, as well as the importance of its three towns: Ceuta (*Sebta*), Ksar Es-Seghir and Tangier, all of which exercised naval activities and maintained direct links, political as well as cultural, with al-Andalus. It was thus that during the height of the Moroccan-Andalusian civilisation, particularly during the $7^{th}/13^{th}$ and $8^{th}/14^{th}$ centuries, these towns enjoyed an economic prosperity and cultural development that was without precedent. Ceuta, which no longer has on its soil any material traces of its glorious past, and which one cannot but disassociate from its western counterpart, Belyunesh, had played a dominant role in the region as a very active cultural centre.

Eminent scholars, works by whom we still have, such as the celebrated Qadi 'Ayad, and Abu 'Abbas al-Sabti – who was one of the seven patrons of Marrakesh – did their medical and astronomical training there, as well as the study of religious sciences.

This radiance unfortunately began to wan the moment the Iberian nations threw themselves into conquering the Strait at the beginning of the $9^{th}/15^{th}$ century for the sake of protecting their maritime routes against pirates. The Portuguese capture of Ceuta in 817/1415 was the beginning of the end for this region. It was then that the Strait became the scene of armed conflict which lasted for over a century. The area of Ceuta became depopulated and collapsed. The ports of Ksar Es-Seghir and Tangier fell a little later under Portuguese domination, as did Asilah, a port on the north Atlantic, which is historically, economically and culturally attached to the zone of the Strait.

Walls and bastions which encircle the medina, Asilah.

185

ITINERARY VII   *The Ports of the Strait*
Tétouan

The Moroccan victory, in the 11th/17th century, in reclaiming the occupied territories, with the exception of Ceuta, brought renewed energy into Tangier and Asilah, but life was still far less sumptuous than it had been during the period of the Merinids. Despite all the trials and tribulations they went through, as well as having to endure the various changes which affected them for nearly two centuries, Tangier and Asilah regained their strengths to become Muslim towns once more, with a traditional urban framework, small alleyways, and public and private institutions built in pure Moroccan-Andalusian tradition.

VII.1 **TÉTOUAN**

VII.1.a **Archaeological Museum**

Situated at 2, rue Ben Hussaien.
Open from Monday to Thursday from 08.00–12.00 and 14.30–18.00; Fridays from 08.30–11.30 and 15.30–18.30. Closed Saturday, Sunday and Tuesday mornings.

Situated close to al-Jala Square, the museum was built in 1943. Displaying the prehistoric and pre-Islamic sites of North Morocco, it holds magnificent small mosaics and diverse objects or instruments like prehistoric utensils, bronzes or potteries dating, for the most part, from the first century. One of the museum's specialities lies in its collection of ancient Iberian and Jewish tombstones exhibited in the garden together with ancient Arab steles from the 10th/16th century. The funeral steles from Jabal Dersa have also been added to the museum's collection, which includes Spanish Renaissance and Baroque art.

VII.2 **BELYUNESH**

Located about 50 km. from Tétouan. A sublime route along the Mediterranean and across

Archeological Museum, principal path of the garden bordered by funeral steles, Tétouan.

the mountainous ridge of Hauz. Estimate between three and four hours for this part of the itinerary.
Leave Tétouan via avenue Martil, heading in the direction of Ceuta. Arriving in Fnidq, head towards Tangier. After about 5 km., take a right in the direction of Belyunesh. Continue for a further 12 km. on an extremely winding road across the Ridge of Hauz. Belyunesh is at the foot of the Jabal Musa.

Belyunesh, an archaeological site, where a village of fishermen and border merchants had rooted itself, was during the Mediaeval times the orchard and water tower of Ceuta, and came under the jurisdiction of the *Qadi* of the Strait's city.
Situated in a deep verdant valley which descends steeply towards the sea, amply watered by the water from its natural sources, it was considered during Mediaeval times to be an idyllic place, sung of by poets such as the famous Qadi 'Ayad. Dominated by the Jabal Musa, known also as the "Mount of monkeys", on which stood, so mythologers believed, one of the columns of Hercules (the antique Abyla), and which was covered in a thick forest, the area of Belyunesh served as the hunting ground for the inhabitants of Ceuta, the *Sebti*s. This enchanting corner, which strikes the imagination, is also where the sorceress Circé is said to have held Ulysses prisoner.
In the 5th/11th century, under the reign of petty King Saqut – a contemporary and equal of the Prince of Seville, al-Mu'tamid Ibn 'Abbad, whose reign marked out one of the most glorious periods in Ceuta's history – notables possessed beautiful mansions placed at the centre of gardens in which the most evolved techniques of irrigation were employed. These holiday villas or *munia*s,

Archeological Museum, funeral stele of Jabal Dersa, Tétouan.

constructed and ornamented with great care, were in fact agricultural centres which fulfilled the same functions as Roman villas. The valley produced an abundance of fruit, and fine-quality coral could be fished from the waters in the bay which, after being treated in the specialised workshops of Ceuta, were exported to the sub-Saharan continent, in particular to Ghana and the Sudan.
This opulence, which lasted until the end of the 8th/14th century, disappeared completely by the 9th/15th century with the Portuguese occupation of Ceuta. The Portuguese nonetheless failed to exploit Ceuta and its surrounding environment due to the difficulties involved in reaching it. Abandoned, it thus fell into ruin, and was only visited by fishermen.
Archaeological excavations, undertaken in recent decades, have enabled certain

ITINERARY VII   *The Ports of the Strait*

Belyunesh

Tower and remains of the rampart, Belyunesh.

remains of the town to be discovered and have brought the famous *munia*s to light, with their countryhouse towers and dancing water fountains as described in texts.

VII.2.a Tower and Residential Area

Take the route which runs along the sea; the tower is on your right, on the seafront.

Although in ruins, the tower is the only element which still stands on this rich archaeological site, allowing us to imagine the splendours of long ago.

This tower dominated an architectural compound of which it was an integral part. This compound, revealed through excavation work, whose ground plan one can still guess at, incorporated a house, a bath and a small oratory, all placed at different floor levels.

The house consisted of a patio surrounded by a portico which opened onto to various rooms, and onto a main room in particular which was adorned with a basin and flanked by alcoves. An oratory was adjoined to the house, as was a private bath whose floor was covered with *zellij*. The tower was rectangular in design. Two vaulted levels were supported above its massive foundations, and the walls of the vaults still show traces of ochred decorations. The tower falls within the tradition of towers set by the enclosure surrounding the Alhambra. This compound informs us on the architecture of *munia*s, these rural holiday villas, which were just as prominent in Muslim Spain. These examples reconfirm again the cultural and artistic links that existed between Nasrid Granada and Merinid Morocco.

It is possible to continue by car and to park 800 m. further down, to descend the small creek, occupied by fishermen, on foot.
In the opposite direction, pass the taxi rank again, and the Spanish border lies 500 m. ahead; Ceuta is situated behind the mountain.

ITINERARY VII *The Ports of the Strait*
Ksar Es-Seghir

VII.3 **KSAR ES-SEGHIR**

Situated 25 km. from Belyunesh. Cast your gaze along the Spanish coast, and in good weather you should be able to see very distinctly the Rock of Gibraltar.

Situated not far from the Spanish coast, facing Tarifa on the opposite side, this site, placed deep within a bay, by the mouth of a river, offered a safe shelter for ships. This is why a fortress was erected there in 89/708–90/709, at the start of the campaign of Islamisation, under the orders of Azziani. It was named *Ksar Masmuda*. However it was equally known as *Ksar al-Awwal*, "First Castle", and as *Ksar al-Majaz* "Passageway Castle" during the era of the Almoravids, after having fallen to the port of *Marsa Musa*, west of Ceuta, a port used exclusively for the embarkation of Muslim troops heading for Spain. In about 588/1192, the Almohads rebuilt and embellished it, re-christening it *Ksar Es-Seghir*. They established shipyards there and transformed it into an important industrial centre by moving in numerous artisans, weavers, carpenters and gunsmiths.

By keeping Ceuta as their commercial centre, they turned *Ksar Es-Seghir* into their military centre, through which Muslim troops came and went to and from the Iberian Peninsula.

In the 8th/14th century, the Merinids built a circular enclosure around the town, which one can still follow traces of today, and erected public and private buildings. The second port after Ceuta to have been conquered by the Portuguese in 862/1458, it remained under their rule until 956/1549. The Portuguese reinforced the enclosure wall and built a fortified hideout linked to the sea via a long channel, *Curaça*. They transformed Muslim monuments into churches, and adapted the public buildings to suit their needs. After its Portuguese evacuation, the site served, in the beginning of the 11th/17th century, as a debarkation port for the Moriscos thrown out of al-Andalus.

Excavations undertaken in the 1970s revealed Portuguese remains as well as certain sections of monuments dating from the Merinid era. A significant collection of both Muslim and Portuguese objects were discovered there.

VII.3.a **Gate of the Sea and Enclosure**

Having arrived in Ksar Es-Seghir, leave the car on the main road (the only road). The gate and the enclosure can be found on the seafront, at the mouth of the river. Ruins are all that is left of the monument.

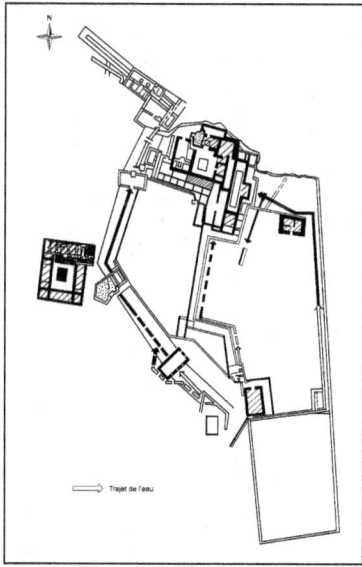

Condominium, general plan, Belyunesh.

ITINERARY VII *The Ports of the Strait*
Ksar Es-Seghir

Enclosure, detail of wall with the Gate of the Sea at its center, Ksar Es-Seghir.

Excavation works, undertaken on the archaeological site of the small town of Ksar Es-Seghir – a town that experienced all the events of Western Mediterranean Mediaeval history – brought to light important remains of the Merinid era which were hidden under Portuguese remains. These included an enclosure with its bastions; a dozen houses; a market; a mosque; and a *hammam*. Some of them are still standing in elevation, whereas only the foundations of others remain.

The enclosure opened to the outside world via three gates: two monumental gates, one of which stood on the western side – the Gate of the Sea – and the other of which stood on the eastern side – the Gate of Ceuta. A third, more modest gate, stood on the southern side – the Gate of Fez.

Gate of the Sea

The Gate of the Sea is the gate which has best been conserved. Although hemmed in by Portuguese buildings and partially destroyed, it retains enough features to understand its layout and reconstruct its décor.

It was flanked on the outside by two massive towers which, on their upper levels, consisted of blockhouses from which the coasts could be surveyed. The gate opened onto a foiled-arch bay above which decorative panels, decorated with a web of interlacing geometric patterns on a coating of painted plaster, were placed.

This bay lead to a vaulted room where, on the south wall, a staircase was built which lead to a covered passageway and onto the upper level. The vaulted room itself looked out onto an open space above which a parapet was placed and which led towards the town entrance. The interior facade of the gate was far more elaborately decorated than its exterior one. The décor, divided into various levels, was formed of polygonal stars and geometric interlacing. The sum of these features allows us to describe this gate as dating from the Merinid era.

It is also useful to note that the architectural plan of the *hammam*, whose walls are still in elevation, consists of a series of rooms, a design which is characteristic of Merinid *hammams* and of Nasrid basins in Granada.

Enclosure

The wall is one of the rare examples in Morocco, being circular in design. This type of layout, considered ideal by Arab urban planning theorists, was not, until now, known of outside the examples present in the first Baghdad of the Abbassids and in the Tunisian town of the Fatimids, Sabra-Mansuriya. The circle sketched out by the wall is more or less perfect and has a diameter of about 200 m. The walls, constructed in rubble and mortar brick joints, have a thickness of about 2 m. and are about 8 m. high. They were reinforced by 29 circular towers placed equidistantly from each other. Two of these towers, situated on the western side, remain standing, allowing us to discover their structure. They are composed of two rooms, one superimposed onto the other. The room on the ground floor, which is vaulted, links to the inside of the town, and would have served as a depot. The upper room, accessed via a covered passageway, served as the guard's quarters.

Before leaving Ksar Es-Seghir, it is possible to buy fresh fish from the fisherman and have it cooked there and then taking the road on the right which leads to the fishing port. To leave Ksar Es-Seghir, head in the direction of Tangier. The road is bordered by deserted beaches, where it is possible to swim. At the mouth of the Wadi Salliam, a track leads to a magnificent and safe beach.

ITINERARY VII The Ports of the Strait
Ksar Es-Seghir

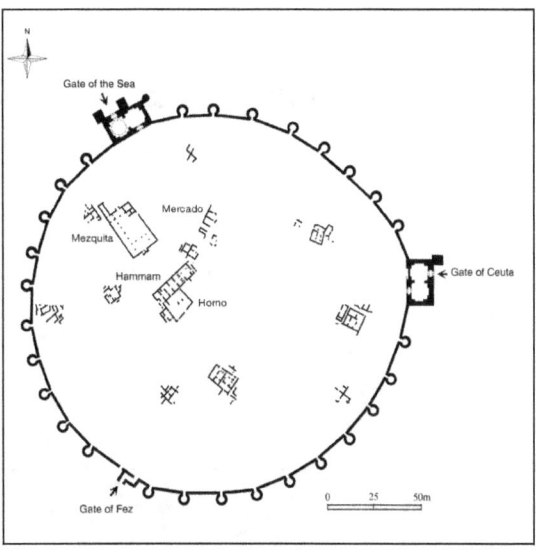

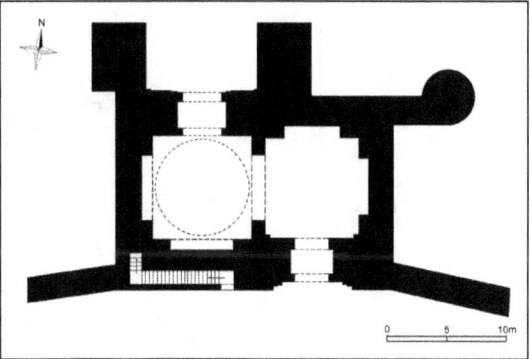

Plan of circular enclosure, Ksar Es-Seghir.

Plan of the Gate of the Sea, Ksar Es-Seghir.

ITINERARY VII

The Ports of the Strait

Naïma El-Khatib Boujibar

Second day

VII.4 TANGIER
- VII.4.a Kasbah
- VII.4.b Mosque of the Kasbah
- VII.4.c Sidi Bu 'Abbid Mosque
- VII.4.d Saint Andrew's Church
- VII.4.e Great Mosque
- VII.4.f 'Aissaua Mosque

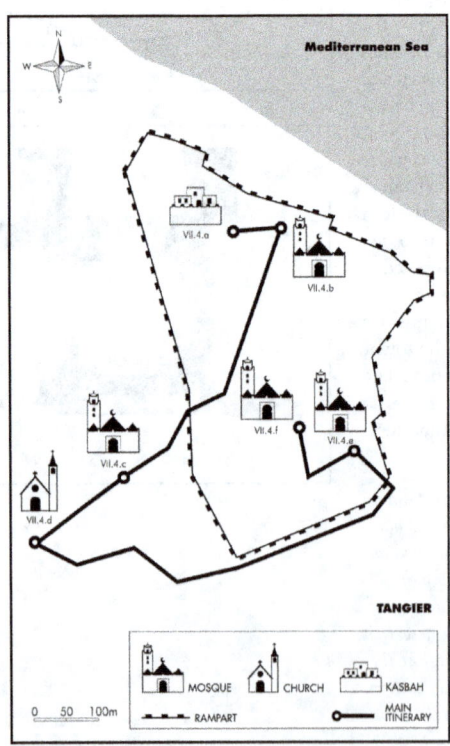

VII.4 **TANGIER**

History teaches us very little about what the ancient capital of Roman Mauretania, Tingitania, was like when Musa Ibn Nusayr seized it in 86/705 to convert it to Islam.

Becoming a few years later the county-town of a large province, it was administered by governors under the Umayyad Caliphs of Damascus. The Governors had to confront a rising of Berber tribes of the Rif who, angered by fiscal exactions, had joined the schismatic Kharijite movement.

In escaping the Abbassids, Idriss Ibn 'Abd Allah arrived there in 171/788, but only stayed for a short while before moving on to *Walili* (Volubilis).

On the death of Idriss II, the founder of Fez, the principality of Tangier was passed on to his sons, first Qassim, then 'Umar. During the second half of the $4^{th}/10^{th}$ century, the town was at stake in the disputes between the Umayyads of Spain and the Idrissids, and ended up falling into the hands of the Fatimids of Ifriqiya in 346/958.

The Almoravids became masters of Tangier in 467/1075, followed in 543/1149 by the Almohads, who preferred Tangier's rival Ceuta, establishing there their seat of command over the north of Morocco as well as making it their place of residence.

The Merinids seized Tangier in 672/1274 and devoted all their efforts to it. Thanks to the concern of these monarchs, the town experienced a period of great splendour during their reign ($7^{th}/13^{th}$ and $8^{th}/14^{th}$ centuries). They endowed it with a grand mosque and a *madrasa*, which display the refinement of Moroccan-Andalusian architectural and decorative arts.

It is interesting to note that the founding stone of this *madrasa*, of which there is no actual remaining evidence, was discovered by the English in 1084/1674 in the wall of a Dominican convent which the Portuguese had built on the site of this *madrasa* during their occupation of the town.

The Merinids also developed economic activities by signing commercial treaties with merchants from Italian towns such as Venice, Pisa, and Genoa, as well as with Marseilles. Its port thus became the turning point of Mediterranean and Saharan commerce. The town imported cloth, spices and metals, and exported hides, leather, rugs and sugar cane.

It was certainly in these *caravanserai*s, which received and lodged foreigners from all over, that a young man from Tangier, who would go on to become the famous Ibn Battuta, was inspired to be a voyager, and where his desire to visit far-off places was born.

In 875/1471, to secure their position in the Strait, the Portuguese seized the town after many fruitless attempts. They transformed it, rebuilding the mosque into a cathedral and the *madrasa* into a convent. They resurrected the walls they had torn down, reinforcing them with bastions and forts and constructed in the higher region, to the west of the bay, a fortress which would bare down over the town.

After the death of King Dom Sebastião, which took place in 985/1578 during the famous Battle of the Three Kings, the crown of Portugal was passed on to Philip II of Spain and the town thus came under Spanish control.

In 1071/1661, having become Portuguese again, it was offered to England

ITINERARY VII   The Ports of the Strait

Tangier

as part of the dowry belonging to the Infanta Catherine of Bragance who married the English Prince Charles II.
On his accession to the throne, the 'Alawite Monarch Mulay Isma'il besieged Tangier in 1089/1679. The English, before evacuating, destroyed the port's pier as well as most of the town.
Mulay Isma'il then put the pasha 'Ali Ibn 'Abd Allah Errifi in charge of restoring the ramparts and reconstructing the town. Thus, in rebuilding the ruins, houses, in traditional Moroccan style, were erected; mosques, as well as a *madrasa*, were raised; and a *kasbah* was constructed on its heights, endowed with a palace, and mosque and its adjoining buildings. The son of the pasha, Ahmed Ibn 'Ali, continued his father's work, having taken over his duties. In 1196/1782, Sultan Sidi Mohamed Ibn 'Abd Allah, who wanted to gather all diplomatic representations into the same town, chose Tangier to act as the seat of the European consulates. During the 19th century, the town was officially promoted to being the diplomatic capital of the kingdom, and a permanent delegate of the Sultan, the *na'ib*, was nominated as part of the consular administration in Tangier. From then on, aided by the presence of its diplomats, merchants, men of letters and artists came flocking to the town. The latter of these, subjected to the beauty of the place and the charm of its Islamic architecture, with its narrow and mysterious streets, sang through their writings, or through their painted canvases, of its fairy-like magic, which still emanates from this town today.
In 1906, Tangier was endowed with a special status which placed it and its surroundings under the authority of an international commission. In 1956, it was returned once more to the country.

VII.4.a **Kasbah**

Follow the sign saying "Kasbah / Musée", which are one and the same monument. The museum is located at the far northern end of the medina. Parking provided. The itinerary is done on foot.
Entrance fee. Open daily from 09.00–13.00 and 15.00–18.00. Closed on Tuesdays.

The site on which the *kasbah*, dominating over the *medina*, is built, was, ever since the time of the Almohads, always chosen as a citadel in which to house the seat of government and residence of the Governor. It is of no surprise then that the King Mulay Isma'il had ordered his Governor, 'Ali Errifi, to erect a *kasbah* at the site on which the English had built their Upper Castle and the Portuguese their *Domus Praefecti*.
The remarkable palatial complex which was built remains well-conserved and in good condition, and offers a beautiful example of palaces which were erected in the same period but which today no longer exist. The complex comprised the Governor's residence together with its outbuildings; prisons; the mosque; stables; the treasury and the court room. It was delineated on its western side by a square, the Square of the Tabors, onto which spilled the only route serving the *kasbah* that was actually open to horses. Streets running alongside the rampart enclosed it on both the north and the south sides. On the eastern side, it opened out onto a vast rectangular square, which separated the walls of the prisons from those of the stables. The stables no longer exist today; instead the site they occupied now serves as a car park.
The court room, or little *mechuar*, is composed of a series of small rooms, preceded by a marble dual colonnade, which are

ITINERARY VII The Ports of the Strait
Tangier

closed off by an iron fence. The columns which support the arcades are surmounted by composite capitals of Italian influence. This building, situated south of the square, has actually been converted into an exhibition room to display works of arts and crafts. Initially it was used as a court room for the "*khalifa*s of the pasha". The *Bit al-Mal*, or the "Treasury Room", is a raised room on the west side of the square which is preceded by a staircase. Its facade is pierced by three pointed horseshoe arches supported on two complete columns and two engaged half-columns. These marble columns are crowned by Tuscan-style capitals. The interior of the room is divided into three spans by a triple colonnade, and is flanked on each side by little cubbyholes on a raised level, lit by finely worked windows. These cubbyholes served as offices for the agents of the Treasury, the *'umana'*. A vaulted cave, which held the money boxes, nestles under the floor boards of this room.

This small, well-balanced, colonnaded room is a rare example of its kind in Morocco. It seduces the visitor through the purity of its lines and its elegance. It is a welcome innovation which was put into action by the Governor Ahmed Errifi. It is now in fact a part of the Kasbah Museum.

Palace of the Kasbah

Erected by Ahmed Errifi, the Palace, completed in 1122–23/1710–11, underwent various changes and restorations,

Kasbah, room of treasure, outside entrance, Tangier.

ITINERARY VII   The Ports of the Strait
Tangier

Kasbah Museum, fountain and three-arched portico of the patio, Tangier.

the most recent of which dates from 1889, on the occasion of the visit paid by Mulay Hassan I to Tangier.

The palace consisted of a large house, *Dar al-Kebira*, a small house, *Dwirat qubbat Sidi al-Bukhari*, kitchens, two gardens, a bath and a storage room disguised as a treasury or *Bit al-Mal*. A Regional Folk and Archaeological Museum now occupies the site.

Dwirat Qubbat Sidi al-Bukhari

This small house is situated on a raised level to the left of the angled passage which leads to the patio of the large house. A veritable little gem, it encloses two rooms and a patio, all finely decorated with a web of sculpted plaster and *zellij*. An inscription in cursive characters of an extract of poetry, engraved onto excised *zellij*, separates the plaster panels from one another. The decoration of this house and the delicacy with which it has been executed is reminiscent of the Merinid and Nasrid ornamentation of the $8^{th}/14^{th}$ century.

Dar al-Kebira

A marble columned portico surrounds a vast patio paved in *zellij*, in the middle of which stands an octagonal basin containing a marble bowl. The columns' capitals, which share similarities to those of a composite order, are embellished with a crescent moon motif, the crescent being an Ottoman emblem which until then had not been used in Morocco. It would seem that these capitals, imported from Italy by Ahmed Errifi, were produced by a workshop which usually supplied Ottoman provinces and thus was in the habit of adding this motif.

The arcades in the north and south wings of the portico are surmounted by *zellij* panels. It is under these porticoes that the two main rooms of the house, which has seven, pan out. Lengthy in shape, they are flanked here and there by alcoves, and their centres are hollowed out by a recess, *bhu*, whose decoration is more accentuated. Surmounted by a wooden arcature cut in the shape of stalactites, the *bhu* is covered by a dome, also made of wood sculpted as *muquarnas*.

The walls of these rooms are covered in mosaics and plaster carved into geometric and epigraphic motifs. The chiselled plaster work of the cloisters is, in particular, remarkable; the bands carrying inscriptions eulogise repeatedly: *"Eternal Salvation"* and *"Wealth belongs to God"*.

An inscription in black *zellij* on a white background, written inside the *bhu* of the northern *qubba*, is of great interest. It celebrates in verse the beauty of the palace, and, at its centre, three words written in blue *zellij*, which are the chronograms of 1122/1711, stand out. This marks the completion date of the palace, a time when the era of Ahmed Errifi was at its peak.

Collections of archaeological and ethnographic objects pertaining to Tangier and other parts of Morocco are displayed in these, as well as in the remaining five rooms.

The Ceremonial Room

This room is found on the right of a patio which is situated north of the hallway. Preceded by a portico consisting of three arcades, it is closed off by a Dutch door with iron bars which replaced the original richly painted and ornate wooden door. Its walls, today stripped bare of all decoration, were covered in *zellij* panels.

A frieze of stalactite sculpted wood, *muquarnas*, crowns the walls. The room is topped by a magnificent wooden dome painted in dodecagonal shapes, decorated with an interlace of polygonal stars. It is a beautiful example of 'Alawite woodwork.

The café Hafaa, the mythical café in which one could meet poets and writers, offers a direct and unique view onto the sea. From the promontory of the kasbah's *square, take the path which runs along the seaside and the exterior wall of the* kasbah, *then walk along rue Assad Ibn Farrat. Pass the stadium on its left, and take the path on the right which leads to the café.*

Kasbah Museum, detail of a composite capital in the patio, Tangier.

ITINERARY VII   *The Ports of the Strait*

Tangier

Minbar of the Mosque of the Kasbah, Tangier.

Ahmed, who endowed it with a minaret and a decorated door. Its prayer room was also enlarged and rebuilt during the time of Sidi Mohamed Ibn 'Abd al-Rahman (1859–1873). It was restored again for the visit of Mulay Hassan in 1889.

It was around 1921 that a *nadir* of the *habus*, the regional representative of the endowment administration, had the idea of covering the decorations with unfortunate colours. This renovation project was generalised to incorporate all the mosques and *zawiya*s of the town.

With the exception of the entrance portal, the only decorated element worthy of any interest is the minaret. Octagonal in form, it resembles those which Ahmed Errifi had built in Chefchaouen and Tétouan. This form which is unusual for Morocco, where the majority of minarets are square-shaped, was probably inspired by the Ottoman minarets of Algeria, reminiscent of the Almohad design of the "Torre del Oro" in Seville.

This small minaret of alluring elegance and slender skylights displays, across the levels of its facade, blind polyfoiled arcatures and geometric interlaces whose interior areas are coated with *zellij* tiles. The delicate colouring of this wall tiling harmonises itself well with the ochre colour of the corner brickwork. At the centre of this symphony, the only colour that looks out of place is the intense dark blue of the tiles which cover the skylights, no doubt the work of this famous *nadir*.

> *Retracing your steps back to the headway of rue Assad Ibn Farrat, you will find the Forbes Museum in rue Shakespeare, housed in the old residence of American millionaire Malcolm Forbes. This museum contains a collection of 115,000 military figurines. More important however, is the exceptional view of the Strait of Gibraltar and the Spanish coastline, which can be seen from the museum gardens that are planted with palm, orange and eucalyptus trees.*

VII.4.b Mosque of the Kasbah

Situated in rue Ibn Abu, next to the museum. Access restricted to Muslims.

The mosque of the *kasbah* is located in the south of the palace. It was linked to the latter via a small gate. It was built by 'Ali Errifi and enlarged by his son

> *At the end of this road, on the bend, one can see a marabout who is known for having been immortalised by Matisse.*

ITINERARY VII *The Ports of the Strait*
Tangier

VII.4.c Sidi Bu 'Abid Mosque

Located on rue Bu 'Abid. At the end of rue Ibn Abu, take a left, and, at the second intersection, take a left again. Descend the steps which lead to Kasbah Street ("rue de la Kasbah"). Follow this street until it comes to an end at Grand Socco Square (Place du Grand Socco). The mosque is on your right in rue Bu 'Abid. Access restricted to Muslims.

The mosque is located at the western extremity of the Grand Socco or Suq Berra, which is towered over by its minaret. Its main gate, which opens onto a side street, is decorated in wall tiles imported from Spain, which were introduced to Morocco at the beginning of the 20th century.

This mosque was built in 1913 on the site of a tomb belonging to a saint of the same name, who was a descendant of Sidi Ahmed or Musa Essemlali, the patron of people from the Sous region. It was built with the help of contributions from benefactors who originated from the Low-Atlas in the Sous region. New motifs were added to the older traditional Andalusian ones in the tile mosaic decoration of the sides of the minaret; these included a shell-like, scaly motif on the lower tier and concentric diamond-shapes on the upper tier.

These innovations, which render the minaret unique, were, more than likely, taken from the diamond-shaped motifs featured in the carpets of the Uawezguits, a tribe of the High-Atlas, which were appreciated by the people of Sous.

Grand Socco Square, where all the town buses converge, is one of the liveliest places in Tangier. On Thursday and Sunday, when the weekly market takes place, farmers wearing striped futa (a traditional textile) and straw hats descend from the Rif mountains to sell their produce.

VII.4.d Saint Andrew's Church

Situated in rue d'Angleterre, which branches off Grand Socco Square. No opening times, ask the guard on duty to open the little church.

This is an Anglican church, situated not far from Grand Socco, within the English cemetery. Built at the end of the 19th century by Moroccan workers, and decorated by craftsmen, *m'almin*, sent by the Sultan Mulay Hassan I to the English community for the completion of this work, it was thus treated as if it were a traditional Moroccan building.

Sidi Bu 'Abid minaret, Tangier.

ITINERARY VII *The Ports of the Strait*

Tangier

Church of Saint-André, bell-tower and entrance door, Tangier.

Its square-based bell tower looks like a minaret without lanternes. Its sides are covered in plaster sculptures, in which geometric interlacing is mixed inside the polyfoiled blind arch.

In its interior, the colonnade separating the naves is supported by columns gemeled in marble that are headed by capitals similar to the Sa'adian ones found in the pavilions of the Qarawiyin Mosque.

The arch which bares over the chancel is a horseshoe, festooned arch. It is surmounted by a floral decoration, and is framed by a band along which reads an inscription in Arabic *kufic* characters which transcribes the words of the gospel. The niche behind the altar is decorated in a lace of sculpted plaster in which the motto of the Nasrids of the Alhambra is revealed: *"There is no victor but God"*.

The ceilings are blanketed with painted panelling depicting a web of polygonal stars.

This architectural endeavour, which reflects the Moroccan's spirit of tolerance, and which owes all its beautiful decorations to late 19th-century artisans, highly deserves to be considered amongst notable monuments of Moroccan-Andalusian art in Tangier.

10 m. on your right is the Grand Hotel, a hotel of mythic status in Tangier, having been host to a number of artists, which now stands empty. From the central window of the second floor, Matisse painted one of his most celebrated works.

ITINERARY VII   The Ports of the Strait
Tangier

VII.4.e **Great Mosque**

Situated on rue de la Grande Mosquée. Retrace your steps in order to return to the old medina, this time via rue Siarrin (or Semarin) which leads to Little Socco Square. The mosque can be found in the extension of the square that is rue de la Grande Mosquée – (Grand Mosque Street). Access restricted to Muslims.

Overlooking "rue de la Marine", the Great Mosque was founded by the Merinid Dynasty, but has since undergone a number of metamorphoses. When the Portuguese seized the town of Tangier, their first move was to convert this mosque into a cathedral. Then, when the town was liberated by Mulay Isma'il, the order was given to the town's Governor, 'Ali Ibn 'Abd Allah Errifi to return this monument to Islam.

Ever since then, this mosque, which was the object of concern of all 'Alawite sovereigns, was enlarged, restored and rebuilt at several intervals. The last great transformation that occurred dates from the time of Mulay Sliman, and the inscription engraved on top of the entrance door commemorates this project, undertaken in 1233 of the *Hijra* (which corresponds to 1818 in the Gregorian calendar). The only part of the facade that is elaborately decorated is the entrance portal, which is finely ornamented and displays certain innovations of Mulay Sliman's time, for instance the floral cartouches in the corners of the door. Unfortunately, these decorations were debased with layers of

Church of Saint-André, central nave, Tangier.

ITINERARY VII The Ports of the Strait

Tangier

'Aissaua Mosque, entrance and minaret, Tangier.

Square on which one can find the mosque. Access restricted to Muslims.

One falsely associates this mosque with the name of the 'Aissaua brotherhood, as it is only due to the proximity of their *zawiya*, on the same square, that the mosque is called so.

This mosque is particularly interesting in terms of the decoration of its minaret. It was founded by Mulay Sliman in about 1230/1815, and restored in 1860, the date which corresponds to the *Hijra* (1276) inscribed on its portal. Although square in plan, which is the classic design of a Moroccan minaret, this one is, through its decoration, similar to the polygonal minaret of the *kasbah*, built during the time of Ahmed Errifi. Indeed it harmonises the ochre colour of the bricks to the polychrome of the *zellij*s. This decoration and colour are typical of Tangier, which seems to have adopted, for the minarets of its town, a type of decoration which suits it and which is unique to it, whilst remaining within the classical norms of Moroccan-Andalusian art.

clashing-coloured paint. The decoration of the minaret was more jolly and more uniform. Softer tints, reflecting a palette of subtle greens, catch and charm the eye.

VII.4.f 'Aissaua Mosque

Situated on Little Socco Square (Place du Petit Socco). Take the street on the left which runs along Hotel Fuentes. Then take the first street on the left which directs you to 'Aissaua

Cape Spartel and the Caves of Hercules.
Cape Spartel, 14 km. from Tangier, defines the north-western extremity of Africa's Atlantic coast. From the Place de France in Tangier, exit the town via rue de Belgique and follow the sign La Montagne, Cap Spartel. The Caves of Hercules, 4 km. from Cape Spartel, offer a magnificent view over the Atlantic. Entrance fee.

ITINERARY VII

The Ports of the Strait

Naïma El-Khatib Boujibar

Third day

VII.5 ASILAH
- VII.5.a Great Mosque
- VII.5.b Rampart and Bastions
- VII.5.c Raissuli Palace
- VII.5.d Naval Cemetery
- VII.5.e Alleyways

VII.6 MEHDIA
- VII.6.a Kasbah

Ibn Battuta

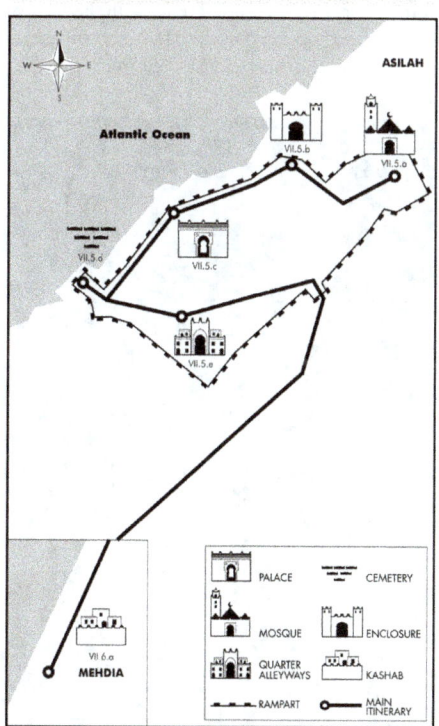

ITINERARY VII *The Ports of the Strait*

Asilah

VII.5 ASILAH

Situated 46 km. south of Tangier, on the Atlantic coast. From Tangier go towards Rabat. Follow the sign saying Centre Hassan II. The itinerary is based within the old town inside the ramparts.
Outside the walls, there is supervised parking.

Asilah was founded by Arab conquerors, probably at the beginning of the $3^{rd}/9^{th}$ century, near a harbour and on a reef, but far from Zilil, a town from the period of antiquity from which it derives its name. It experienced a turbulent history throughout the Middle Ages and modern times which was linked to that of Tangier's.

Mentioned by the Arab geographer al-Bakri, it had to endure two Norman invasions during the second half of the $3^{rd}/9^{th}$ century due to the attractiveness of its agricultural wealth. Rebuilt by the Umayyad Caliph of Cordoba, al-Hakam II, it needed to surround itself with an enclosure to protect it from further attack. It was provided with a mosque composed of five naves which were *"reached by the waves when the sea was stormy"*. Its port, which offered an effective shelter for ships, had a jetty built of ashlar stones which were positioned in an arc to protect the mooring.
The town, which seems to have existed peacefully during the $6^{th}/12^{th}$ century, opened itself up to trade with the West at the accession of the Merinids, and experienced a certain amount of prosperity.

Great Mosque, entrance and minaret, Asilah.

ITINERARY VII   *The Ports of the Strait*
Asilah

Portuguese rampart and bastion, Asilah.

The Wattassids turned it into one of their main footholds in their struggle for power.

It was stormed by the Portuguese in the same year as Tangier (875/1471) and remained under their control until 957/1550. The latter rebuilt the ramparts in stone, fortifying them with solid bastions, and erected a donjon to serve as a surveillance tower. The garrisons entrenched in this fortress suffered continuous assaults over many long years led by the Wattassid Sultans, and by the famous Prince of Chefchaouen, Mulay Brahim. Liberated in 957/1550, the town was reoccupied in 984/1577 by King Dom Sebastião in return for becoming an ally of the Sa'adian Prince Mohamed al-Maslukh. It was in Asilah that the last of the Portuguese Kings of the Avis Dynasty, having dreamt of reoccupying Morocco, stayed with his army before heading into the fields of the Wadi al-Makhazin Battle near Ksar al-Kebir, a battle which would cost him his life. The town was reinstated back to the Sa'adian King al-Mansur in 997/1589, then reclaimed by Spain for several years towards the end of the $11^{th}/17^{th}$ century. It was stormed by Mulay Isma'il and liberated in 1102/1691. Populated by people from the Rif, it was given two mosques, a *madrasa* and bathhouses, and from then on began to live a modest existence. In 1906, it fell to the forces of Mulay 'Ali Ibn Raissul who became the town's pasha, before being occupied by the Spanish from 1912 until 1956.

Today, Asilah is known for its annual international festival during which cultural exchanges bring together men of

ITINERARY VII   *The Ports of the Strait*

Asilah

Raissuli Palace, entrance gate of palace enclosure, Asilah.

letters, philosophers and artists from all four corners of the globe.

It has preserved, behind the high ochre walls of its ramparts which encase it like a jewel, the immaculate whiteness of its houses and the authenticity of its architecture.

VII.5.a **Great Mosque**

Situated in front of the Hassan II Centre. Access restricted to Muslims.

The Great Mosque was built during the time of Mulay Isma'il. Following the town's liberation, the governor of the *Gharb* region (Kenitra and Larache) and of the northern region, 'Ali Ibn 'Abd Allah Errifi, was put in charge of building a place of worship, as he was in Tangier. However, judging by its octagonal minaret, it seems that this mosque was in fact built by his son, Ahmed Errifi, who was the first to introduce this shape. In contrast to the minaret of the mosque in Tangier's *kasbah*, this one has simplified décor, drowned under various coats of whitewash. The entrance to the mosque is equally simple in its decoration.

VII.5.b **Rampart and Bastions**

The wall surrounds the old town. At Place Ibn Khaldun (Ibn Khaldun Square), take a right onto rue Sidi Mohammed Ben Marzouk and follow the wall which runs alongside the mosque.

The first enclosure built in Asilah dates from the Almohad era. It was restored during the Merinid era and reinforced by the Wattassids. But this first enclosure was unable to resist the assaults of the Portuguese who were in possession of heavy artillery. On seizing Asilah they began working, on the one hand, on reducing the surface area of the town in order to have better control over it, and on the other, on reinforcing the walls with bastions, circular in shape, which were armed with loopholes and machicolations.

Hence one can view most of the actual enclosure walls, as well as the majority of the bastions, as having been built by the Portuguese, except perhaps those which are situated on the seafront and are rectangular in shape.

ITINERARY VII   *The Ports of the Strait*
Asilah

VII.5.c Raissuli Palace

Situated in rue Sidi Ben Marzouk, the entrance door can be found in a recess on the left. Currently undergoing restoration work.

The palace, situated on the seafront in the centre of the town, occupies a key strategic position. It was constructed by the famous Mulay 'Ali Ibn Raissul, who came to seize power in north Morocco proclaiming himself pasha of Asilah. With the resources he had accumulated, he had a palace built with disconcerting speed. This palace, more like a large residence, has all the outbuildings which come with this kind of a building: a large house with a patio, a garden, *riyad*, kitchens and so on. On the first floor of the house there is a very beautiful salon decorated with *zellij*, painted wood and chiselled plaster, which opens out onto a vast loggia from where one discovers a stunning view onto the sea and the *medina*.

Instead of being covered in glazed tiles from Fez, the execution of which would have demanded far more time, the walls of the ground floor are decorated with industrially manufactured glazed tiles imported from Spain, which started, from

Navy Cemetery, Marabout Sidi Ahmed Ibn Musa and ceramic-covered tombs, Asilah.

207

ITINERARY VII *The Ports of the Strait*
Mehdia

Alleyways, Marabout's Gate, Asilah.

the beginning of the 20th century, to compete with the far more beautiful but considerably more expensive ones from Fez.

VII.5.d Naval Cemetery

Situated at the far end of rue Sidi Ben Marzouk. Access restricted to Muslims. Possibility of seeing the whole of the monument from the bastion at the far end of the street.

Right next to the Portuguese bastion, which stretches an arm out to the sea and is known as *Curaça*, lies a small cemetery placed near the marabout of Sidi Ahmed Ibn Musa and his sister Lalla Mennana.

This cemetery and its marabout were laid out on a platform that was constructed outside the Portuguese ramparts. The imported ceramics which cover the tombs brighten up this austere place.

VII.5.e Alleyways

One can veer off, without any risk of getting lost, into the alleyways of the medina, *which is very small.*

The town of Asilah has not kept the rectilinear urban plan of the Portuguese town. The Moroccans, in repossessing their town, redressed the size of the streets to enlarge them once more, created *derb*s and impasses, and returned to the town its Islamic character, through incorporating a *qaysariya*, winding roads, *hammam*s and bakers' ovens as well as craft, and in particular, weaving workshops.

VII.6 MEHDIA

From Asilah, take the motorway up to Kenitra. From there, take the exit marked sortie Centre-Ville, then drive towards Mehdia, 12 km. from Kenitra. After a further 8 km., take a left in the direction of the kasbah, *which is marked by a signpost. It is necessary to go via the guard for the site to be opened.*

No other site in the Atlantic coast of Morocco incited as much desire as did the estuary of the Sebou, which in fact dominates the ruins of the *kasbah* of Mehdia. It became, during the centuries, the thoroughfare of populations and nations who surged into Moroccan cities, thus becoming the stage for the country's important historical events.

ITINERARY VII *The Ports of the Strait*
Mehdia

The first locality established, in the Middle Ages, close to the mouth of the river was called *Marsa al-Ma'mora*. It was founded at the end of the 4th/10th century, and, in the 6th/12th century, the Almohad Monarch 'Abd al-Mumen established a shipyard there.

During the 5th/11th century, *al-Ma'mora* was a small but active commercial centre frequented by European merchants. Having become, by the beginning of the 6th/12th century, one of the main centres of North African piracy, it turned itself into an autonomous Republic. The Spanish stormed the fort in 1022/1614, and built a fortress on the hill overlooking the mouth of the river, whose main enclosure constructions constitute the backbone of the perimeter of Mehdia's *kasbah*. After 67 years of occupation, the fortress was finally conquered by Mulay Isma'il in 1092/1681. Liberated, it took the name of al-Mehdia, and the name Ma'mora was restricted to describing the large forest of oak trees to the north-east of Salé.

Mulay Isma'il restored the enclosure, inserting a monumental elbow-shaped gate. He erected a large palace with all its outbuildings and established shipyards and warehouses along the river.

VII.6.a **Kasbah**

The *kasbah* is situated near the edge of the cliff which looks over the mouth of the Sebou, thus occupying a strategic position which suits this defensive compound perfectly.

The enclosure which encircles it on all sides as well as the bastions were built by the Spanish.

The 'Alawite Sovereign Mulay Isma'il, in taking hold of the *kasbah*, rechristened it Mehdia, "The Submissive". He introduced certain modifications to the enclosure, and transformed the interior of the *kasbah* completely.

The Gate

The main gate, Bab Jdid, is the work of Mulay Isma'il. A monumental gate, it is flanked on each side by two rectangular towers crowned by triangular sections separated by slits, just like the central body of the gate, and the towers are pierced, on two levels, by embrasures and loopholes. The entrance bay, in the form of a horseshoe arch, is itself defined by an arch of interlacing festoons. It is framed by a sculpted

Alleyway, Asilah.

Mehdia

band carrying a *kufic* inscription eulogising the founder. Above it sits a pretty window. The mini-column of the gemeled window is topped with a twisted capital, a characteristic form of this period.

The gate is made of stone boulders positioned in an alternating bond, with one thick layer of stones above a thin layer. This technique, which appeared during the Almohad era, was used and maintained throughout the Merinid era. It was employed frequently during the time of Mulay Isma'il in the stone architecture of the Moroccan coast.

The *kasbah* is entered through an angled passageway, as is the form of all traditional gates in Moroccan towns. The bedrooms and benches are found in the first area, and the side corridors are used as the guardrooms.

A staircase serving the upper floors also gives access onto a platform, from where the defenders could overpower the assailants who had entered the courtyard.

The Palace

The Governor's House, or *Dar al-Makhzen*, is the most important building in the *kasbah*. It must have been strikingly beautiful if one judges it by the care with which it was constructed and decorated. It was built by the Governor 'Ali Ibn 'Abd Allah Errifi, who exerted his duty over the north of Morocco and had several constructions in Tangier, Tétouan and Chefchaouen to his name. One enters this residence, in the south-east, via a long alleyway furnished with a finely decorated sculpted stone gate, similar in proportion and ornamentation to the gate of the Merinid *madrasa* in Salé. After crossing a courtyard, one enters an angled covered passageway which leads into the house, having beforehand walked along a long corridor emphasised by arcades.

The house, overshadowed by a square tower which looks like the Andalusian towers of Granada, was equipped with an upper floor. On the ground floor, the rooms were spread around a vast patio paved in polychrome *zellij*, at the centre of which stood a basin. The four large rooms with alcoves are each flanked by two smaller rooms. The doors to these rooms are sculpted as polyfoiled arches surmounted by smaller three-bay arches which are of the same pendentive design. An angled passage in the north-west corner of the patio leads to a small garden and little bath.

The Silos

At the edge of the river, and occasionally on the road itself, stand impressive buildings 3 m. wide and 40 m. in length. They consist of a series of square or rectangular compartments, each one isolated from the other and protected by thick clay walls, from 8 m. to 10 m. in height.

These buildings were incorrectly identified as a naval shipyard. These walls seem more likely to have been used for the storage of wheat or other foodstuffs, built as they are like Mulay Isma'il's *heri*s in Meknès.

The Lake of Sidi Bourhaba
Situated inland, 2 km. from Mehdia's beach, the lake of Sidi Bourhaba is one of the largest bird sanctuaries in the country. Over 200 species, coming to stay the winter, were listed, including the marbled teal, a bird which can be recognised by the dark circles around its eyes. To tour round the reserve, bearing in mind the lake covers over 200 hectares, there are three signposted paths, the trails of which take between 30 and 90 minutes.

ITINERARY VII   *The Ports of the Strait*
Mehdia

Belghazi Museum
Located in Bouknadel, which is off the Kenitra/Rabat Road, about 17 km.
Open daily from 08.00–19.00.
The museum belongs to a family of master craftsmen from Fez who have for generations specialised in woodwork and have various beautiful works to their name in Morocco as well as abroad.
Built over 5000 sq. m. the museum encloses an important collection of about 40,000 traditional artifacts, thus offering a nearly complete selection of all the Moroccan decorative arts.

This collection, exhibited in rooms on the ground and first floors, includes everything from architectonic features in wood – ceilings, domes, lintels, doors and windows from the different regions of Morocco (mainly from old houses in Fez and Meknès) – to furnishing and accessories: beds, coffers, rugs, tapestry, embroidery, jewels and ceramics, some of which are exquisitely made. It also houses Arabic and Hebraic manuscripts as well as Jewish liturgical furniture.

IBN BATTUTA

Naïma El-Khatib Boujibar

Ibn Battuta, his true name being *Shams al-Din Ibn 'Abd Allah 'Allawati al-Tanji*, was born in Tangier in 703/1304. After finishing his legal and religious studies at the *madrasa*, he left his hometown aged 22 to make a pilgrimage to Mecca to fulfil his duty as a believer. He was only to return in 749/1349 to go and meditate at his mother's grave before going on to complete what he considered to be his voyage (crossing the Islamic countries) by visiting Andalusian Spain and the regions south of the Sahara. It was only in 753/1353 that he settled in Fez, where, on the insistence of the Merinid sultan Abu Inan, the great patron, he dictated his memoirs to a well-read writer, Abu Juzay, who completed the work in 766/1365.

During his 30-year pilgrimage, Ibn Battuta, this extraordinary voyager, perhaps even the world's first globe-trotter, covered 120,000 km. alone, visiting the Muslim communities of many countries in Africa, Asia and Europe.

This was an incredible undertaking at a time when the majority of the countries he crossed were unstable and quite dangerous, not to mention the precariousness of his means of locomotion.

However Ibn Battuta, who had made travel his main vocation, had as his motto: *"To cross the earth and go where no one has been before"* and *"never come back on the same road"*.

He thus accepted to endure the harshness of climates, to endure snow as well as the torrid heat of deserts, the howling storms of the Indian Ocean and China Seas. He experienced every possible practical and financial situation, the best and the worst, the richest and the poorest. He sometimes lived in palaces as a privileged guest of Hindu princes, sometimes in the keep

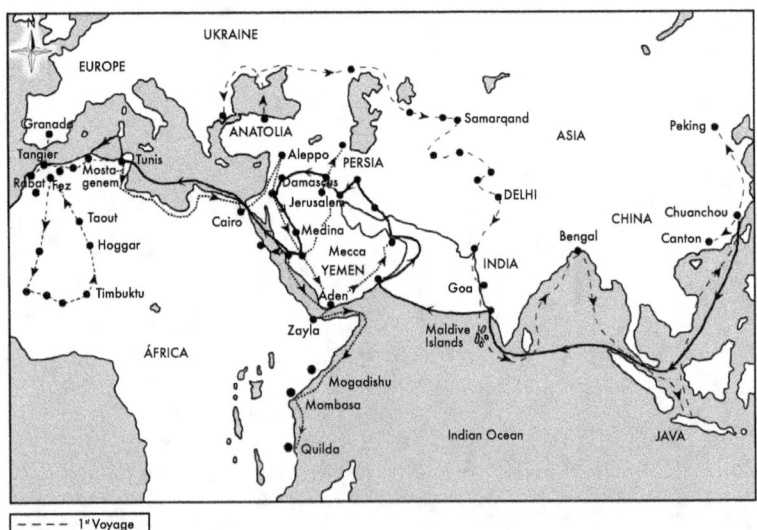

Map detailing the voyages of Ibn Battuta.

of judges, *qadi*, in the Maldives, and sometimes off the offerings of convents belonging to religious brotherhoods.

But the grounded humanist education which he received in Tangier, as well as his solid faith in God and his exemplary piety, had prepared him for such events. Thanks to the important status held by the Arabic language, the language of religion and civilisation, which during this time was also the international language of commerce and communication, he was understood wherever he went. His faith gave him confidence in his own destiny, and the tranquillity and serenity needed to face the difficulties he encountered on his way. Furthermore, his tolerant spirit enabled him to be accepted by the non-Muslim communities of Africa and Asia, giving the historians of today precious information on Hindu values and Nigerian customs as well as on local traditions of the Turkestan populations, all of which he related in his memoires.

His curiosity did not stop at the ways of life led by the populations he visited. Nature interested him too. Endowed with a gift for observation worthy of a naturalist and a geographer, he took note of and wrote down all the information he acquired pertaining to flora and fauna. This is why his memoirs are of great value and remain so today.

ITINERARY VIII

Ebb and Flow, Shine and Eclipse

Kamal Lakhdar

First day

VIII.1 RABAT
        VIII.1.a Archaeological Museum
        VIII.1.b Royal Palace
        VIII.1.c Almohad Ramparts and Gates
        VIII.1.d Mulina Mosque
        VIII.1.e Esplanade of the Tower of Hassan
        VIII.1.f Mohamed V Mausoleum
        VIII.1.g Chellah

Zellij

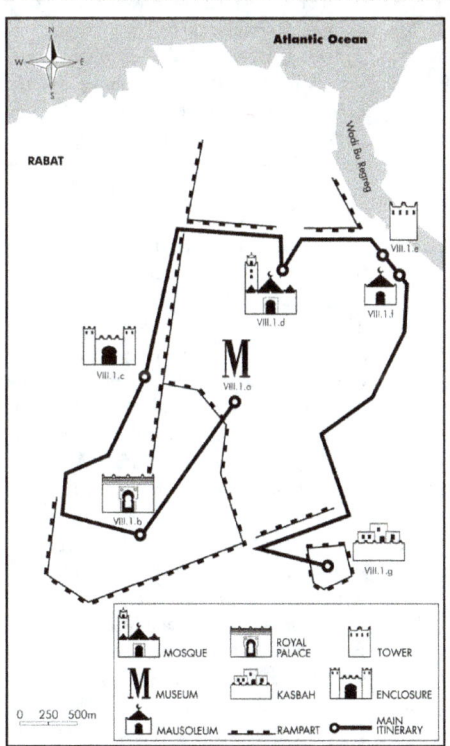

Esplanade of the Hassan Tower, Rabat.

ITINERARY VIII   Ebb and Flow, Shine and Eclipse

Chellah, Mosque of the Necropol, galleries, Rabat.

Rabat and Salé, situated opposite one another, on each side of the mouth of the Bu Regreg river, were rivals and allies in turn. Today they compose a single administrative entity and a single indissociable tourist compound.

Capital of the kingdom since 1912, the agglomeration of Rabat-Salé experienced, throughout the centuries, a single destiny composed of radiances and eclipses, of feverish activity and profound lethargy, of ambition and dashed hopes.

This see-sawing trajectory is charted by the monuments and remains which lend the two riverbanks of the Bu Regreg their aesthetic charm, their tourist appeal and their historical and cultural interest.

The "site of Bu Regreg", as termed by historians after the name of the river that flows between and separates the twin towns, was biased towards Andalusian culture and civilisation in the two following terms:

1   In terms of the transfer of Islam and Arabic-Berber culture towards Spain under the Almoravid, Almohad and Merinid Dynasties, as the site was mid-way between Marrakesh – the Almoravid and Almohad capital – and the Mediterranean ports from where the expeditions towards al-Andalus were launched.

2   In terms of the transfer of Muslim and Jewish populations from al-Andalus (Morisco populations) –with their weapons and luggage, ways of life and techniques– towards North Africa. Following the Christian Reconquest of al-Andalus, the Bu Regreg estuary was a navigable port and possessed a sparsely populated agglomeration (*kasbah*) which could welcome a good number of immigrants.

This dual facet of Rabat-Salé's relation with Muslim Spain is reflected perfectly in the monuments and remains of the site: those of the Almohad conquerors, stripped bare, imposing and extrovert in style (Hassan Tower, ramparts, Chellah), those of the Merinid and those of their successors, refined, personalised and introverted in style (*zawiya*s, mosques, residences).

The first type is represented by the architecture of the Almohads (second half of the $6^{th}/12^{th}$ century) whose relations with al-Andalus became more and more direct. In fact the Hispanic-Moroccan style expanded rapidly and blossomed within Almohad architecture, and their constructions, whether military, religious or of public utility, are imposingly noble and grand, such as the great enclosure of Rabat with its monumental gates, or indeed the remains of the Hassan Minaret and Mosque.

Erected in a single casting, according to simple and stripped down designs, often in colossal dimensions in which freestones play an important role, these monuments possess a majesty about them, leaving an impression of a strong faith nourished with vast ambitions, whilst at the same time intimating to man the qualities of self-effacement and anonymity. This explains why none of the names of princes and *afortiori* of architects figure on these monuments.

In contrast, the art of the Merinids, in all its fluidity, still reflects the constant worry of uniting beauty and utility, to force the sense of admiration upon the viewer whilst perpetuating the memory of great builders.

Indeed, faith is kept alive but the enjoyment of earthly pleasures is not scorned. Thus it is not about haughty majesty and severe elegance, but about refined voluptuousness and soft harmony. The freestone and the marble give way to more manageable and malleable, softer materials: clay, brick, wood, plaster, and tile. These materials, associated with a rare sense of delight, allow for seductive variations, constantly renewing themselves. For the realisations of such works, craftsmen of all kinds were treated with respect and good favour, and one has attributed the following saying to the Merinid Sultan Abu Inan (752/1351–759/1358): *"What is of beauty is of no expense, however high the price. One can never pay too much for what gives pleasure to man".*

Andalusian art is thus a plural art, and some people, in a sound attempt to form links, have compared Almohad art to Roman art, and have wanted to draw a parallel between Merinid art and the flamboyant Gothic style of the same era. The quality and originality of this Andalusian heritage make Rabat and Salé one of the major keys to apprehending and understanding this inestimable heritage which continues as always to be very much alive. Nevertheless the most important inheritance that Rabat received is without doubt its human heritage. With respect to this, it is interesting to underline that whilst the

Esplanade of the Hassan Tower, complete view from the Bu Regreg, Rabat.

site of Bu Regreg received waves of Andalusian emigrants ever since the 7th/3rd century up until the 11th/17th century, it seems that a great number of them were disappointed with the welcome they received from the natives, particularly from the inhabitants of Salé. This phenomenon of rejection was particularly strong and obvious towards the Moriscos expelled from Spain in 1017/1609, who had a renegade reputation, having had, at a certain point, to renounce their faith in order to stay in their homeland. This explains why the latter immediately adopted a defensive attitude and an insular position within the new ramparts which they erected short of the Almohad ramparts. This "Andalusian" rampart is in fact practically the only remains (of historical interest) left to us by the Moriscos. This is because deep down they always secretly hoped to be able to return one day to their homeland: al-Andalus.

However, far beyond a legacy left in stone, the Andalusians left their mark on the riverbanks of the Bu Regreg through the legacy of their traditions, habits and customs, through their ways of being and of appearing.

Weddings, funerals, dress, music, songs, and children's cradles – all hold traces from al-Andalus. Similarly, the survival of certain seasonal festivals like *nayer*, the winter solstice, and *ansra*, the summer solstice, appear to trace back to Andalusian origins, even Christian inhabitants. *"Andalusian culture gives the* Rabtis *a particular cachet, turning them into a distinct group, with its own myths of excellence and of ancestry".* (Mariette Hayeur).

Thus, Rabat-Salé, which in turn had been Phoenician Sala, Roman Sala Colonia, Almoravid Mehdia, Almohad *Ribat al-Fath*, Ancient Sala and New Sala, or even the Republic of the two Moriscos riverbanks, never stopped being receptive to outside influences and had, particularly with Arab-Muslim Spain, a relationship of exchange and mutual interest which lasted from the start of the Muslim Conquest

Kasbah of the Udayas, patio inside the museum, Rabat.

ITINERARY VIII *Ebb and Flow, Shine and Eclipse*
Rabat

Salé, fortifications, general view.

to its reoccupation by the Catholic kings or there about.

It is this element of interaction, of ebb and flow, and finally of symbiosis which the visitor should keep in mind, in order to appreciate not only the architecture, craftsmanship and decoration, but also the ways of life of *Rabti*s families and their mentality, which in turn was traditionalist and open, simple and refined.

The visitor should also bear in mind that this itinerary, spread over two days, is devised in a specific order: the first day relates to the first period, that of the Muslim "ebb" towards the Iberian peninsula, starting at the pre-Islamic period which forms its historical and archaeological background; the second day relates to the second period, that of Andalusian "flow" towards Morocco, whose background consists of the unusual adventures of the privateers of Salé.

VIII.1 **RABAT**

It was during the $4^{th}/10^{th}$ century that the Orthodox Muslim warriors, fighting against heretic tribes, built a fortified basecamp, *ribat*, on the left bank of the mouth of the Bu Regreg, not far from the remains of the Roman city of antiquity, Sala Colonia. The latter was itself built on the site of a small agglomeration which served, from the 10th century BC, first as a Phoenician, then as a Carthaginian stopover at a time when the western Maghreb, from Algiers to the Atlantic, and from the Sahara to al-Andalus, was unified under the Almoravids (447/1056–542/1147). These *Murabitin*s, "men of the *ribat*", endowed the *ribat* of Bu Regreg with an element of sanctity, making it the spearhead of their battle against the Berghuata, who had been responsible for the death of 'Abd Allah Ibn Yassin, the founder of their dynasty. When the Almohads succeeded the Almoravids, the *ribat* of Bu Regreg, instead of losing its defensive and military role, entered into the history books during the reign of the first Almohad Sovereign 'Abd al-Mumen (524/1130–558/1163) under the title of "*Ribat al-Fath*", "The Camp of the Conquest".

In fact, it was around 540/1146 that 'Abd al-Mumen, the founder of the greatest

219

ITINERARY VIII   Ebb and Flow, Shine and Eclipse
Rabat

Muslim Empire of the West that ever existed, gave the order for the creation of a *kasbah* including its palaces, its mosque and its compensating reservoirs. He christened it *Mahdiya* at first, meaning the town of *Mahdi* in reference to Ibn Tumert, promulgator of the Muslim reformist movement which called itself *Mahdi*, that is to say "*God's Chosen One*", chosen to preach the Good and fight Bad. According to witness accounts by Hassan al-Wazzan, known under the pseudonym of Leon the African, the Almohad Caliph became particularly attached to the new *kasbah*, and grew into the habit of residing there each year between April and September, as well as from time-to-time holding large reunions there, gathering round him all provincial governors and army chiefs. Additionally, the *ribat* gained a military aspect to it by becoming an assembly point for the troops, a step on the way to the Conquest of Spain where Muslims faced an increasing Christian opposition. 'Abd al-Mumen thus enlarged the *ribat*, fortified the *kasbah*, Salé and the Ma'mora, and constructed an important naval shipyard. The towns of the Bu Regreg entered the history books at full steam.

The Almohad Empire experienced its true Golden Age under the reign of 'Abd al-Mumen's grandson, Abu Yusuf Ya'ub al-Mansur (579/1184–595/1199), who defeated the Castillians at Alarcos in 591/1195, this time gaining an enormous war booty which enabled him to produce great works as a builder. It was thus that he decided, in particular, to erect a veritable Almohad capital, following the Idrissids in their building of Fez and the Almoravids in their building of Marrakesh. Having in spirit what his empire had in terms of its Andalusian destiny, he chose the site of the *ribat* of the Bu Regreg, which opened directly onto the ocean, to house, in his view, one of the greatest Muslim towns in the world. He undertook the construction of a massive mosque, the largest in Islam after the Samarra Mosque in Iraq. But in 595/1199, as the minaret stood already 40 m. high above ground, Ya'qub al-Mansur died, and the building work stopped, and was not to be taken up again, on the same site, until seven and a half centuries later when the mausoleum of Mohamed V was built.

Thus, after *Ribat al-Fath* had become a charming city, of which geographers of the time spoke highly on its beautiful houses, attractive coastline, varied and lush orchards, and numerous boats which assured the navigation between the two riverbanks which were in any case linked by a wooden bridge, as well as on the prosperity of its inhabitants and the safety of its streets, it progressively became depopulated after the death of al-Mansur, especially after the defeat of Las Navas de Tolosa in 608/1212, which blew a hole in the Muslim conquest of al-Andalus. It nevertheless retained a certain economic prosperity, derived from fishing and agriculture, which grew when it began to take advantage of the new techniques brought over by the Andalusian refugees. With the demise of the Almohad Empire, *Ribat al-Fath* entered a morose era of abatement, even though the river's estuary retained its sacred status. It was this mythical and mystical prestige which incited the founder of the Merinid Dynasty, Abu Yusuf Ya'qub (656/1258–685/1286) to bury his wife, al-Horra Umm al-'Izz, at the antique site of Chellah in 682/1284, and to have himself buried there as well. The various sovereigns belonging to this

ITINERARY VIII   *Ebb and Flow, Shine and Eclipse*
Rabat

Royal Palace, al-Fas Mosque, Rabat.

dynasty kept this tradition going, and in 739/1339, Abu al-Hassan had a rampart and *zawiya* added. Even when Abu Inan, the son of Abu al-Hassan, revolted against his father, who was then killed in the ensuing battle, his own body was brought back to Rabat to be buried in the necropolis.

As soon as the Hafsids of Tunisia created troubles for the Merinids, forcing them to leave the mouth of the Bu Regreg, the left bank experienced a kind of hibernation period, during which the Chellah watched over its dead in silence. However, Salé continued to have a booming agriculture and to be an important harbour, welcoming in several migrating populations including the Berbers, the Andalusians and even the Tunisians.

VIII.1.a Archaeological Museum

Situated on rue al-Bihri close to the headquarters of Moroccan Television.
Open daily from 09.00–11.30 and 14.30–18.00. Closed Tuesdays.

VIII.1.b Royal Palace

One can only enter up to the mechuar, *an avenue 1,200 m. long which runs across the Royal Palace, as the palace cannot be visited. One enters via the Gate of the Ambassadors, which opens onto Boulevard Mulay Hassan.*

The Royal Palace is situated in the enclosure of the *mechuar* which covers an area of about 50 hectares. This area, where delegations waited before being received by the Sultan, is also called the Enclosure of the *Tuargas*, after the warriors from the south brought here by Sidi Mohamed Ibn 'Abd Allah (1170/1757–1204/1790). In 1864, Sultan Mohamed Ibn 'Abd al-Rahman had a new palace built which has since undergone 20th-century reconstruction and extension work.

The palace is flanked by a number of administrative buildings, the Royal Protocol, the Royal Cabinet, the First Ministry (Prime Minister's Office), the *Habus* Ministry, and the Royal College, all of which are recent constructions, but which luckily

ITINERARY VIII *Ebb and Flow, Shine and Eclipse*
Rabat

Almohad rampart, enclosure and square towers, Rabat.

reflect the endurance of Andalusian architectural and decorative art.

The palace and its adjoining buildings all have very beautiful gates, including that of the Throne Room, which is very elaborately decorated, and that of the First Ministry, in front of which the daily ceremonies of the raising and descending of the colours, in the presence of a number of Royal Guards in uniform, takes place. There are several gates through which the enclosure can be entered into, of which the Gate of the Ambassadors, built in 1941, is the only one which remains open at night. The *al-Fas* –"the people of Fez"– Mosque, sober in appearance but well-balanced in proportions, can be found half-way between the Gate of the Ambassadors and the palace. A number of traditional religious ceremonies take place here, in particular the morning prayers of the *'Id al-'Adha*, *'Id al-Kebir*, after which the king proceeds with the ritual sacrifice of a sheep, in commemoration of Abraham's sacrifice.

The enclosure also holds an equestrian arena for the Royal Guard to practise their horse-riding skills, as well as a vast paved area, embellished with water fountains, where the locals gather during ceremonies, royal appearances or indeed concerts of the group "55", a musical band dressed in richly coloured clothing who play themes from Andalusian music on percussion and wind instruments.

VIII.1.c **Almohad Ramparts and Gates**

The ramparts run alongside the Royal Palace and reach as far as the Bab al-Alu, Gate near the Sea.

The Almohad Empire experienced its Golden Age during the reign of Abu Yusuf

ITINERARY VIII Ebb and Flow, Shine and Eclipse
Rabat

Ya'qub al-Mansur (579/1184–595/1199) who had the idea of constructing an Almohad Capital on the left bank of the Bu Regreg. He thus encircled an area of 450 hectares with a strong enclosure-wall flanked by 74 square towers, which spanned 5,263 m. and which defended the western and southern sides of the town, which on other sides was protected by the cliff, the river and the sea. Although it is over eight centuries old, the wall, built in 593/1197, has admirably resisted the tests of time and bad weather, due to the quality of cement with which it was built; the cement was made of crushed brick as opposed to plain earth, of small rolled stones and a third-part limestone, a mixture which gave it the hardness and durability of stone. Standing, nearly 2 km. in length, between Bab al-Had and Bab Ruah, and running alongside the Bu Regreg, the rampart has a mean thickness of 2.4 m. with a height varying between 7.55 m. and 8.4 m.

The Almohad gates of Rabat emit a vivid impression of grandeur. They count, along with the great Almohad minarets of the Kutubiya of Marrakesh, the Giralda of Seville and the Hassan Mosque of Rabat, as being amongst the masterpieces of Andalusian modelling.

The Almohad enclosure of *Ribat al-Fath* originally had only five gates: namely, starting with those closest to the sea; Bab al-'Alu, Bab al-Had, Bab Ruah, Bab al-Hedid and Bab Zaers. Bab al-Hedid, "The Gate of Iron", was incorporated into the Royal Palace's enclosure and is not open to the public. All the others can be seen, sometimes only from the outside as they no longer fulfill their past function. Other more important gates were opened around them to allow for the flow of motorised traffic.

Bab Zaers

Situated at the far end of the mechuar, *on the exterior of the Royal Palace, opening onto Boulevard Musa Ibn Nusayr.*

Called thus because it faces the road which leads towards the Zaers tribe, about 20 km. from Rabat, this gate was the only one incorporated into the southern side of the ramparts by the Almohad builders. It is 9.7 m. in height and 18.25 m. in depth; while measuring 12.6 m. in width on its interior side, its exterior facade attains a width of 18.6 m. The Gate of the Zaers looks particularly like Bab al-'Alu in its design, even though it is less uniform. The central section of its exterior facade looks itself like that of Bab al-Had in terms of its composition. Its detailing seems to have been restored quite a few times: two successive arches superimpose

Almohad rampart, square tower, Rabat.

ITINERARY VIII *Ebb and Flow, Shine and Eclipse*
Rabat

Almohad rampart, general view of Bab Ruah, Rabat.

and fold over each other, one recessed from the other, composed of alternating keystones, which jutt out and remain undecorated. A third arch, semicircular and raised above the ground on stilts, was added rather clumsily later on. A similar addition was made on the interior façade of the gate, whilst doorways opening onto the parapet and the small room on the terrace were installed. These transformations date from the $12^{th}/18^{th}$ century, when Sidi Mohamed Ibn 'Abd Allah proceeded in consolidating the ramparts.

The Gate of the Zaers is both the smallest, the least looked after and the most altered of the five gates of Ya'qub al-Mansur's wall.

Bab Ruah

From the Gate of the Zaers, walk through the Royal Palace and exit onto Avenue Mulay Hassan. The gate is situated at the far end of the avenue and opens onto Avenue al-Nasser.

The "Gate of Departure", Bab Ruah, 28 m. wide, 27 m. deep and 12 m. high, is the largest gate belonging to the Almohad enclosure. It is also the most elaborately decorated, even though its military purpose is more strikingly evident. The gate povides access to four square rooms, each 5.65 m. in length and width, which are interlinked through the presence of two hallways each measuring 4.2 m. x 2.2 m. The entrance archway, slightly pointed and raised on stilts, was added during the reign of Sidi Mohamed Ibn 'Abd Allah in the second half of the $12^{th}/18^{th}$ century.

Flanked on the outside by two bastions, the door's archway is decorated with a festooned interlace, interwoven covings and yet another row of festoons; its floral arabesque corners are marked on each corner with a large relief of a shell; a band of

ITINERARY VIII *Ebb and Flow, Shine and Eclipse*
Rabat

kufic writing frames the arch, and, in the corners, small columns with sculpted capitals support foiled corbels. The interior bayonet passageway runs under a series of domes of which one, which is puckered, rests on a pendant. The four guard rooms in the interior of the gate have been transformed into exhibition rooms, whilst other entrances were created to allow for a fluid through-wall traffic. Placed practically at the centre of the enclosure's western wall, it possesses – along with the importance of its passageways, the certainty of its design and the ingenuity of its ornamentation – a majestic quality for which it can compared to the most beautiful of the Almohad gates: that of the Udayas' Kasbah and Bab Aghnaua in Marrakesh.

Bab al-Had

From Bab Ruah, follow the wall, heading towards the sea. The gate stands at the intersection of Boulevard Hassan II and Boulevard Misr.

The "Gate of Sunday", Bab al-Had, thus called due to the weekly market held in its surroundings, has undergone numerous repairs and changes:
– during the 13th/19th century, under the reign of Mulay Sliman, in 1229/1814, as an oval medallion carrying the following inscription is evidence thereof: *"Praise be to God. This blessed gate was rebuilt by the Commander of Believers of the Worshipful, Mulay Sliman. 1229."*
– during the French Protectorate: the angled gate of four twists and turns was transformed into a straight, more direct one in order to facilitate traffic;
– and finally, in 1995–96, restoration and refurbishing work was carried out within the framework of a patronage scheme.

The entrance bay of the external facade, which measured 6.35 m. in height prior to the work undertaken in 1229/1814, is today only 3.7 m. high. Despite those transformations which destroy the elegant line drawn by the arch of this simple entrance, Bab al-Had remains a good-looking monument, far less severe than Bab al-'Alu.

Bab al-'Alu

Continue walking along the wall in the direction of the sea. It is the last gate on your right before you reach the sea.

The "Gate of the Hill", Bab al-'Alu, which stands shoulder to shoulder with the entrances which were opened up in the 20th century, is built protruding outwards on both sides of the wall. Measuring 19.2 m. across, 20.92 m. deep and 10.85 m.

Almohad rampart, Bab Ruah, detail of the arcatures, Rabat.

225

ITINERARY VIII   *Ebb and Flow, Shine and Eclipse*
Rabat

Mulina Mosque, general view, Rabat.

high, it contains four angled bends and two turrets which frame the entrance bay, each jutting out by 3 m. and measuring 5.3 m. across. The entrance bay consists of a pointed horseshoe arch made completely of stone, whose keystones remain undecorated, which opens onto two parallel rooms, one of which originally had an open rooftop. A solid monument which has kept to its original design, Bab al-'Alu is truly representative of Almohad art, being at once both imposing, bare and a little frosty in appearance.

VIII.1.d Mulina Mosque

Go back to Boulevard Hassan. The mosque is situated 300 m. from Bab Buiba, at the south end of the Triangle de Vue park which sits between Boulevard Hassan II and rue al-Mansur al-Dhahbi. Access restricted to Muslims.

Situated between the small enclosure and the large enclosure of Rabat, the Mulina Mosque draws its name from the owner of the orchard at the centre of which it stood hidden, Mulin being an old al-Andalus family from Rabat. According to popular tradition, this mosque is as old as that of Chellah, and was erected during the reign of Yusuf Ibn Tashfin. However, in the absence of any sort of indication, reference or inscription, one could, in comparing it to the *Jama' Sunna* Mosque, when it was in its original state, more reasonably attribute it to the reign of Sidi Mohamed Ibn 'Abd Allah during the $12^{th}/18^{th}$ century.

The monument, built on a square surface area, consists of a courtyard, a minaret, two naves, a *mihrab* and five small rooms. The monumental door made of large stone bolders, outlining a horseshoe arch, is surmounted by an entablature covered in green tiles. The minaret stands in the north-west corner of the courtyard, blocked in on both sides by the enclosure walls. It is made of solid brick, covered with a plaster coating. The tower, square in cross-section and robust, is crowned by a series of jagged triangular stone slabs, 11 on each side. The lantern, which sits above the tower, is also crowned with five such slabs on each side, and is furnished with a small dome. This sanctuary, modest in its dimensions, indeed just a simple oratory, remained for a long time in ruins, before its structure and original appearance were completely brought back to life between 1970–1980.

VIII.1.e Esplanade of the Tower of Hassan

Follow the sign Mausolée Mohamed V. It is possible to park in rue Bu Regreg.
Entry Free. Open daily from 09.00–19.00.

Apparently, it was impossible to find, during the time of the Almohads, a sufficiently prestigious character after whom what was intended to be one of the largest places of prayer and of worship of the Muslim world could be named, and of which only an unfinished minaret remains. This gigantic project, for which a headland was chosen which was situated 30 m. above sea-level, north-east of the ramparts, there to protect the great Almohad capital which was still in construction, employed an enormous number of technicians, craftsmen and workers, including 700 Christian captives. Initiated in 592/1196 during the reign of Ya'qub al-Mansur, the construction of the mosque – which was intended to house a prayer hall over 2.5 hectares in size, as well as a roof supported by 300 columns and 100 pillars, and a minaret 64 m. in height but over 80 m., in fact, with the addition of its lantern – was interrupted after the monarch's death in 595/1199. The unfinished building then deteriorated severely, due to its being dismantled so that its materials could be re-used, after it was pillaged. It was also victim to an earthquake which hit Lisbon in 1168/1755 whose shock waves decapitated the minaret, as well as being damaged by a serious fire which destroyed the wooden structures, traces of which were discovered when the

Esplanade of the Hassan Tower, view of the facade which faces the Bu Regreg, Rabat.

ITINERARY VIII   *Ebb and Flow, Shine and Eclipse*
Rabat

Hassan Tower, detail, Rabat.

Mohamed V Mausoleum was constructed. The Hassan Tower in fact rises up to a height of 44 m. and, with its square base of 16.2 m. and its 2.5 m.-thick walls, appears majestic and forceful, dominating the valley of the Bu Regreg as well as the sea front. Each of its four large stone sides have developed various different sheens over time, ranging from silver-grey to dark-red ochre, and these are perforated with elegant apertures which light up the interior ramp, up which one could ascend on horseback. They are, at various levels, adorned with arcatures which are crowned by a classical interlacing-web design, and with a motif of arches supported by small columns, made both of marble and stone, capped with capitals, a few of which, originating from al-Andalus, date from the 4th/10th century, from the time of the Caliph of Cordoba. This is the third Almohad creation of its kind, the previous being the Kutubiya of Marrakesh and the Giralda of Seville.

Its 183 m. x 139 m. enclosure was to be punctured by the insertion of 12 gates, and its immense hall was to contain 19 naves and 21 rows.

The Roman-Byzantine styled columns, made of superimposed drum-shaped sections and topped with capitals that had hardly any shape, form an exception within the realm of Almohad religious art.

VIII.1.f **Mohamed V Mausoleum**

Situated in front of the Hassan Tower. Entry Free. Open daily from 09.00-19.00.

Inside the enclosure of what was the Great Mosque, opposite the Hassan Tower, is the Mohamed V Mausoleum, which keeps alive the memory of the sovereign (1927–1961) who regained his country's independence. This monument, built between 1961 and 1969, draws its inspiration from traditional royal *necropoli*. Placed on a 3.5 m.-high plinth, it is sheltered by a pyramidal green-tiled roof. One can access the funeral room in which Mohamed V's tomb is located via a "gallery-balcony"; his mortal remains, along with that of his son's, who died in 1983, were transferred in 1971. The entire wealth of Moroccan decorative art of Andalusian origin is present in this monument: the 12-piece dome composed of sculpted mahogany and stained glass, the great bronze chandelier measuring 2.3 m. in diameter and weighing 1.5 tons, walls covered in *zellij* and in stucco, white onyx tombstones engraved by the great *m'allem* Ibn 'Abdelkrim, and granite floors, so thoroughly and perfectly polished, that the royal sarcophagus looks as if it is floating on a turquoise lake.

ITINERARY VIII   *Ebb and Flow, Shine and Eclipse*
Rabat

Below the paved square of Hassan Tower, a new mosque, with a surface area covering 2,200 sq. m., adjoins the mausoleum. Its floor was set 1.2 m. into the ground in order to provide its prayer hall with sufficient height (7 m.) without overshadowing the majestic quality of the neighbouring mausoleum. This mosque contains two prayer rooms: one for men and one for women, which are separated by *mashrabiyya* and an interior courtyard paved in marble and framed by a portico of sculpted stone. The entire monument, dedicated to the memory of Mohamed V, is completed by a museum whose surface area amounts to 1,500 sq m., which traces the history of the 'Alawite Dynasty from the $11^{th}/17^{th}$ century right up to the reign of Mohamed V. This museum contains a portico, unique of its kind, made of colonnades and arcades exposed to all kinds of winds; a completely novel idea, although conceived in a very traditional style. This portico is built on an esplanade identical to that on which the mausoleum is built, and access to the museum is provided by four staircases which lead to various exhibition rooms decorated in *zellij*, wood and plaster, each with its own particular character.

The Hassan Tower and the Mohamed V Mausoleum, both situated on this same esplanade, cover between them over eight centuries of history.

VIII.1.g **Chellah**

Situated opposite the Bab Zaers. Take the small road at the intersection of the Grand Avenue which runs along the wall (Avenue Musa Ibn Nusayr) and the avenue which leads into the Royal Palace.
Entrance fee. Open daily from 09.00–18.00. Parking available.

Situated outside of the walls, at about 2 km. from the centre of town, the necropolis of Chellah sits on the antique site of Sala Colonia, a prosperous Roman city which could be reached directly by river before it was deserted in the $2^{nd}/8^{th}$ century, becoming a field of ruins by the $4^{th}/10^{th}$ century. The Merinid Sultans, of the $7^{th}/13^{th}$ to the $8^{th}/14^{th}$ centuries, turned it into a royal necropolis and it is from this period that most of the Arab-Muslim constructions date. Unfortunately, only the ruins of these constructions remain today, as they were destroyed by an earthquake in 1168/1755.

The enclosure is of an irregular quadrilateral form, about 300 m. long on each side. One can penetrate it through a rich-

Mohamed V Mausoleum, general view, Rabat.

229

ITINERARY VIII   *Ebb and Flow, Shine and Eclipse*
Rabat

ly ornamented gate which is flanked by two semi-octagonal bastions, whose upper corners are crowned with merlons projecting out of corbelled corners which are constructed in the form of stalactites. A staircase leads to an upper platform; inside, on the left, one can see an ancient guard post and the remains of a inn.

The *kufic* inscription which adorns the frame of the gate tells us that the construction of the ramparts was begun by Abu Sa'id 'Uthman (709/1310–731/1331) and completed by his son Abu al-Hassan in 739/1339.

A path leads downwards to the lower part of the enclosure, marked by the presence of a spring, where in all likelihood stood an ablutions room from the Merinid period, next to which several marabouts lived, including Sidi Yahya Ibn Yunes among others. On the left stands an enclosure which encompasses an old sanctuary, housing:

– a mosque whose gate is still surfaced in magnificent tiled mosaic, and a spring sheltered in the shadow of a sacred fig tree;

– the tomb of the Merinid Emir Abu al-Hassan, "The Black Sultan" (731/1331–752/1351), whose exterior is adorned with a canopy of stalactites; the south-east facade, of beautifully cut stone, structured and sculpted, with lead joints, and coated with an attractive ochre sheen; the tomb holds a marble headstone carrying Abu al-Hassan's epitaph. Close by, another marble stone carries a dedication to his wife, Shems al-Duha, "Morning Sun", a European who converted to Islam, and who was the mother of Abu Inan;

– a *zawiya*, unearthed in 1930, consisting of a courtyard with a central basin still embellished with its ceramic paving, surrounded by small rooms set back from galleries upheld by elegant columns and pretty marble capitals, and equipped with an oratory whose *mihrab* is surrounded by

Chellah, gate and rampart, Rabat.

ITINERARY VIII *Ebb and Flow, Shine and Eclipse*
Rabat

a semi-circular corridor. Legend has it that the Prophet prayed in this mosque, and that there was a time when it was enough to walk round the *mihrab* seven times in order to be accoladed with the title of *haj*, which was given only to pilgrims who had made the journey to Mecca;

– a minaret 15 m. high, surmounted by a lantern decorated in multi-coloured tiles;

– a stele known as the Lalla Chellah, who became the patron saint of the surrounding area. Lower down, a garden runs along the ruins, irrigated by a neighbouring spring, *'Ayn Mdafa'*, "The Source of the Canons", which is full of eels considered to be sacred, bred under the orders of King Mulay Ya'qub, who are reputed to be guardians of considerable treasure buried within the sacred enclosure.

Excavations have also revealed an entire ancient Muslim Quarter, with its squares, houses, public places and *hammams*, which was established at an unknown date on the site of the Roman town Sala Colonia, and which thus demonstrates that the site was a veritable funeral city as opposed to merely a simple necropolis.

The Bu Regreg
The Bu Regreg river is a historical, as well as natural, site, which the twin and rival cities of Rabat and Salé both lay claim to with the same sense of pride and selfish jealousy. It is listed by the historian al-Marrakshi as the Wadi al-rumman, *"River of the Pomegranates", appearing in the 7*th*/13*th *century under the name of Bu Regreg, a name derived from 'Ali Rakrak. Does it refer to the Berber term* ragag, *seagull, the emblematic animal of Rabat?*
Both a witness of and a player within a history that is both age-old and diverse,

the Bu Regreg carries with it streams of souvenirs and dreams, of exploits and dramas, of joy and anguish, with its marketeers, its producers, its bourgeoisie, its men of power, and, as always, with its praiseworthy river mouth which offers an extraordinary panoramic view, as charming and attractive on the right as it is on the left. It is this panorama which the visitor can admire at leisure, looking out from one of the local boats which sail between the two riverbanks or which on demand undertake small excursions. A journey on the water allows one's eyes to embrace 20 centuries of History!

Chellah, minaret and entrance to the zawiya, Rabat.

ZELLIJ

Kasbah, museum, mural paving in zellij, polygonal star motif, Tangier.

Zellij is enamelled fired clay, tinted different colours and cut by hand into various shapes which are used to decorate walls, columns and occasionally, paving stones.

The art of *zellij* appeared in Morocco, as it did in al-Andalus, during the $4^{th}/10^{th}$ century and began to blossom in the $8^{th}/14^{th}$ century. Having originated most probably from Byzantine mosaic, it was certainly influenced by Italian *majolica* (from Mallorca) and Andalusian *azulejo*. It is important to note on this subject that the Arabs had, in general, the great idea of borrowing from the arts of the lands they had conquered: in fact, while branding its character on everything it touches, Arab-Muslim art has borrowed from Hindu, Persian and Byzantine artforms. That is how, after having borrowed from the latter the technical processes involved in the making of mosaics, the Arabs knew how to create, in al-Andalus, as early as the $4^{th}/10^{th}$ century, a new art of enamel wall tiling which no longer used uniform square pieces measuring 1cm. on each side, but pieces which varied in shape. In the beginning, clay squares were used which were 10 cm. in length, covered in enamel and fired in a traditional manner (drying, first firing, enamelling, second firing). They are then manually shaped with the help of small, heavy hammers called *menqash*.

The designer of *zellij* works in a sitting position, arms resting on knees, and with the help of his *menqash*, which is sharpened at both ends, he cuts the pieces one by one, in a continuous and precise movement, following the pattern traced beforehand onto the enamelled tiles. The diverse shapes of *zellij*, each of which has a specific name that corresponds to it, can be fitted together to form motifs which obey the traditional rules traced out by the regulating patterns.

ITINERARY VIII

Ebb and Flow, Shine and Eclipse

Kamal Lakhdar

Second day

VIII.1 RABAT
        VIII.1.h Kasbah of the Udayas
        VIII.1.i Medina
        VIII.1.j Andalusian Wall
        VIII.1.k Bastions of the Andalusian Rampart

VIII.2 SALÉ
        VIII.2.a Bab Mrissa
        VIII.2.b Merinid Madrasa

        The Rugs of Rabat

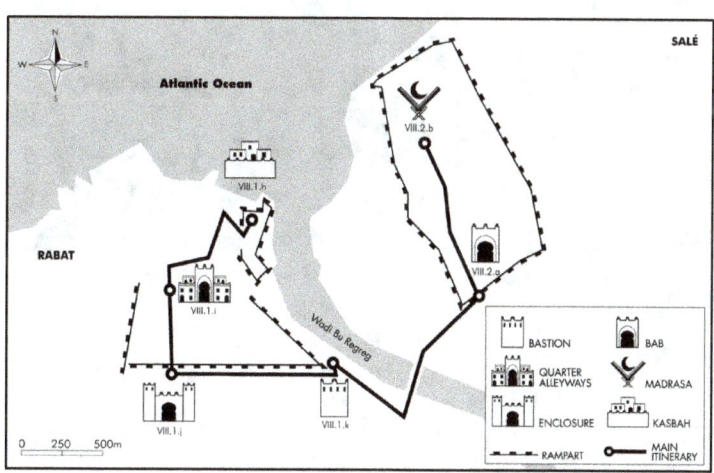

ITINERARY VIII   Ebb and Flow, Shine and Eclipse
Rabat

VIII.1.h Kasbah of the Udayas

Follow the sign saying Kasbah of the Udayas. One can park opposite the kasbah *on Place Suq al-Ghezel. The museum is located within the* kasbah's *enclosure.*
Entrance fee. Open from 09.00–12.00 and 15.00–18.00. Closed Tuesdays.

The Udayas were an Arab tribe from the Sahara among whom Mulay Isma'il (1082/1672–1139/1727) recruited numerous warriors, some of whom were placed in a garrison stationed in Rabat to protect it from its turbulent tribal neighbours. The actual *kasbah* is not very expansive, but is picturesque nonetheless. Its upper part was founded by the Almohads, its lower part by the 'Alawites, in the 12th/18th century. The Almohad wall which surrounds the *kasbah*, 2.5 m. thick and 8–10 m. high, is built of rubble, and is bordered by an inclining esplanade on which old canons still stand. The monumental gate, built of red-ochre freestones, stands on a mound and overlooks the town. The *kasbah* is the first *ribat* to have been erected in this area and is mentioned as early as 366/977 by the geographer Ibn Hawqal, who assures the reader that it could hold up to 100,000 soldiers.

In 534/1140, the Almoravids built themselves a *kasbah* in their fight against the Almohad menace. The Almohads managed to destroy it before rebuilding it in 544/1150 with the inclusion of a palace and a mosque. 'Abd al-Mumen named it *Mahdiya*, and stayed there frequently, where he received, both in 545/1151 and

Kasbah of the Udayas, rampart, Rabat.

ITINERARY VIII *Ebb and Flow, Shine and Eclipse*
Rabat

in 553/1158, delegations sent by the Andalusian government.

Following Ya'qub al-Mansur's death in 595/1199, who had wanted to make the *Ribat al-Fath* the grand capital of the Muslim West, the *kasbah* was practically deserted. When Philip III decreed in 1017/1609 the expulsion of nearly half a million Moriscos from Spain, 2,000 *Hornacheros* came to settle in Salé, and then in Rabat, to which they attracted between 5,000 and 14,000 other emigres who went onto become fearsome pirates, setting up an "Autonomous Republic" which existed independently of the central power until 1076/1666, when the 'Alawite Sultan Mulay Rashid placed them under his authority.

The Gate of the Udayas, composed of an archway flanked by two towers, was built in the $6^{th}/12^{th}$ century by Ya'qub al-Mansur. Of majestic proportions, it displays a sculpted repetitive decor on its inward facing facade. When festooned arches were first created, motifs representative of snakes or eels constituted a one-off curiosity within the realm of Moroccan decorative art.

The oldest mosque in Rabat can be found within the *kasbah*: *Jama' al-'Atiqa*, which was built in 544/1150 by 'Abd al-Mumen. Its minaret, adorned with arcatures, was restored in the $12^{th}/18^{th}$ century by an English convert, Ahmed al-Inglizi.

Tower of the Privateers

The rue Jama' leads to a platform which towers over the mouth of the river Bu Regreg and the town of Salé, and on which stands a semaphore signal from the $11^{th}/17^{th}$ century as well as a warehouse from the $12^{th}/18^{th}$ century which now in fact houses a school and a rug workshop. The rue Laalami ends in a cul-de-sac at the Tower of the Privateers. Still refered to as "Tower of the Pilots", this *burj* dates from the $12^{th}/18^{th}$ century. Squat, massive, and at water level, it is furnished with openings to hold four canons, aimed at the *wadi* and at Salé. It is situated 25 m. uphill from the Sqala. It has a circumference of 13 m., and its platform lies 3 m.

Kasbah of the Udayas, door of the kasbah, detail of corners decorated with palm leaves and mini palm leaves, Rabat.

above water level. Concealed at the entrance to the port, on the bend of the *wadi*, it was used for the attack on ships which, having broken through the barrier and penetrated into the port, had thought themselves to have entered a safe haven.

The rue Bazzo leads to the Andalusian garden, created between 1915 and 1918. The stairs lead to two jagged-edged towers endowed with ancient canons, and to a round path which prevails within the *medina*s of Salé and Rabat.

Museum of the Udayas

The *kasbah* also holds Rabat's Museum of Moroccan Arts, established in the Prince's Pavilion which Mulay Isma'il had built at the end of the 11th/17th century. The building was transformed into a *madrasa* before becoming a museum. Today, three rooms are open to the public. In the first room of the Museum of the Udayas one can see a reconstruction of a traditional Moroccan interior, with its walls covered in gold brocades and Persian silk.

In a second room, paved in marble, a collection of pottery from Fez is on display, together with some Berber musical instruments, some pieces of Berber or Hispanic-Arab jewellery, and a display of Qur'ans and illuminated manuscripts, the oldest of which date from the 6th/12th century. One of these was written by the brother of the Almohad Caliph al-Sa'id 'Umar al-Murtada whilst he was governor of *Ribat al-Fath*. The site's ancient mosque holds a collection of rugs which come from all over Morocco. The oldest among the rugs from Rabat and from Mediuna date from the 11th/17th century. A further room is dedicated to Moroccan dress and costumes from the regions between the Rif and the Sahara. Behind the Andalusian garden one can find a "Moorish" café, which, as it is built on the ramparts, offers a panoramic view onto the Bu Regreg.

THE RUGS OF RABAT

Related to the Islamic rugs traditionally produced in cities, the *rbati* rug is considered to be one of the most sumptuous wollen rugs available in Morocco and indeed in the Arab-Muslim world. In contrast to Berber rugs which employ the traditional motifs prevalent in tattos and henna decoration, the rugs of Rabat display floral, zoomorphic or geometric elements of Turkish origin. They are made using a crafts technique most probably introduced into Rabat at the time of the privateers of Salé and the multiple traffic of visits, exchanges and alliances which took place in the 12th/18th century between the Ottoman Empire and the Kingdom of Morocco, in particular with the cities along the Bu Regreg. Legend has it that, several centuries ago, a seagull carried in its beak a piece of rug from the Orient and dropped it in Chellah. The inhabitants did not rest until they had found it, and having done so, began to copy the techniques used in the creation of this miraculous piece, which had truly been "heaven sent". The Austrian explorer Oskar Lenz, who stayed in Rabat from January 29 to February 3 1880, spoke of the rugs of Rabat in the following terms: *"Long ago, Rabat was in a class of its own, set apart from the rest of Morocco, and even today remains one of the most important places for the production of indigenous crafts. Magnificent rugs, original in design and very vibrant and very varied in colour, which are pleasing to the eye, are created on a grand scale. The wool and colour are produced in situ, and the rugs themselves are not created in large workshops, but independently by workers, both fathers and sons, devoted to this industry. One can often find, within these ancient rugs, colour tones which are worthy of appreciation, particularly the diverse hues which can be gained from red. The rugs from Rabat are distributed all over the Empire; they are rarely exported to Europe, where truly Oriental products dominate the market".*

The *rbati* rug, of a close-cropped velvet and fine texture, is made on a weaving loom which runs very smoothly, stands vertically and is affixed, which enables several people to work on the rug at the same time. The threads of the horizontal framework, which determines the width of the rug, are passed through the threads which run vertically, and which deter-

Floral patterned rug with framed centre of two diamond shapes superimposed, Museum of the Udayas (Inv. No. 5125).

mine its length. A very strict rule states that there must be a minimum of 50,000 stitches per sq. m., although there can be as many 160,000 stitches within a single sq. m. The overall design of the layout and the motifs, as well as the colours, which originally were limited in number, is based, both schematically and symbolically, on the design of a traditional Moroccan house, with its patio, its central water fountain, its rooms, its corridors and canopies, as well as its wall decorations (plaster and *zellij*).

Traditionally, the *rbati* rug has a bright red, brick-red or dark pink background with a triangle in each corner; occassionally only one of the two endwidths of the rug has a single triangle at its centre, providing the rug with the element of a *mihrab*. This type of motif features particularly on small prayer rugs. At the centre of the rug lies, invariably, a rose, whose designation depends on its general appearance. Thus it is either a *limuna buarqha*, "orange with its leaves", a *siniya*, "tray", a *mdal al-sultan*, "the sultan's parasol", or a *hzam Sidna Suleyman*, "King Solomon's belt". This rose is also sometimes surrounded by little motifs called *kchiuchat*, "little utensils". Continuous bands, of various widths, outline the border of the rug, and they are richly decorated but the colours they display obey strict rules: the colours are normally restricted to seven – red, green, blue, black or brown, yellow, orange and white. Nevertheless, it is not unusual for there to be up to 13 shades present within finely crafted, evocatively-named motifs, for example *halwa*, "cake", *chajra*, "tree", and *warda*, "flower".

ITINERARY VIII *Ebb and Flow, Shine and Eclipse*
Rabat

VIII.1.i **Medina**

From Place Suq al-Ghzel, opposite the kasbah *of the Udayas, take the rue des Consuls which is situated below on the left.*

On leaving the Kasbah of the Udayas, one ends up on *Place Suq al-Ghzel*, "Spinners' Market", where captives of the privateers were sold during the $10^{th}/16^{th}$ and $11^{th}/17^{th}$ centuries and where now twice a week rugs are sold on auction. This square leads to the Street of the Consuls, along which foreign delegates were compelled to reside until 1912, and which was built during the era of the "Republic of the Two Riverbanks" which existed from 1018/1610 to 1076/1666. The first section of the street is totally occupied by a succession of craft stalls and shops selling rugs, copper, leather crafts, clothes and fabrics. Two *funduq*s are to be found at numbers 93 and 109, old "inn-warehouses" for commercial travellers; leather craftsmen now use them as workspaces. Another *funduq*, of a modern construction, houses a *qaysariya*, a gallery for textile merchants.

The dwellings on *rue des Consuls* are more European in style than the others in the *medina*, and each have a multitude of windows which look onto the street, whilst more traditional housing is more introvert, with blind facades and rooms opening onto an interior patio instead. *"L'impasse du consulat de France"* is a narrow alleyway at the end of which lies the Consulate's Palace, where, as the French Consul from 1180/1767 to 1196/1782, Louis Chénier, father of the poet André Chénier, stayed.

At the far end of the rue des Consuls, one can either turn left to exit the *medina* via the Quarter of the Blacksmiths, *Haddadin*, heading towards the river through the Gate of the Sea, *Bab al-Bhar*; or one can turn right, crossing over the shoe market, *Suq Sebbat*, which is shielded in a canopy of reed mats, and is permanently swarming with activity, as a hub where both modern and traditional shoes, and leather items and crafts, are sold, as well as traditionally made gold and silver jewellery. On entering the *suq*, one sees to one's left the Great Mosque, *Jama' al-Kebir*, built by the Merinids but subsequently forever reshaped, whose very solemn, bland ochre minaret was rebuilt in 1939. By taking a left, one reaches Bab Chellah and, in so doing, walks past a beautiful

Medina, shoe market, Rabat.

239

frieze of blind arcatures and sculpted curving interlace. It can be found on the pediment (front wall) of an old Merinid fountain whose archways are now occupied by a bookseller.

VIII.1.j **Andalusian Wall**

The wall runs along the Boulevard Hassan II. Exit the medina *via Place du Mellah, or instead through the central market opposite; the wall links these two furthest points of Boulevard Hassan II.*

Under the Sa'adians (961/1554–1069/1659), the more or less deserted town of Rabat received, from 1017/1609 onwards, a contingent of Muslims expelled by Philip III of Spain, who settled in the *Kasbah* of the Udayas. These were known as the *Hornacheros*. Another group underwent the same fate in 1018/1610, and occupied the perimeter of the actual *medina*.

Living in fear of being attacked at any moment, the Andalusians hastened to build a wall to protect themselves against both external and internal enemies. This enclosure remained, known under the name of the "Andalusian wall". Note that this migratory movement occured during the reign of the Sa'adian Sultan Mulay Ahmed al-Mansur (985/1578–1011/1603).
Measuring 1,400 m. in length, the wall contains five gates. *Bab Teben*, "Gate of Hay", which no longer exists today due to urbanisation, was composed of three bays: a central one, larger and higher than its two sides ones. Of this gate, which to this day is called *Bab Jdid*, there remains only one room, which was in fact used as a police station.
Bab al-Buiba, "the Small Portal", which opens onto boulevard Hassan II, derives its name from its size, its height not exceeding that of a man's. Bab Chellah was itself completely rebuilt in 1228/1813 by the 'Alawite Sultan Mulay Sliman. Its decoration is the exception to the rule of

Andalusian Rampart, general view, Rabat.

gates built at the same time. Whilst it lacks the grandeur of Almohad gates, it reveals interesting architectural elements such as its pointed entrance arch composed of bare but finely constructed keystones, and its cornerstones overridden by floral and geometric motifs. Measuring 11.28 m. in length, 6.82 m. in width and 7.4 m. in height, it is adjacent to one of the wall's *burjs*. The final two, Bab al-Mellah, the gate which leads to the old Jewish Quarter, and Bab Diuana, transformed into the entrance gate of a mosque, are not worthy of any particular attention.

VIII.1.k Bastions of the Andalusian Rampart

At the far end of the Andalusian Wall which runs along Avenue Hassan II, on Place Sidi Makhlouf, the Sidi Makhluf Burj can be found. Continuing on from the wall, one finds the Qadia Burj, which borders Boulevard Tariq al-Marsa along the river.

The Andalusian rampart is flanked by 26 towers and one round bastion called Burj Sidi Makhluf after the patron of ferrymen at the time.

Burj Sidi Makhluf

This bastion dates from the $11^{th}/17^{th}$ century. It offered look-outs a view of the harbour, which had been built by the *Qa'id al-Caceri* during his visit to Salé, and which was bombed in (1046/1637) by an English squadron lead by Admiral Rainsborough. Within the *burj*'s enclosure resides the marabou of Sidi Makhluf, Jewish in origin, from where a small path leads to the *wadi*.

Burj Qadiya

This bastion derives its name from the tomb close by in which Lalla Qadiya was buried. It was here that ferrymen crossed the *wadi*, embarking and disembarking passengers. At high tide, the water rose as far up as to reach the foot of this tower, which was never a fortified bastion but a look-out tower. It was built in the $11^{th}/17^{th}$ century.

VIII.2 SALÉ

Salé is 3 km. from Rabat, separated from it by the river Bu Regreg. It is possible to cross the river by ferry.

Whilst it only took three years (154/771–156/773) for Spain (al-Andalus) to submit to the Arabs, it took the Euro-Christian Reconquest several centuries, from the Almohad defeat at Las Navas de Tolosa in 608/1212 to the expulsion of Muslims edicts signed by Philip III in 1017/1609, via the capitulation of Granada in 897/1492. A wave of Andalusian immigration towards Morocco is attached to each of these fateful dates. But the one which is of particular interest to the Bu Regreg riverbanks is the most recent one listed (Philip III's expulsion edicts), which chased the Moriscos out of al-Andalus at the beginning of the $11^{th}/17^{th}$ century, making the town of Salé a globally renowned name. This town, situated on the right bank of the Bu Regreg, and whose establishment date remains unknown, was probably in the $4^{th}/10^{th}$ century the capital of the Kingdom of the Beni Ifren. It became, at the end of the $6^{th}/12^{th}$ century, a lively port

ITINERARY VIII *Ebb and Flow, Shine and Eclipse*

Salé

town which in the 7th/13th century wetted Spain's appetite and political ambitions. Thus, taking advantage of the conflict between the Almohads and the Merinids, Alphonse X of Castille pillaged it in 658/1260 on the day of *'Id al-Fitr*, "Feast of the rupture of the youth of Ramadan", and 14 years then went by before Abu Yusuf Ya'qub was able to seize it back. This Merinid sovereign then raised a wall to protect the city, and built a *madrasa*, a *zawiya*, a School of Medicine and an aquaduct within the enclosure.

The Merinids were just that: defenders of the arts and humanities. Like their contemporaries, the Kings of Granada, they embellished the principal cities of their kingdom. During that time, Salé became the main port of the Kingdom of Fez, and the most important commercial depot of the west coast, frequented by merchants from the whole of the Christian world: Mediterranean, Flemish and English, all of whom attracted the commercial aptitudes and hankerings of the merchants of Salé, who sold hides, wool, textiles, rugs, ivory, wax and honey and who in return bought fabrics and manufactured items from merchants from Pisa, Catalonia, Genoa and Venice. When the Moriscos (both Muslim and Jewish) were expelled from Spain, entire families from Castille, Catalonia, al-Andalus and Murcia settled on the *ribat*s of Bu Regreg: ancient Salé, actual Salé and new Salé, Rabat. Under the impetus of the *Hornacheros*, wealthy merchants from the Bajadoz area who were out of touch with the techniques of maritime navigation, they decided to specialise in a new form of *Jihad*: buccaneering, to which they dedicated themselves wholeheartedly for over half a century, to earn their fortunes as well as to avenge themselves against the Christians who had robbed them of their homeland. The arrival of these Moriscos coincided with fratricide wars between the Sa'adian Princes, wars which brought the dynasty to an end and which rendered the central political authority very weak. Having stood their ground against Christian Spanish power, by refusing to abandon the Arab-Muslim element of their cultural heritage, they showed themselves, on the other side of the Mediterranean, to be equally resolute against a Moroccan government in a state of decay, against which they refused to abandon the European elements of this same cultural heritage. In the space of 10 years, more than 1,000 ships were captured, and *"These Andalusian Sirs, Governors of the Castle and its outbuildings"*, as they were referred to by their captives, decided to break themselves off from the authority of the Sultan of Marrakesh. They stopped giving him a tenth of the profits they were making, and set up an autonomous City-State headed by a Governor elected for the period of a year, who was to reinforce the defensive barrier against Europe's general instinct for war and domination. In tandem with these buccaneering activities, Salé sustained fruitful commercial relationships with various European nations (Spain, France, Holland, Italy), and signed, along with some of these countries' delegates, non-aggression treaties, or truces that had been carefully negotiated.

In the meantime, the 'Alawite Dynasty had replaced that of the Sa'adians, and this "Republic of the Two Riverbanks" ended up being considered by the 'Alawite *shorfa*s, the country's new masters, who took over the banks of the Bu Regreg in 1076/1666, as a first-class centre of excess and debauchery. They put the privateers under their supervision,

ITINERARY VIII *Ebb and Flow, Shine and Eclipse*
Salé

Bab Mrissa, general view, Salé.

entrusting them occassionally with diplomatic missions, like that undertaken by Ra'is 'Abd Allah Ibn 'Aicha to Louis XIV in 1109/1698.

It is within this period, as noted by Charles-André Julien, that one finds the origins of modern Morocco, a Morocco which would continue to come against the Imperial ambitions of European states who did their utmost to dominate and fragment it. Mulay Isma'il (1082/1672–1139/1727) put members of the nomadic Udayas tribe in charge of guarding the fortress, and it was their successors who consolidated and fortified it, developing its armoury.

After having been one of the main centres of commercial trade with foreigners, and having contributed to Morocco's exposure to the outside world, the port of Bu Regreg saw a decline in its activities with the creation, in 1177/1764, of the great port of Essauira (Mogador). Both Bu Regreg towns gradually turned their backs to the sea, but remained a mandoratory thoroughfare between Fez and Marrakesh.

Rabat became the Royal City during the reign of Sultan Sidi Mohamed Ibn 'Abd Allah, who built the Sunna Mosque, opened in 1199/1785. But the plague epidemic, which spread rampantly from 1211/1797 to 1214/1800, decimated over a third of the country's population, which at the time was estimated at five million, reducing the number of Rabat's inhabitants to less than 20,000, heralding a new Dark Age. In 1248/1833, Sultan Mulay 'Abd al-Rahman placed members of the Udayas tribe between Rabat and Témara to create a shield against the fierce tribes of the Zaers.

It was the French occupying forces that chose Rabat as the kingdom's capital in 1912, so as to establish the seat of their Protectorate at a distance from Fez, Marrakesh and Meknès, which stood as sym-

ITINERARY VIII — *Ebb and Flow, Shine and Eclipse*

Salé

bols of Morocco's great Empires. The Kasbah of the Udayas was thus restored and turned into a museum and embellished with an Andalusian garden, and Salé dedicated itself to activities of a more pacifistic nature: religion, and arts and crafts.

However, the peaceful bourgeois agglomeration of 20,000 persons quickly became the cradle of a new Nationalist movement for independence. The town expanded significantly following the establishment of independence in 1956, and it was this that, in particular, perpetuated the deep imprint of Andalusian Arab-Muslim civilisation, as much in the form of religious as well as government buildings, as in the form of certain noteworthy residences, on both sides of the Bu Regreg River.

VIII.2.a Bab Mrissa

Having reached Place Bab Rih, head towards the rampart which surrounds the medina. Bab Mrissa lets one into the medina through an opening onto rue Ach Charid Ahmed ben Aboud.

Without doubt the most ancient monument that is known to us from the Merinid period, this monumental gate was built between 658/1260 and 668/1270, allowing boats to pass through the enclosure via a canal which linked the Bu Regreg to a naval dockyard which is now silted up. Having partially eroded, it remains none the less striking, through the sheer scale of its arch, as wide as it is high, with an 8 m. diagonal rib entrance. Its construction was designed by a Sevillian architect, who knew how to adapt the structure of a traditional Moroccan gate in order to give it a new function, notably avoiding the angled bends which characterise gates used for defence. Flanked, in the same way as Almohad gates are, by two rectangular towers, but without a single arcature lining its smooth keystones, it features, on one of its facades, a rich floral decoration, whilst the other facade is totally bare.

If Daniel Defoe's novel *Robinson Crusoe*, published in 1719, is not considered a work of fiction, then it can be said that its hero was captured before the gates of Salé, and entered the town through Bab Mrissa, before escaping to then run aground on a desert island.

VIII.2.b Merinid Madrasa

From the Bab Mrissa Gate, take rue Haddadine (Street of the Blacksmiths) which leads to the Suq al-Kebir, an old slave market. Take rue Kechachine which stops at the square on which stands the Great Mosque and the madrasa. Entrance fee. Open daily from 09.00–12.00 and 14.30–18.00.

This educational institute, which specialised in the teaching of theology, philosophy and linguistics, was founded around 733/1333

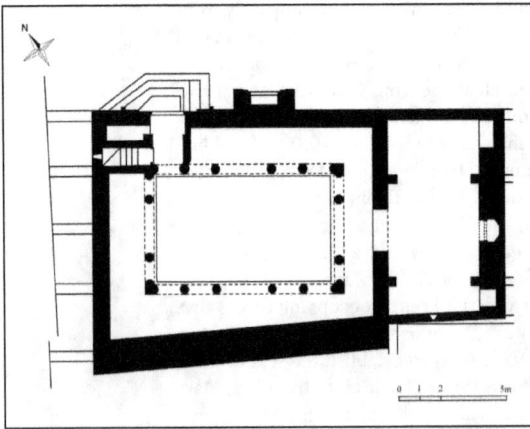

Merinid Madrasa, ground-floor plan, Salé.

by Abu al-Hassan, the famous "Black Sultan" whose tomb can be found in the *necropolis* of Chellah. The *madrasa* remained active for nearly six centuries due mainly to *habus* endowments left behind by its founder. Placed facing the Great Mosque which dates from the Almohad period, it highlights the differences between the two dynasties: powerful Almohad sobriety versus delicate Merinid finesse. In fact, inscriptions engraved in stone bear witness to this wish for studied refinement: *"The wonders of this madrasa perturbs the faculty of reason and captivates both ascetics and the pious alike"*, affirms one inscription, whilst another states: *"I am constructed like a tiered palace and sparkle like the rows of pearls on the neck of one that is engaged to be married"*.

The elegant entrance gate is distinct for its pointed horseshoe arch which fits into a rectangular frame, displaying, within its upper half, a text written in *kufic* script, and surmounted by a very beautiful sculpted cedar canopy protected by varnished green tiles. One then enters the *madrasa* via an elaborately decorated hallway, which leads onto a rectangular courtyard, bordered by galleries supported by columns surfaced in *zellij* and decorated with stucco in the shape of honeycomb. The decor, which is specifically Merinid in style, leaves nothing untouched, time and time again making use of *zellij* ornamentation (black and green), chiselled plaster and carved wood. The prayer hall, small in scale like the rest of the building, possesses a finely decorated *mihrab* niche.

Via the staircase in the hallway, one can reach the student accomodation and then the terrace, from where one can enjoy a gripping view of Salé, Rabat and the Bu Regreg estuary.

Bab Mrissa, floral pattern and corner of arch, Salé.

ITINERARY VIII Ebb and Flow, Shine and Eclipse
Salé

Museum of Ceramics
Situated in the north-western burj of the ramparts, the Museum of Ceramics, opened in 1994, holds a collection of rare examples of pottery from Fez, the Rif and the Middle-Atlas. Another attraction is the spectacular view which the monument offers over the rooftops of the medina. To get there: from the madrasa, cross the Muslim cemetery, and the museum is next to the rampart.

The Feast of the Candles
The Feast of the Candles consists of a solemn ceremonial but popular procession which happens in Salé on the eve of Mawlid, the day celebrating the birth of the Prophet Muhammad. During the ceremony, richly decorated, monumental chandeliers in wax are carried by tobji (a turkish term for naval artillerymen) and are paraded in a fanfare across town until the sanctuary of Sidi Ahmed Ibn Achir is reached, who was the town's first Patron Saint, a doctor of medicine and a mystic who had emigrated from al-Andalus in the $8^{th}/14^{th}$ century. This tradition was introduced at the end of the $10^{th}/16^{th}$ century by the Sa'adian Sultan Mansur al-Dhahbi, the victor of the Battle of the Three Kings (30th Yumada 986/4th August 1578), who had taken part in a similar ceremony in Istanbul. The sovereign wanted for a procession of candles to be organised in his capital, Marrakesh, as well as in the main towns of his kingdom, for the occasion of Mawlid. However, it was only the town of Salé which continued this tradition, thanks to Sidi 'Abd Allah Ibn Hassun, a great mystic who was a contemporary of Mansur al-Dhahbi, as he had decided to turn a part of his endowments into Waqf or Habus (endowments in perpetuity), providing annually for the production of the candles. It is within his mausoleum, which dates from the 19th century, that in the afternoon the incantation candle dances take place to the sound of Andalusian music, and it is also where the candles are stored. There are different stages to the preparation of the ceremony, and several weeks of work are required, involving carpenters, paper-makers and wax craftsmen who pass their know-how on from generation to generation. The wax takes the form of chandeliers, real three-dimensional representations composed of thousands of pieces of sculpted wax, in shimmering colours, with architectural motifs (arcades, columns, domes), as well as geometric and calligraphic motifs, which makes the whole composition look like a scaled-down sanctuary, erected in hommage to the Prophet of Islam and to the Patron Saints of the town.

DAHIR (ROYAL DECREE) PROMULGATED IN THE HEGIRAN YEAR OF 637 (1239) BY THE ALMOHAD SOVEREIGN AL-RASHID WHICH PUTS THE SITE OF *RIBAT AL-FATH* TO THE DISPOSITION OF EMIGRANTS OF AL-ANDALUS

French translation: Kamal Lakhdar

This prestigious decree was created under the orders of the Commander of the Worshipful, son, grandson, great-grandson, and great-great grandson of the Commander of the Worshipful – may God bless and help them – for the benefit of emigrants of Valencia, of the islands of Shakd and of Shabta, as well as for the benefit of all those who, in the same way, have come from the countries of the East after having undergone similar bad times. Therefore, and only after the holder of two *vizier* hoods, the very noble, very considerate, very respectful and very generous Shaykh Abu 'Ali, son of the very noble and very generous Abu Ja'far Ibn Khalas – may God maintain his wealth and generosity – had spoken of the throes of the exile they had been subjected to, and of their bad treatment in the hands of their enemies; and only after they had sought for themselves, in the name of being good neighbours, the granting of a safe haven where they could at last abandon their walking stick, he wanted to give the order – may God gives rise to his orders and prolong his glory – for them to render themselves, with their weapons and belongings, to *Ribat al-Fath* – may God develop its repopulation – and take possession of lodgings and of lands to replace their own lodgings and lands, and erect a welcoming and convivial city – and they are certainly worthy of the warmest welcome and capable of the greatest joy.

The amenities they gain from the earth and the sea are available to them each and every season, allowing the inhabitants to enjoy a life of comfort and without worry. The beneficiaries of the binding arrangements outlined here – may God forever prolong its effects – will come to know a fate as favourable as the one they had known in better days, the kind in which the powerful will have the opportunity to increase their power, and in which the weak will benefit from so much kindness from which they will be able to acquire affluence and wealth.

They will have the opportunity to dedicate themselves to the cultivation of the land, as the plots are both large and abundant, and be able to practise all sorts of lucrative and profitable activities, to plant fig trees and other trees according to the customs of their countries.

They will be in a position to acquire property in their own name and in the name of their children and in turn of their offspring, all kinds of farming, residential and real estate, which they will have gained in view of their taking on official, permanent and paternal roles, without them being liable to pay any sort of compensation or payments other than the legal dues which God has commanded to be taken from the wealth of Muslims. In this respect, they will be trusted in the declarations they make regarding the amount they should pay in dues, in the same way as they should trust that their wishes, and those of their successors, will be fully granted.

The *walis* and the governors – may God protect them – are responsible for guarding them against any grievance which could affect them in one way or another or that might prevent them from accomplishing whatever task, however big or small. They are similarly responsible for honouring their scholars and their nobles, and equally to show proof of being hospitable and friendly neighbours, preventing them from having any nostalgia for their country, to help them forget the injustices they were subjected to and to make them rejoice at the same time over the rights they acquired by becoming natives and the privileges that are due to them as inhabitants. His magnaminity will apply — may God glorify his power and fill him with gratitude — to the whole of their group and of their elite, and will bring them to live according to the arrangements outlined in this eminent decree — may God prolong its effects and goodwill. Whoever it may refer to, be it student or governor — may he be full of generosity — should conform to it and respect its generous advice, with the help of the Almighty, Him to whom we call upon for support, him the only God.

Written on the 21st *sha'ban* of the year 637.

Quoted by A. Kriem in "*Ribat al-Fath, Assimat al-Mamlaka al-Maghribiya*" (1988).

GLOSSARY

'Abid	Converted slaves.
Adan	Summon to prayer.
'Adwa	Riverbank.
'Alim	(Pl. *'Ulama'*): Scholar, doctor of law and Islamic theological science.
'Alj	Renegade.
Amir al-Mu'minin	Prince of Believers.
Amir al-Muslimin	Prince of Muslims.
Anza	Wooden kiosk.
Bab	Gate, door.
Bestella	Filo-pastry tart stuffed with chicken or meat.
Berchla	Granaries.
Bhu	Alcove.
Bled	In North Africa, countryside region, inland area.
Bokhari	Algerian copper, originates from Bokhara (Central Asia).
Burj	Bastion.
Caravanserai	Hostel along main travelling routes to accommodate travellers and safeguard their goods.
Dar	House.
Dbagh	Tanner.
Derb	Alley or impasse or by extension a neighbourhood.
Darih	Mausoleum.
Funduq	In North Africa, a hostelry for merchants and their pack-animals; a warehouse for merchandise and a commercial centre, equivalent to *caravanserai* or *khan* in Oriental Islam.
Futa	A piece of fabric which is tied around the waist instead of an apron, specific to the Rif region. A towel.
Fqih	(Pl. *Fuqaha'*): Jurisconsult versed in the code of Islam.
Habus	Gift bequeathed in perpetuity, usually by the deceased. See *waqf*.
Hadith	(Lit. "sayings"). Tradition related to acts, sayings and attitudes of the Prophet Muhammad and his companions.
Hammam	Public or private bathhouse.
Hanta	Corporation.
Heri	Provisions granary.
Hisba	Prefecture of markets. Post held by *muhtasib*.
Horm	Sacred space.
Imam	One who presides Islamic prayer; a guide, chief, spiritual model or cleric, and sometimes, also, a politician in Muslim society.

249

Glossary

Jabal	Mountain or mountainous terrain.
Jama'	Main mosque where daily prayers and Friday prayers are celebrated.
Jbalas	Persons originating from the region of Jebala, North Morocco.
Jdid	New; *Fas-Jdid*, Fez "Newtown".
Jellaba	Traditional undergarment, long robe with long sleeves and a hood, worn by both men and women in North Africa.
Jihad	Striving towards moral and religious perfection. It can lead to fighting "on the path to God" against dissidents or pagans. Holy war undertaken to protect and defend Islamic territories. *Ijtihad*: (same etymology as *jihad*) a personal effort of interpretation of Islamic law.
Kasbah	Fortress, citadel.
Khalifa	Administrative role: lieutenant, priest, representative, successor. Caliph.
Kharraz	Babouche maker.
Lahri	Grain silo.
Lekbir	(Fem. *lekbira*.) big, large, great.
Madrasa	Islamic school of sciences (theology, law, Qur'an, etc.) and lodgings for students during the Mediaeval Age in Morocco; today, a school.
M'allem	(Pl. *m'almin*.) Master of craft.
Makhzen	The government belonging to the Sultan; comes from *makhzen* (grain silo).
Maq'ad	Open rooms without doors, situated on the sides of a patio.
Maristan	Hospital.
Marrano	Those who in fear of persecution practised their religion secretly.
Mashrabiyya	Wooden lattice screens made of turned pieces of wood assembled together to form a window grille.
Matmora	Underground room, by extension underground prison.
Mechwar	Place in which delegations wait before being received by the Sultan.
Meda	Ablutions hall.
Medina	Town. In North Africa the old part of an agglomeration in opposition to the European extension to towns.
Mellah	Generic term used in Morocco to designate the Jewish Quarter.
Menqach	Hammer used by *zellij* craftsmen.
Mesria	A separate room generally used to lodge guests.

Mihrab	Niche in the *qibla* wall, indicating the direction of Mecca towards which worshippers face when praying.
Minbar	Pulpit in a mosque from which the *imam* preaches his sermon (*khutba*) to the faithful.
Minzah	Pavilion with garden. Characteristic element of the *riyad* of large urban residences in Morocco.
Muhtassib	Employee responsible for *hisba*, overseeing markets and commercial transactions, for checking weights and measures, preventing fraud and for overseeing public hygiene and urban buildings, etc. Alderman.
Munia	Holiday villa.
Mussem	Patronal celebration.
Mruzia	Mutton cooked with a seven-spice mix called *ras al-hanut*, almonds, dried raisins and honey.
Muezzin	Religious Muslim administrator, in charge of announcing the five daily prayers from the top of the mosque's minaret.
Mufti	A Muslim legal expert who is empowered to give rulings on religious matters.
Muqarnas	Stalactite or honeycomb ornament that adorns cupolas or corbels of a building.
Nadir	Administrator in charge of the control and management of *habus*.
Noria	Mechanism used to draw water. A serrated horizontal wheel pulls a vertical wheel carrying flasks that spill into a recipient vessel that is in place for this purpose. Chain pump.
Qadi	Muslim judge.
Qa'id	High ranking military officer, chief administrator of a province.
Qaysariya	Covered market.
Qibla	Direction of *Ka'ba* towards which believers turn to face for prayer. Wall of mosque in which the *mihrab* is situated.
Qubba	Dome. By extension a monument or chamber built over the grave of a saint. Marabout.
Qsar	(Pl. *qsur*.) Palace.
Riyad	Garden within residential housing.
Ribat	Fortresses built on the border zones, from where religious warriors who dwelled there went to fight the Holy War. The town name Rabat comes from *Ribat al-Fath*, Ribat of the "Conquest".
Sabat	Covered passageway.
Sahn	Open patio or courtyard of a mosque.

Glossary

Sahrij	Large basin of water.
Seffar	Bookbinder.
Serraj	Saddler.
Shaykh	Elderly man, respected for his age and knowledge. Tribal chief or leader of a brotherhood.
Shkayri	Leather craftsman.
Sherif	(Pl. *shorfa*.) Descendant of the Prophet Muhammad.
Suq	Market-(place).
Sufism	Derived from *suf*, wool, which is the fabric in which ascetics (*sufi*) clothe themselves. Since the $2^{nd}/8^{th}$ century, term denotes Islamic mysticism.
Tal'a	Ascent. *Tal'a Lekbira*, "Grand Ascent"; principal axis of the *medina* of Fez.
Taleb	(Pl. *tolba*.) Student.
Tawhid	Unicity, uniqueness.
Toshabim	Moroccan Jews.
Wadi	Watercourse, often temporary, in arid regions.
Waqf	An endowment in perpetuity, usually land or property, from which revenues were reserved for the upkeep of pious foundations.
Wudu'	Ablutions practised before prayer.
Zawiya	Establishment under the authority of a brotherhood reserved for religious teaching designed for training *shaykhs*; includes mausoleum of a saint, built on the site where he lived.
Zellij	Small enamelled ceramic tiles used to decorate monuments and interiors.

HISTORICAL PERSONALITIES

'Abd al-Malik
Sa'adian Sultan, reigned from 983/1578 to 986/1578.

'Abd al-Mumen Ibn 'Ali
First monarch of the Almohad Dynasty, reigned from 524/1130 to 558/1163.

'Abd Allah Ibn Yassin
Almoravid Sultan, Malikite propagandist, died in 450/1059.

'Abdelkader Achache
Governor of Tétouan, reigned from 1261/1845 to 1267/1851 and from 1862 to 1864.

Abu al-'Abbas al-Sabti
Scholar, one of the most important representatives of *Sufism* during the Almohad period, protector of the blind and one of the actual patrons of the city of Marrakesh.

Abu al-Hassan
Merinid Sultan, reigned from 731/1331 to 752/1351.

Abu Bakr al-Qurayshi
Andalusian doctor.

Abu Juzay (721/1321–757/1356)
Writer for Ibn Battuta, secretary of the Merinid Sultan Abu Inan.

Abu Inan
Merinid Sultan (son of Abu al-Hassan), reigned from 751/1351 to 759/1358.

Abu Sa'id 'Uthman
Merinid Sultan (father of Abu al-Hassan) reigned from 709/1310 to 731/1331.

Abu 'Ubayd al-Bakri (431/1040–486/1094)
Historian and geographer. Author of *Books of Routes and of Kingdoms (Kitab al-Mamalik wal-l-masalik)*.

Abu Ya'qub Yusuf
Almohad Sultan, reigned from 558/1163 to 579/1184.

Abu Ya'qub Yusuf
Merinid Sultan, reigned from 684/1286 to 706/1307.

Abu Yusuf Ya'qub
Merinid Sultan, reigned from 656/1258 to 684/1286.

Abu Zakariya
Wattassid Sultan, reigned from 831/1428 to 852/1449.

Ahmed al-Mansur al-Dhahbi
Sa'adian Sultan, reigned from 985/1578 to 1011/1603.

Ahmed Errifi (Ahmed Ibn 'Ali Errifi)
Governor of Tangier, Larache and Tétouan from 1124/1713 to 1155/1743, son of Governor 'Ali Errifi.

Al-Bukhari
Traditionalist, author of the *Sahih* (collection of authentic *hadith*s).

'Ali Errifi ('Ali Ibn 'Abd Allah Errifi)
Governor of Tangier, Larache, and Tétouan from 1090/1680 to 1124/1713.

'Ali Ibn Yusuf
Almoravid Sultan, reigned from 500/1107 to 537/1143.

Al-Nasiri (1250/1835–1314/1897)
Letter writer, historian and *sherifian* administrator. Author of "General History of Morocco", *Kitab al-istiqsa' li-akhbar duwal al-Maghrib al-aqsa*.

Alphonse X, referred to as Alphonse the Wise (1221–1284)
King of Castille and Leon, from 1252–1284, and Germanic emperor from 1267–1272; he re-established the University of Salamanca and instructed the drawing up of astronomical tables, called "Alphonsine Tables".

Aurillac (d'), Gerbert (938–1003)
Pope from 999 to 1003, promoted under the name of Sylvester II.

Bulughin (Ibn Ziri)
Zirid Prince of Fez around 369/980.

Chénier, Louis
French Consul in Rabat in the 18th century.

Defoe, Daniel (c.1660–1731)
English writer, adventurer, tradesmen, and political agent. Author of stories, essays, pamphlets and of an adventure novel whose reputation remained global, *Robinson Crusoe* (1719).

Fatima al-Fihri
Daughter of a wealthy Kairouan negotiator, she founded the Qarawiyin Mosque in 242/857.

Foucauld (de), Charles (1858–1916)
Explorer and French missionary. Author of the *Renaissance of Morocco*.

Ibn al-Khatib (712/1313–775/1374)
Andalusian chronicler, writer, doctor and minister in Granada. Author of *Mi'yar al-Ikhtiyar*.

Ibn Marzuq (born in Tlemcen in 709/1310)
Writer and poet of the court of the Merinid princes Abu al-Hassan and Abu Inan. Author of *Musnad al-Sahih al-Hassan*.

Ibn Rushd referred to as Averroës (520/1126–594/1198)
Illustrious Arab philosopher, *vizier* and doctor to the Almohad sovereign Abu Ya'qub Yusuf. Author of *Discovery of the Method*.

Ibn Tofail (503/1110–580/1185)
Master of Ibn Rushd. Author of *The Autodidactic Philosopher (Risalat Hayy Ibn Yaqzan)*.

Ibn Zidan
Historian of the 'Alawite Dynasty. Author of *Al-Ithaf*.

Idriss I (Idriss Ibn 'Abd Allah)
Idrissid Sultan, reigned from 171/788 to 174/791.

Idriss II
Idrissid Sultan, reigned from 192/808 to 213/828.

Imam Ahmed Abu Bakr
Zenet Governor Sultan, died in 479/1087.

Julian, comte
Governor of Ceuta in 710.

Khayr al-Din, Barbarossa (880/1476–952/1546)
Corsican of Greek origin and Governor of Algiers. Was nominated "Grand Admiral of all Ottoman Fleets" by Sulayman the Magnificent.

Louis XIV referred to as the Sun King
King of France, reigned from 1643 to 1715.

Lyautey (1854–1934)
Marshal of France, resident General of the French Republic in Morocco.

Maimonides (Moshe Ibn Maimun) (529/1135–600/1204)
Author of *The Epistle on Persecution*.

Historical personalities

Meryem al-Fihri
Sister of Fatima al-Fihri, founded the Andalusian Mosque in 244/859.

Mohamed al-Nassir
Almohad Prince, son of Ya'qub al-Mansur, reigned from 595/1199 to 609/1213.

Mohamed al-Muttawakil
Sa'adian Sultan, nephew of 'Abd al-Malik, reigned from 981/1574 to 983/1576.

Mohamed Ibn Idriss
Idrissid Sultan (son of Idriss II), reigned from 212/828 to 221/836.

Mohamed Ibn Tumert (472/1080–524/1130)
Almohad Sultan, *fqih,* thinker and *mahdi* of the Almohads who called him "The Impeccable Imam".

Mohamed III
'Alawite Sultan, reigned from 1170/1757 to 1204/1790.

Mohamed IV
'Alawite Sultan, reigned from 1859 to 1873.

Mohamed V
'Alawite Sultan, reigned from 1927 to 1961.

Mulay 'Abd Allah
'Alawite Sultan, reigned from 1140/1728 to 1170/1757.

Mulay 'Abd al-Rahman
'Alawite Sultan, reigned from 1237/1822 to 1275/1859.

Mulay 'Abd al-Salam Ibn Mshish
Idrissid *Sherif* of the Bani 'Arus tribe, died in 622/1225.

Mulay Hassan
'Alawite Sultan, reigned from 1873 to 1894.

Mulay Isma'il (1055/1646–1139/1727)
'Alawite Sultan, reigned from 1082/1672 to 1139/1727.

Mulay Rashid
'Alawite Sultan, reigned from 1076/1666 to 1082/1672.

Mulay Sliman
'Alawite Sultan, reigned from 1206/1792 to 1237/1822.

Musa Ibn Nusayr (19/640–98/717)
Governor of Ifriqiya in 78/698.

Naqsis, al-Moqadem Abu al-'Abbas Ahmed Ibn 'Aissa
Tétouanese warrior chief, reigned during the 11th/17th century.

'Umar Lukash
Andalusian, descendant of the Umayyad Caliphs. Was first the secretary of Mulay Isma'il, then chief of Customs and then the Caliphate of Governor Ahmed Errifi.

Phillippe II (1527 - 1598)
Son of Charles Quint, King of Spain from 1556 to 1598; and King of Naples, Sicily and Portugal from 1580 to 1598.

Salah al-Din al-Ayyubi referred to as Saladin (531/1137–589/1193)
Sultan of Egypt and Syria, founder of the Ayyubid Dynasty.

Sebastião, Dom
King of Portugal, reigned from 1557 to 1578.

Sidi al-Mandri
Originally from Granada, founder and symbol of the town of Tétouan, died in 916/1511.

Tariq Ibn Ziyad (1st/8th century)
Freed slave of the Umayyad General Musa Ibn Nosayr.

Ya'qub al-Mansur
Almohad Sultan, reigned from 579/1184–595/1199.

Yusuf Ibn Tashfin
Almoravid sovereign, reigned from 453/1061 to 500/1107.

FURTHER READING

AFRICAIN, L., *Descriptions de l'Afrique*, 2 vols., Paris, 1956.

AZZIANI, *Turjuman al-murib 'an duwal al-Machriq wa-l-Maghrib, Le Maroc de 1631 à 1812*, French translation and edition by O. Houdas, Paris, 1886.

BEL, A., *Inscriptions arabes de Fès*, Paris, 1938.

BUSNOT, A., *L'histoire du règne de Moulay Ismaïl, Roy du Maroc, Fès, Tafilalet, Sousse*, Rouen, 1714.

GAILLARD, H. , *Une ville de l'Islam, Fès*, Paris, 1905.

AL-GHAZALI, *Le livre du licite et de l'illicite (Kitab al-halal wa-l-haram)*, French translation by R. Morelin, Paris, 1981.

IBN BATTOUTA, *Récits de voyages (Rihla)*, French translation and edition by C. Defrémery and B. R. Sanguinetti, 4 vols., Paris, 1853–1859.

IBN HAWQAL, *Livre de la configuration de la terre (Kitab surat al-ard)*, French translation by G. Wiet, Paris-Beirut, 1964.

IBN KHALDOUN, *Prolégomènes*, French translation by de Slane, Paris, 1863.

IBN QUZMAN, *Le Diwan d'Ibn Guzman*, text, French translation and commentaries by D. de Gunzburg, Berlin, 1896.

AL-IDRISSI, *Livre de Roger (Kitab Rudjar)*, French translation by A. Jaubert, 2 vols., Paris, 1836–1840.

JULIEN, CH-A., *Historoire de l'Afrique du Nord*, Paris, 1956.

MARÇAIS, G., *Architecture musulmane d'Occident: Tunisie, Algérie, Maroc, Espagne et Sicile*, Paris, 1954.

— *L'Art musulman*, Paris, 1962.

MÁRMOL CARVAJAL, *Descripción general de África*, Granada, 1573.

MIÈGE, J. L., *ThLes activités maritimes et commerciales de Tétouan XVIIIe, XIXe siècles*.

— *Le Maroc et l'Europe (1830–1894)*, Paris, 1961.

MIÈGE, J. L., BENABOUD, M., ERZINI, N., *Tétouan: ville andalouse marocaine*, Tétouan, 1996.

MOÜETTE, M., *Relation de la captivité de S. Moüette dans les royaumes de Fès et du Maroc*, Paris, 1682.

PIDOU DE SAINT-OLON, *État présent de l'Empire du Maroc*, Morocco, 1694.

TERRASSE, H., *Histoire du Maroc*, parts I and II, Casablanca, 1950.

— *Islam d'Espagne. Une rencontre de l'Orient et de l'Occident*, Paris, 1958.

ZAFRANI, H., *2000 ans de vie juive au Maroc*, co-edited by Eddif and Maisonneuve and Larose, Casablanca, 1998.

COLLECTIVE WORKS

Fès médiévale, Autrement, Série Mémoires, n°.13, 1992.

Histoire du Maroc, Hatier, 1990.

AUTHORS

Naïma El-Khatib Boujibar
Archaeologist and art historian, Naima El-Khatib Boujibar has occupied various positions within the Ministry of Cultural Affairs before becoming the Director of Morocco-Lusitanian Heritage (1997).
Author of *Deux mille ans d'art au Maroc*, Charpentier Editions, Paris, 1963, she has also collaborated on various articles in archaeological journals and has published a number of articles on Moroccan furniture, the architecture of antiquity as well as on the art and traditions of Morocco, notably the following:
Mémorial du Maroc, Nord Organisation Editions, Rabat, vol. 1, 1983, 128–167 and 177–189 and vol. 8, 1985, 228–249.
"Les fouilles de Dchar Jdid 1977–1980", *Bulletin d'Archéologie Marocaine*, Moroccan and International Editions., Tangier, 1984, vol. 14, 169–2454.

Mhammad Benaboud
Research Fellow at the University of Tétouan, Mhammad Benaboud is a historian and a specialist on the town of Tétouan. He is the author of a number of works, notably:
Tétouan, ville andalouse marocaine, CNRS Editions, Paris, 1996.
Kalila wa dimna, Rabat, 1996.

Kamal Lakhdar
Historian, member of the Ribat El-Fath Association, he was for a long time a high-positioned civil servant of Public Administration in Morocco. Kamal Lakkhdar is the author of the book *Rabat: le temps d'une ville*, Eddif Editions, Casablanca, 1991.

Mohamed Mezzine
A Doctor in Modern History at the University of Paris VII-Jussieu, Mohamed Mezzine is in fact the Dean of the Humanities faculty of Fez-Saiss. He was awarded the Moroccan Prize for the Social Sciences for his book *Fès et sa campagne 1549–1637. Contribution à l'histoire du Maroc Saadien,* Dar al-Maarif al-Jadida Editions, Rabat, 1986. He is also the co-authored of the volume *Histoire de l'Encyclopédie du Maroc*, 1988, with the following inclusions:
"Les Saadians: XVIe et XVIIe siècles", pp.83–96.
"L'avènement d'une nouvelle dynastie, les Alaouites, 1660–1727", pp.98–108.

Abdelaziz Touri
A Doctor in Archaeology and History of Art at the University of Paris-IV Sorbonne, Abdelaziz Touri is Director of Heritage at the Ministry of Cultural Affairs. A Director of numerous archaeological research projects in Morocco, he has written various articles on Moroccan and western Islamic archaeology, as well having co-authored certain works such as:
Abdelaziz Touri, M. Ameziane Hassani and Gian Carlo Barbato, *Le projet pilote de restauration et réhabilitation du palais Dar Adiyel à Fès (un exemple de coopération internationale tripartite)*, Diagonale Editions, Rome, 1999, 25–41. "L'oratoire de quartier", *Fès Médiévale. Entre légende et histoire, un carrefour de l'Orient à l'apogée d'un rêve*, directed by Mohamed Mezzine, Autrement editions, Séries Mémoires, n°.13, Paris, 1992, 100–109.

ISLAMIC ART IN THE MEDITERRANEAN

This cycle of Museum With No Frontiers Exhibition Trails permits the discovery of secrets in Islamic Art, its history, construction techniques and religious inspiration.

ALGERIA

LEGACY OF ISLAM IN ALGERIA: The Art and Architecture of Light* introduces the varied and richest forms Islamic art assumed in Central Maghreb (Algeria), an important artistic heritage related to crucial events that marked the country's history, from the rise of dissident religious movements to the influence of great dynasties, and the roles played by trade and pilgrimage routes and by the Ottomans in the Mediterranean cities. The synthesis of Arab and Berber, African, Andalusian and Eastern influences shaped the artistic and architectural models, the purity and harmony of Ibadid architecture, Almoravid mosques, Ziyanid monuments and Ottoman palaces on the Mediterranean shore.

Five itineraries invite you to discover 70 museums, monuments and sites in Biskra, Ghardaia, Bani Isguen, Algiers, Tlemcen, Nedroma and Tamentit (among others).

EGYPT

MAMLUK ART: The Splendour and Magic of the Sultans tells the story of almost three centuries of political security and economic stability achieved by the sultans' successful defence against Mongol and Crusader threats. The intellectual, scientific and artistic currents that flourished then are manifest in Mamluk architecture and decorative arts, almost modern in their elegant and lively simplicity, bearing witness to the vitality of Mamluk trade, to their cultural exuberance and to their military and religious strength.

Eight itineraries invite you to discover 51 museums, monuments and sites in Cairo, Alexandria and the Nile Delta.

ITALY

SICULO-NORMAN ART: Islamic Culture in Medieval Sicily illustrates how the great artistic and cultural heritage of the Arabs who ruled the island in the 10th and 11th centuries was assimilated and reinterpreted during the Norman reign that followed, achieving its acme in the resplendent age of Ruggero II in the 12th century. Spectacular coastal and mountain landscapes provide the backdrop for visits to villages, castles, gardens, churches and Christianised old mosques.

Ten itineraries invite you to discover 91 museums, monuments and sites in Palermo, Monreale, Mazara del Vallo, Salemi, Segesta, Erice, Cefalù and Catania (among others).

JORDAN

THE UMAYYADS: The Rise of Islamic Art presents a journey through the great artistic and cultural flourishing that gave birth to the formative phase of Islamic art during the 7th and 8th centuries. The Umayyads unified the Mediterranean and Persian cultures and developed an innovative artistic synthesis that incorporated and immortalised Classical, Byzantine and Sassanid heritage. The elegant architecture of desert castles and the frescoes, mosaics and masterpieces of figurative and decorative art still evoke the strong sense of realism and the great cultural, artistic and social vitality of the centres of the Umayyad Caliphate.

Five itineraries invite you to discover 43 museums, monuments and sites in Amman, Madaba, Al-Badiya, Jerash, Umm Qays, Aqaba and Humayma (among others).

MOROCCO

ANDALUSIAN MOROCCO: Discovery in Living Art tells the story of the exchanges between the furthest frontier of the Maghreb and Al-Andalus for more than five centuries. Political and social circumstances gave birth to a crossroads of cultures, techniques and artistic styles revealed by the splendour of Idrisid, Almoravid, Almohad and Marinid mosques, minarets and madrasas. The influence of Cordoban architecture and Andalusian decorative models, horseshoe arches, floral and geometric motifs and the use of stucco, wood and polychromatic tiles, display the continuous interchange that made Morocco one of the most brilliant homes of Islamic civilisation.

Eight itineraries invite you to discover 89 museums, monuments and sites in Rabat, Meknès, Fez, Chefchaouen, Tétouan and Tangier (among others).

PALESTINIAN TERRITORIES

PILGRIMAGE, SCIENCE AND SUFISM: Islamic Art in the West Bank and Gaza explores a period during the reigns of the Ayyubid, Mamluk and Ottoman dynasties when numerous pilgrims and scholars from all quarters of the Muslim world came to Palestine. The great dynasties commissioned architectural and artistic masterpieces in the most important religious centres. Attracting the most learned scholars, many centres enjoyed considerable prestige and encouraged the spread of a rarefied art that still fascinates today. The Islamic monuments and architecture of this Exhibition Trail clearly reflect the connections between dynastic patronage, intellectual activity and the rich expression of people's devotion, rooted in this land for centuries.

Nine itineraries invite you to discover 70 museums, monuments and sites in Jerusalem, Jericho, Nablus, Bethlehem, Hebron and Gaza (among others).

PORTUGAL

IN THE LANDS OF THE ENCHANTED MOORISH MAIDEN: Islamic Art in Portugal uncovers five inspired centuries of Islamic civilisation that shaped the people of the former Gharb al-Andalus. From Coimbra to the furthest reaches of the Algarve there are palaces, Christianised mosques, fortifications and urban centres, all of which bear witness to the splendour of a glorious past. This artistic recollection is the expression of a very delicate symbiosis that determined the particularities of vernacular architecture and still permeates the cultural identity of Portugal.

Ten itineraries invite you to discover 76 museums, monuments and sites in Lisbon, Sintra, Coimbra, Evora, Mertola, Faro and Sesimbra (among others).

SPAIN

MUDEJAR ART: Islamic Aesthetics in Christian Art uncovers the fascinating richness of a genuinely Hispanic cultural and artistic symbiosis that became a distinctive element of Christian Spain after the end of Arab rule. Mudejars were Muslims who were allowed to stay in the reconquered territories and Mudejar artists and craftsmen strongly influenced the culture and art of the new Christian kingdoms. Beautifully decorated brick-built churches, monasteries and palaces in Aragona, Castile, Estremadura and Andalusia provide a unique example of the creative preservation of Islamic forms within Christian art in Spain between the 11th and 16th centuries.

Thirteen itineraries invite you to discover 124 museums, monuments and sites in Madrid, Guadalajara, Saragossa, Tordesillas, Toledo, Guadalupe and Seville (among others).

SYRIA

THE AYYUBID ERA: Art and Architecture in Medieval Syria* focuses on the unique artistic and architectural development in 12th–13th century Syria, when Atabeg and Ayyubid military resistance to the Crusaders coincided with a great cultural and artistic revival in the most important Syrian cities. The Ayyubid patrons provided educative, religious and charitable institutions; their intense activity left its mark in the sober elegance of mosques, madrasas, citadels, mausoleums and hospitals, embellished with Eastern architectural and decorative motifs, muqarnas, Kufic inscriptions, carved stucco and wooden minbars, beautifully illuminated manuscripts, pottery, metalwork and textiles.

Eight itineraries invite you to discover 95 museums, monuments and sites in Damascus, Bosra, Homs, Hama, Tartus, Aleppo and Raqqa (among others).

TUNISIA

IFRIQIYA: Thirteen Centuries of Art and Architecture in Tunisia is a voyage through the history of the Islamic architecture of the Maghreb, to uncover a millenary civilisation that made works of art of its most important spaces. The great Islamic dynasties – Abbasids, Aghlabids, Fatimids, Zirids, Almohads, Hafsids, Ottomans – and Islamic religious schools and movements left the mark of their artistic expression over the centuries. Islamic art in Tunisia is a cultural crossroads, widely influenced by local artistic customs, by Andalusian and eastern architectural and decorative elements, by Arab, Roman and Berber traditions and by the variety of its natural landscape.

Eleven itineraries invite you to discover 108 museums, monuments and sites in Tunis, Sidi Bou Saïd, Bizerte, Testour, Al-Kef, Kairouan, Mahdia, Sfax, Tozeur and Gabès (among others).

TURKEY

EARLY OTTOMAN ART: The Legacy of the Emirates presents the artistic and architectural expressions in Western Anatolia and the emergence of the Ottoman dynasty in the 14th and 15th centuries. The Turkish Emirates developed a new stylistic synthesis by blending Central Asian and Seljuq traditions and the legacy of the Greek, Roman and Byzantine past. The architectural schemes of mosques, hammams, hospitals, madrasas, mausoleums and the great religious complexes, columns and domes, floral and calligraphic decoration, ceramics and illumination testify to the richness of styles. The cultural and artistic flourishing that matched the rise of the Ottoman Empire was deeply marked by the distinctive legacy of the Emirates.

Eight itineraries invite you to discover 61 museums, monuments and sites in Milas, Selçuk, Manisa, Bursa, İznik, Karacabey, Çanakkale, Gelibolu and Edirne (among others).

---

* Under preparation.

www.ingramcontent.com/pod-product-compliance
Lightning Source LLC
Chambersburg PA
CBHW070323240426
43671CB00013BA/2347